BEST OF THE DAO OF DOUG

A PUBLIC TRANSIT GUIDE

DOUGLAS MERIWETHER

BALBOA.PRESS
A DIVISION OF HAY HOUSE

Balboa Press books may be ordered through booksellers or by contacting:

Balboa Press
A Division of Hay House
1663 Liberty Drive
Bloomington, IN 47403
www.balboapress.com
844-682-1282

Because of the dynamic nature of the Internet, any web addresses or links contained in
this book may have changed since publication and may no longer be valid. The views
expressed in this work are solely those of the author and do not necessarily reflect the
views of the publisher, and the publisher hereby disclaims any responsibility for them.

The author of this book does not dispense medical advice or prescribe the use
of any technique as a form of treatment for physical, emotional, or medical
problems without the advice of a physician, either directly or indirectly. The
intent of the author is only to offer information of a general nature to help you
in your quest for emotional and spiritual well-being. In the event you use any
of the information in this book for yourself, which is your constitutional right,
the author and the publisher assume no responsibility for your actions.

Any people depicted in stock imagery provided by Getty Images are
models, and such images are being used for illustrative purposes only.
Certain stock imagery © Getty Images.

Print information available on the last page.

ISBN: 979-8-7652-4414-2 (sc)
ISBN: 979-8-7652-4416-6 (hc)
ISBN: 979-8-7652-4415-9 (e)

Library of Congress Control Number: 2023914087

Balboa Press rev. date: 10/22/2024

Reviews for Dao of Doug 1—Finding Zen

"The Dao of things cannot be complete without the Dao of Driving a bus. I'd ride with Doug all the way to the Himalayas just to listen to the art of his wisdom."
—David Biddle, author of *Implosions of America—A Story Collection*

"Nice read. I like the mix of situational context and life lessons."
—Chad Upham, graduate, Art Center College of Design

"Back Door!"

—Brandon Stanton

For my leader and my follower.

Acknowledgments

Ann Delay, Steven Whitworth, and Cyndia Chambers for help with the title of this book: *The Dao of Doug: Finding Zen in San Francisco Transit: A Bus Driver's Perspective*

Any Life worth living is worth writing about.
—Anthony Robbins

Reviews of Dao of Doug 2

Whether you take mass transit or drive, either in San Francisco or elsewhere, this book offers philosophical wisdom beyond the overt advice on how to be a better passenger or driver, and how to deal with traffic jams and difficult personalities. The sequel to the *Dao of Doug* is about the art of remaining peaceful and maintaining dignity when the going gets tough.

—Jackie Cohen, member of the Board of Directors, National Lesbian and Gay Journalists Association

I've been riding Muni for my whole life and, as an *SF Weekly* reporter, delving deep into its inner workings for many years. It's not always a pretty picture. Actually, it's rarely a pretty picture. So that's why Driver Doug's tales are such a pleasure. They're the often painfully honest testimonials of a man who really gives a damn.

A man who strives to achieve Zen while operating a Muni bus is worth getting to know. San Franciscans get on the bus. And then they get off. But Doug is there for the long haul, pulling in, pulling out, and motoring, ever closer, to Zen. May he reach it soon.

—Joe Eskenazi, *SF Weekly* staff writer and columnist

In loving memory: Doug Fritz
5.7.41–12.31.12
For the other Doug. Thanks for listening.
Your broad smile and Cheshire grin—with a laugh—kept
me going those first two years as a bus driver. Thanks!

Acknowledgments

Special thanks to baristas Angela, Chan, Brian, Data, Jaime, Karla, Kim, Luis, Memo, Mike, et al. for providing the dark roast coffee as fuel for writing this book.

Better three hours too early, then one minute too late.
—William Shakespeare

Trolleybus of Happy Destiny: Dao of Doug 3

Driver Doug is a twenty-nine-year resident of the City by the Bay and has been a transit operator for the San Francisco Municipal Railway for almost twenty years. His current run is on the 21 Hayes trolleybus line from the Ferry Plaza to Golden Gate Park. His interests include photography and writing, and this latest essay, *The Trolleybus of Happy Destiny*, is a composition including anecdotes and photo illustrations from his experience behind the wheel of a city transit bus.

Book 3 Summary

I am continually inspired by those who take the bus to work; to play; to get around this exciting city—students, businesswomen, and tourists, all walks and wheels who enter and exit the bus toward their next destination. Here is the answer to the request I get often, "Driver Doug, you should write a book!" Get inside the *Trolleybus of Happy Destiny* and open a page, a chapter, and see what life is like behind the wheel as a transit operator in the City That Knows How—San Francisco!

To all those who take mass transit on a regular basis, those who have encouraged me to write my story, and the hundreds of family and friends who know someone who drives a bus for a living.

Other Books by Douglas Meriwether★
The Dao of Doug: The Art of Driving a Bus or
Finding Zen in San Francisco Transit: A Bus Driver's
Perspective 2013, 2014, 2015 *(Dao of Doug 1)*
The Dao of Doug 2: The Art of Driving a Bus: Keeping Zen in
San Francisco Transit: A Line Trainer's Guide 2015, 2016
The Trolleybus of Happy Destiny 2018, 2022 *(Dao of Doug 3)*

Best of the Dao of Doug—Finding Zen in San
Francisco—A Case for Free Transit KDP upload edited
for Audiobook July 18, 2021 *(Dao of Doug 4)*

Visit http://www.daoofdoug.com.

Contents

Preface

This book is to be read in short doses, such as a chapter a day, like in a meditation book. Some common points come up in more than one chapter and repeat. A common refrain is how paying the fare slows down on time performance. I have condensed my blogs into this fourth installment of the Dao of Doug series: *A Public Transportation Guide.* Nowhere does this become more evident than in a dense city that has more trolleybus wires than any city in the world.

Who is this book meant for? If I learned anything from my grade-school speech teacher, one of the first ups is: *Who is my audience?* I would say I have several groups of people in mind for this book. *First, students in Muni's training division* who have recently applied for a job as a transit operator. *Second, those considering a new career* path in their life. *Third, city transit passengers* who have wondered what we go through and what we do to *Keep the Zen in the Art of Driving a Bus.*

Fourth, the other more passive audience are *those who still own cars or drive* most places to get around but have their car in the shop. My hope is if I can get one more car off the street because of this book, our streets can be clear, such as they were in the 1970s. Coincidentally, the way they are now is due to a planet-wide crisis created by influenza in a world of huge polluting cruise ships and clogged arteries on freeways.

I am happy our cars are becoming more fuel efficient, but this doesn't mean I am going to own one. What I have found here in this dense city is the cost of rent is high, but so are wages. By dumping the car, I found a higher standard of living than the supposed convenience of the suburbs and drive-through culture. A drive-through meal at a suburban chain may be cheaper compared to a boutique restaurant here in the city, but at what cost does that drive-through meal imply? Right now, the stores that have paper towels in stock and have no waiting in line are the smaller, more realistic supply chains, based upon *customers who walk to their corner store*—not in immense parking lots filled with death monsters.

I don't pay for parking. I don't pay for gas, a new car battery, jumper cables, car insurance, deductibles, oil, brakes, or checkups. I have three bikes, and the repair bill rarely goes over $150. For $150, I get all new brakes and cables, and these last for over two years. I just don't see that in owning or caring for a car. I walk or ride to work, and my bus is an electric vehicle without carbon emission. The electricity comes from hydroelectric power. This is clean living. I am trying to breathe deeply and appreciate the fresh air after a rainstorm. Hopefully, this book, too, is that breath of fresh air. Thanks for riding public transportation! Let's lower the cost for everyone and make public transportation more attractive.

Should public transit be free? It would sure cut away a huge loss in dwell time at the fare box and speed boarding. Tagging in with our Clipper card has dramatically reduced all the drama and anecdotal evidence found in most of these essay-style chapters. I realize my humorous food groups of fare box styles are fast becoming a historical footnote. So, too, are the advent of driverless cars—whereby my profession becomes extinct as a job classification.

Douglas Meriwether
October 19, 2024

Why I Wrote This Book

I WAS ASKED ABOUT WHY I WROTE A BOOK ABOUT BEING A BUS DRIVER in San Francisco. The first reason was in answer to why I am here. *We are all here to do what we are all here to do,* as the Oracle tells Neo in *The Matrix* trilogy. Being of service was and is my first motive to get what I learned down on paper—as a guide for those who follow me at the job, to have a higher vantage point with which to see what lies on the road ahead, not just with the drive-camera evidence at a disciplinary hearing! Keeping the fare to, say, one dollar for everybody and making penalties reasonable in cost would go a long way in keeping me at my job.

Where I place the door seems to baffle most intending passengers. The distraction of showing a transfer at an awkward, unsafe moment also causes complaints to arise, from my tone of voice, with a complete lack of understanding about why. My passion about safety is a priority, and the challenge is in trying to relay much experience in a very short attention span. This relay is what this book is all about. I have reasons for why I do what I do, and if this is understood, another angel can be with me on the bus, not in the complaint cue.

When a patron rushes to the door, they are just as unsure about what to expect from me, the bus driver, as am I of them. If anything written here stirs controversy, though not my intent, it would be to get into a conversation about what has worked and that which has not. To see through eyes of interconnectedness, not isolated in our car with the windows up. To end compulsive honking syndrome, with an arm and a hand sticking out with the single middle finger in the air as it passes by the bus, over the double line at an unsafe speed, just missing a head-on with an oncoming car or a person in the next crosswalk up ahead!

It is the "caution and reinstruct" love letter from our superintendent after an incident, without a hearing of the necessary clarity about my part and the riders' part in causing the conflict—or the solution for the next time. I find and keep—not lose and weep—Zen-like mastery to understand the needs for safety without an angry or harsh tone. Preconceived notion or attachment to something else is usually behind a service complaint. Usually, it is not what is said but the tone in which it was said. In the flash of the pan moment, this becomes almost impossible, but on the pages of this tome, a space cushion remains.

This space cushion, which I am trained to always keep around my bus at all times, goes a long way in explaining why I am splitting the lane, driving down both lanes of traffic in the Mission or on Van Ness. I am avoiding car doors, skaters, bike riders, and the person with the door open at their parked car. I can't answer your question right now because I am busy looking at the show in front and up to one to two blocks ahead! *Now sit down and shut up, please. Just do your job.* Surprise. I am, and you're not helping!

I am continually returned to the state of abashment, to destroy the self-possession or self-confidence of my integrity and experience of my job. Someone who enters and alights before I have a chance to answer and complains of discourtesy. A motorist rushes ahead, only to block the lane to wait for a parking space. A "fixie" on his bike who passes on the right, only to block a right turn on red. An assigned penalty in a love letter that proposes no solution. The other reason for this book is to respond to the continual bombardment from the press, the public, and those in authority of our operators' response, "Try a week, *a day* behind the wheel, and *then* tell me what you think!"

In the past twenty-one years, I have received feedback from passengers, coworkers, and other newer operators, and I hope this follow-up compilation sequel answers the questions I still get about issues or topics not in *Finding Zen*. A hearing just used above, for example, is that first part of progressive discipline between manager, the union representative, and self that tries to follow due process in leading to the penalty box. These tales are presented here so you don't have to go through the house of pain.

Fortunately, there are classes on a regular basis in the training department that keep the information fresh. I have collision-avoidance training (accident review), VTT class (verified transit training), and requalification, REQUAL, after not having been behind the wheel for sixty days. This public transportation guide is just another point of information to get me, the bus driver, and you, the riding public, on the same page. To get us empowered to change the system and make it cheaper, easier, and faster. Most politicians in this country do not ride transit and are stuck in their cars. It is no wonder nothing ever changes—they don't understand what path, or Dao, they choose not to take.

When I see the small coincidence of right action and joy around me on the bus and on the street, I get such a smile and a laugh and realize I am in the right place at the right time.

This book and the essays within its chapters are from intense passions released in the never dull moments of driving a ten-ton vehicle under overhead wires in San Francisco. The life of a trolley operator contains so much challenge I don't ever need to look elsewhere to stay on my toes. Being sequestered in my apartment and ordered to stay at home has given me the time to rewrite, edit, and condense my anecdotal stories as a transit operator over the past twenty-one years. This book compiles the best of the Dao of Doug series: 1) *The Dao of Doug: Finding Zen in San Francisco Transit: A Bus Driver's Perspective* (2012), revised (2016); 2) *The Dao of Doug 2: Keeping Zen in San Francisco Transit: A Line Trainer's Guide* (2015), revised (2016); 3) *The Trolleybus of Happy Destiny* (2018).

Thank you for reading! Thank you for riding! www.daoofdoug.com

First Stop and Getting Started

WHEN I PULL OUT IN THE MORNING, I ALWAYS SMILE AND SAY HELLO TO my first customer. I try to make this an important barometer for how the day will go. The greeting gives me an instant check-in to see where I am at in my head and whether I am present to be of service. The job gives great paychecks, but I have always followed the precept *do what you like, and the money will follow.* I do know that placing service first is my best action to create job security. I am not surprised to admit that I may not be following this belief for more than half the time I spend behind the wheel. Most of my actions become subconscious, which is great from a Zen point of view, but it takes considerable effort to get back to a *service-first* mode when I am running late and heavy.

I was jotting down ideas for chapters, and this one popped into my head as I was doing pre-op on track 12. I would add chapter idea headings into a blank notepad in my shirt pocket—then add them to my netbook. If I ever had a block against writing, I could use those notes as a starting point to get my juices flowing.

I had a blank as to what I was thinking when I put it in "Getting Started." It could mean anything—waking up before coffee; getting to the bus stop to take a twenty-two to the barn; signing in on the daily pullout coach assignment; finding the yard starter; calling Central Control and telling them I am blocked on track 4; running back to the tower to see if I could get someone from the shop to stop an air leak; or getting out of restricted mode, just getting the coach to move or getting the doors to open.

I remembered my tears as I was trying to make it to the gate to pull out. My collectors had not been reset when someone dewired pulling on to track 12 last night. I didn't know how much leeway the wheel had against the wash rack, and I cut the turn too fast and too sharp and got caught in the wires. After finally coaxing the poles out of the web, I put them back on the wires, only to dewire again. I needed to be at Eleventh and Mission in five minutes and wasn't going to make it. I began crying because I wasn't even out of the gate and was already an emotional wreck.

A couple of times, maybe three, I went through three coaches before I pulled out. Finding a coach that is okay can be a game of musical chairs. As soon as I remember the wisdom of being Zen is kept when I throw out the schedule or try to maintain the schedule, I immediately relax. You could ask me a question about where I go if I am in the Zen. Thankfully, the SFMTA has purchased an entire fleet of new trolleybuses since this chapter was written in 2012, and there is little hunting and pecking for equipment since 2018. Several chapters in my first book were not included in this *Best of Dao* compilation because hot-body, low-air, reduced performance warnings are gone.

But getting started could be when the alarm goes off in the morning. did I get enough rest last night? Am I too stiff? Waking up with a crick in the neck is just awful—especially if I must turn my head your head to the right to observe boarding passengers. I must check the condition my body is in when I wake up because I have learned the hard way that if I don't take care of myself, I could be in for a bad day. Nothing is worse than being tired behind the wheel of a bus in a busy city. So getting started could actually be about how we approach the day when we first wake up. Getting on a regular sleep cycle, when I don't even need an alarm, is a good indication that I will be in the Zen zone for most of the time in the seat.

The great thing about the first stop and the first passenger is that none of the burdens of being late or overwhelmed usually exist. I always try to find a start time that doesn't put me behind the eight ball from the get-go. There are certain quirks in the schedule that place cut-in coaches at a disadvantage at the first terminal. At the first terminal, I may have to pull poles to let the follower regain leader headway. With the cuts to recovery time (2009, 2010), the leader may not have any wiggle room to relax and break before heading out from that terminal. Recovery time at the outbound terminal doesn't usually allow for enough time to go to the bathroom until after 10:00 a.m.

Sometimes it is easier to trail blaze ahead and keep the follower less busy, so he or she can make better time to arrive at the next terminal with some recovery time. These nuances do influence how I feel when I get to my first terminal and, hence, shorten or lengthen my temper when picking up those first few passengers at the first stop.

I found out that I am not a rush hour downtown bus driver. I am a crosstown guy who avoids being on that inbound trip at 8:30 a.m. or that 5:15 p.m. trip outbound. Crosstown is where it's at for me. The Muni meaning behind "doing homework" means checking out the paddles to see where the run is in the morning and in the afternoon. People always ask me what the bad line is. I say there are no bad lines— only bad leaving times. Would I really like being on a run that leaves the Ferry Plaza at 5:05 p.m., especially if there are tunnel problems? Or would I rather be in Daly City leaving in the nonpeak direction with a few babysitters or house cleaners returning home?

Would I rather be leaving the industrial area near Dogpatch on the 22 after 5:00 p.m. or in the Marina hours after school has let out?

Does my run leave Fillmore and Bay five minutes after the bell rings at the largest middle school in the system, or would I already be on the road ten minutes away from the school, heading up the hill past Union? At Muni, just like in stand-up comedy, timing is key.

Not a Bus—A Person Driving a Bus

ONE OF THE MOST FRUSTRATING ASPECTS IN THE BUSTLE AND TUSSLE OF a large, dense city is just missing a connection. This chapter is for the regular transit rider who may still be missing transfers to another bus that can be averted by one simple rule: your desire to catch that trolleybus hinges not on the caricature of one massive entity called a Municipal Transit Agency but rather on an individual seated behind the wheel of a car. Yes, we call coaches or cars by their number, and it is okay to call a bus a car, such as car number 5505. If you are aware of car numbers, chances are you have a good handle on understanding the system. If your awareness extends to run number, car number, cap number, and line number, then your status is elevated to that of a Muni god. By reading this book, you, too, can be elevated unto that heavenly status. Gods can get angry. Gods can cause major damage. Gods can cause a rush of change. But when they are benevolent as angels, good things can happen!

Most of us have been given the incorrect model on how to effect change. Heck, I can't even spell the distinction correctly! Do you desire an effect or an affect? I believe that expending a burst of loud, hostile energy is a fast way to make change happen—or I can harbor anger for years, yet nothing changes. I become comfortable with my anger and nurse it and polish it into a fine object, such that it can become attractive to all who encounter. I know I have loved my deepest and longest-held resentments against a large organization and telling you about these over happy hour!

Now, however, I write these down on my inventory list with a recovery sponsor. My most exciting challenge is to take this wonderfully polished and shiny resentment about missed transfers into a missive about the approaches to catching a bus and the mistakes people make in doing so.

If you are on a one-shot deal, then all I can give you are the facial expressions or body language that cause me to wait for you and hope that they work on a transfer you may never have to make again.

The Wounded Kitty

Aw, poor baby. Are you all alone on the corner without a warm, dry bus for shelter? This works if I have room and time and I know there is no bus behind me. A smile at the last-minute works great if timed correctly. A Homer Simpson "Doh" or one loud, profane exclamation also works if timed just as the front door passes by. This works great when traffic is light or nonexistent. Twilights and Sundays are good times for wounded kitty. If not young and pretty, a sigh of sadness with quivering cane uplifted to an invisible Kaiser also works. Dropping the shoulders Charlie Brown style after "Lucy" also works wonderfully. But note that these all require the eye contact of acknowledging that it is a person driving a bus and not just a bus.

The Plea Bargain

This was used in the movie *Speed*. Annie makes it to the doomed bus as Sam the bus driver jokes that this boarding point is not at the bus stop. I have expanded this with the train and plane analogy of questions. "Where do you catch a train?" "At a train station." "Where to get on a plane?" "On a jetway at an airport." "And where do we get a bus?" Some of you latecomers are so puffed up with pride you may never get on a bus. But if you pronate yourself as if praying to the Muni god of nigh, the transit operator, grace has been known to open the back door (occasionally). This would be a good chapter for a movie. I wish I could call up some clips on the plea bargain. The plea bargain can come silently with the eyes or with a huge, loud, profane word! The more over the top, the better!

The Dignitary

Only works with blessed folk. Those who attend church regularly and have a comfortable sense of self-righteousness that does not infringe on others. Those who pray regularly without self-centered fear can stop a bus from any location just by a simple turn of the head and a smile. It is always a wonderful rush to pick up someone like this. Quality, not quantity, is the Dao of this pickup.

The Lost Puppy

Unfortunately, these are most dramatic and visceral because of their stand-alone nature. If you are traveling from the East Bay for a job interview, for example, and are new to the system, the time you are allowing for transfers may be inadequate. The image of successfully dashing across the street to a streetcar from a trolley is easy to get, especially if you have heard our service is frequent. As you become familiar with the transfers, transit time can be reduced, such that a trip that may have taken two hours and twenty minutes can be shaved down to forty-five minutes.

I am aware of the places where intending passengers ask me for a destination behind me. On crosstown routes, we see that by a BART station, people board buses going in the opposite direction that they need to reach their destination.

If you have been given an address, it is important to search this on a map system so you have a good idea about which corner you need to wait at. There can be four different lines on each corner, with the same bus line going in two different directions on either side. Such is the case at Jackson and Fillmore, where people chronically wait on Fillmore instead of Jackson to take an outbound 24 to the Castro Station.

Have It Ready

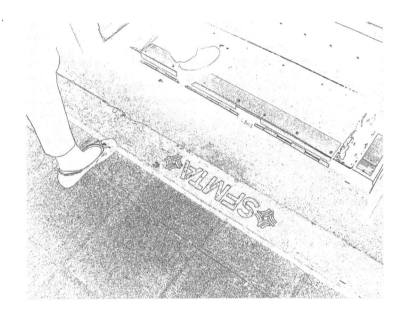

SOME OF THE REGULARLY OCCURRING DELAYS ARE THOSE BOARDING passengers who cannot locate their pass or change. Their fumble to locate the pass takes many forms: unable to pull the pass out of a pocket from behind a jacket; the pass is in a clip or wallet that is too fat for the pocket opening; the pass around their neck on a lanyard is tucked tightly behind a jacket that has tough snaps or zippers. Making transit free would eliminate all these delays.

Some of these flash presentations are hilarious—or frustrating, such as not knowing where the transfer is. True, the transfer paper is extremely thin and very hard to find when you don't remember where you put it. But oh, the drama: not having the fare counted or not knowing the fare; not having a Clipper card with money on it; having more than one Clipper card in the wallet and triggering the shutdown alarm; having a bank card or other magnetic strip rendering the Clipper card inactive; displaying an invalid fare; dropping money or belongings on the floor, down the steps, or out the door; dropping tobacco leaves or clothing threads or hair in the coin drop; placing folded bills in the coin drop—sliding dimes into the bill meter. *What were you doing while you were waiting for the bus to come?*

Having torn, folded, or worn bills that are not accepted by the bill meter. Blocking the passengers behind them that are ready and have the fare. Blocking others trying to ask a question about where I go. Running in to someone trying to tag in behind them. Stopping at the door and blocking by asking questions about where I go or what I do. Having their bag or purse slide down their arm and knock the money out of their hand before finishing paying the fare. Holding too many objects, such as a cane, a shopping bag, and a purse while trying to use one hand to pay the fare. Walking by, saying nothing, showing nothing. And all of these above examples can occur at just one stop, such as Sixteenth and Mission!

The stoplight changes, and a UCSF shuttle pulls in front of the coach to block my pullout—or an ambulance arrives and shuts down the intersection, or fixed-gear cyclists pull past the stop line and block the crosswalk so that the cars that have now passed me turn in front of me and are blocked by the cyclists doing their prance dance, standing on the crank to prevent imbalance. (Being a cyclist myself, I always make sure I am not blocking cars from making a right on red.)

Muni trolleys now have in a tag-in device located to the left of all doors as you enter. Now in credit card form as a plastic Clipper card, monthly fast passes, cash, and other forms of fare can be discarded with a quick swipe or tag in at the door. Right. Sure. And now all forms of fare evasion are healed. Not quite.

I could see early on that with this technology, once it caught on and became familiar with the masses, boarding would be made much easier. Only problem was in the learning curve of the first phase of passengers and operators to become aware of the nuances of using this Clipper card to keep the flow when boarding.

I knew there would be problems, and so when some problem kept coming up frequently, I would choose those moments when Zen pervaded the coach and my attention to ask the passenger what was going on with their card when an unsuccessful tag was being shown on my dashboard screen.

I found out that there were delays in crediting payment. Riders with multiple agency payments, such as BART and Muni, had to tag in more than once to verify ID. If a person was pay as you go on BART and had the non-BART monthly pass on Muni, their card would read as blocked or low funds unless they tagged in again. Since being quick to judge someone who is evading fare has never worked for me at the fare box, I was sure I would take this tag-in message as not necessarily correct with regards to payment. Being wrong at first blush creates an added emotional hassle with passenger relations that need not be.

If I took the position in my mind that all passengers were trying to get one over on the new system and that they intentionally knew that they were trying to get on free, things would not go well, and I would learn nothing. In those rare cases when a boarder tried to explain something or ask a question about the Clipper card, I stayed open to find out what the history was behind their getting the card and why their card was not beeping normally.

Sure enough, when a card had two different payment forms from two different agencies, a second tag was needed; the card reader could only read one payment form at a time, and the default read may not be Muni. Riders who used AC transit in the East Bay fell into this category. There were also delays in payment credit with the cards. Just because someone went to pay their bill online or at a convenience store did not mean it would read correctly at the gate instantly.

Aside from the low funds messages, there were other nonpayment warnings. *Blocked* and *Not Permitted* were two other messages that were warning of nonpayment. When in Zen, I waited to choose my battles wisely. I found out what was really going on. *Not Permitted* was from a passenger that purchased a paper card reader from the underground Metro system and had already tagged a second time on a surface coach. The paper card issued from the underground system would not allow a pass back message after one transfer had been used. This jibed with what I knew about the older turn style receipts issued before the new gate system was installed. *Blocked* came up when a card was reported lost or stolen or a newer card by the holder was issued.

I found out why people had more than one card in their wallet. The problem was that when they had more than one card in their wallet and they tagged in without taking a single card out of their billfold, the system went down or sounded a loud alarm. When they tagged in again, everything was okay.

I found out the second tag was from another card. I started looking at what they were doing when the second tag was okay. Getting the mirrors just right took some doing because most folks would block a direct view of where their hands and card were by standing between me and the reader. New riders were the best at showing me what they were doing. Blocking my view is a characteristic of fare evaders, so it took some doing to find out if blocking my view was intentional or not. By asking those who were open and friendly, I found out that they carried two cards because they were having problems with low funds warnings on the first tag-in. They also realized that having more than one payment option from two separate agencies like BART and Muni created problems with the tag in.

So now I had most of the reasons why a bad tag in was occurring and why there were plausible reasons why the passenger did not know why an error was occurring. I could move on to the problem of people bumping in to one another when they paid the fare and moved back down the aisle.

As a rule of thumb, each trip we make on a line is about forty-five minutes long, with a ten-minute recovery. On longer lines, such as the 14 Mission trip, the length is fifty-five minutes with a five-minute chance to go to the bathroom. So each lap down and back takes an hour. Our transfers are printed so that a rider has two hours from time of purchase to use the transfer to take another bus on another line that crosses the bus line on which they start.

Since our trips only last for half of this time, there should be ample time to take another bus even if you board at terminal A and go all the way to terminal B. A two-hour transfer time is double the time it takes us to make one trip from Daly City to the Ferry Plaza, or from Dogpatch to Marina Green. No brainer, right? Nah.

Many riders believe that they should be able to board, get off, run errands, go to a meeting, see a friend, and then have the time to go back for a round trip. If the time spent at a meeting or errand is an hour or more, it becomes clear one transfer won't hack it in making it back to the original boarding point. I usually ask them to consider buying a fast pass—no change, no looking for coins, no running out of time. The response is, "I don't ride enough to make it worthwhile."

"Fast track on the right, please. Clipper on the left. Please form two lines." This is a good announcement to make at big stops and transfer points to get the flow going and reduce boarding times. Exact change folks at the fare box to the right of the steps, and Clipper card taggers to the left of the steps gets two lines going and cuts zone delays in half.

Holding the transfer becomes an artform. How riders hold the transfer is immediately read by the operator and is key to how fast you board and whether or not you will be asked for your fare. Most people obscure part of the transfer when they hold it so it is impossible to tell if the fare displayed is valid. Add to that, most people don't show the transfer in a reasonable zone to see it, much less read it.

The first trick of evasion is holding the transfer, wrapping your hand on the bottom like a flower in a vase, so the cutoff time is not visible. The second trick is to thumb over the date so an expired day is not visible. And my favorite is the use of two transfers together, both expired but held together between the thumb and pointer, so that the day and time are displayed and appear correct. The big challenge is to call this one correctly, especially at a big stop where there are many boarders. I always get a charge out of catching this one—not by being tripped up by the clowns who try to make it look like they are doing the two-step but have a valid fare. This is the downside. The holder is hoping you call them on the fare so they can browbeat you by being discriminatory. When I state, "Three dollars please." The neutral tone of voice quells the battle for the fare.

When buses are missing and headway or waiting time increases, it can become very unclear to those standing at or near multiple-line bus stops why the bus passes by. All the frantic yelling and screaming is moot if you are no longer in the scanning range of the operator or outside the zone. *The scanning range of an operator is one to two blocks ahead of the direction of travel.* Once the front door passes by where you stand, lucky is the day that the bus stops. And I do appreciate your thanks when I do stop. But stopping is the exception to the rule when I am late and full.

If no one rings to get off and the bus is full, the bus doesn't stop. It becomes important to see how full a bus is as it approaches. Looking away on a cell phone or talking to someone else and facing away from the direction of travel all compound the chance of a bus not stopping if no request to stop is made on board on a crowded bus. *These are the unwritten rules of not wanting a bus:* if you are not facing the operator as the bus is a half a block away, and you are alone, and you are on Van Ness or Mission, we usually will not stop. In San Francisco, there are so many passing by, or standing, or sleeping (or whatever) in the shelter; we have learned to look at your hands to see if you are holding the fare. This is called *looking for those who are ready.*

So baby stops, not at a light or far side from the cross street, are not equal to major transfer points nearside at a stoplight. Increasing your odds for pickup become relevant if no bus is seen coming or you see the taillights of a bus just having gone by.

So as to having it ready. As this is just one stop on one line at one light, it doesn't take much to see that paying the fare really slows things down and leads to buses bunching together and running off of schedule. Getting to this understanding helps me and those at the door get into the Zen of Muni.

Crunch Zone

I PICKED UP A MAN IN A WHEELCHAIR NEAR DOWNTOWN AT THIRD Street outbound and was amazed at how smooth and fast he boarded and locked in. I could tell he was a regular rider. Instinctively, I knew he was going to get off at Sixteenth and Mission, and sure enough, when I asked, he stated he was going to Sixteenth. I told him I was glad to have a regular rider who knew how to ride Muni. He talked about his learning curve on how to work the flip-up seats and about where to get on and get off. If there was any heartfelt strength of purpose to distribute this book to the masses, it is not about the money or the power in the vanity of being an author but *to get out the wisdom in how to ride so that the bus system moves faster and creates less headache* for those in getting around. Nowhere is this wisdom needed more than in the crunch zone.

I at first wanted to call this chapter "Crunch Time," such as the operation of a bus from 3:30 p.m. to 6:30 p.m. However, the pattern of movement between two stops was as predictable as the time frame, and I realized a more accurate description of gridlock was in certain zones between stops. The idea for this chapter was born in the conversation with this wheelchair rider as he glided away from downtown with me in a coach that was calm and roomy. I found out he wanted to go up Van Ness to Geary but was passing up the transfer point by four blocks. I know why. He was avoiding having to board Muni in the *crunch zone*.

On the 14 line Mission bus, the crunch zone exists between Sixteenth Street and Seventh inbound—and Fourth and Eleventh outbound. The sequence of events is so repetitive and coincidental that one could plot a graph of predictability on an actuarial table for an insurance company. Come to think of it, the city of San Francisco *is* an insurance company for Muni! I don't know how this would help with claims, but like this man who was on my coach, avoiding the problem areas makes for an easy ride, even if it means traveling beyond the shortest distance between two points.

Indeed, I found this out as a rider in my thirties, new to the city in the 1980s. In getting to my warehouse in Hunter's Point and Bayview from the Tenderloin, the shortest route was the 19 Polk. But the fastest way was to go inbound on the Geary bus to catch a 15 Third. I made a large check mark inbound to outbound rather than go crosstown direct. This is true of the crunch zones between the 49 Van Ness and the 14 Mission. Especially for a rider in a wheelchair, carrying a large, cumbersome object, or using a grocery cart. Also, if riders have difficulty in getting up the stairs or need a seat right by the door, oddly enough, the best offense is the defense of traveling beyond the closest stop to your destination—backtracking to board where the bus is less crowded.

The crunch zone for the 49 Van Ness builds as the bus moves inbound to the streets numbered in the teens, until at Fourteenth Street, where room runs out and there is nowhere to sit or stand. Cyclists, walkers, and those receiving food bank items filling a grocery cart all wait in the crunch zone. If there are two coaches bunched together, usually all is well. But if there are gaps between buses, frequently a pass-up prevents crowding problems.

On the 49 line, the crunch zone lies between Sixteenth Street and Eddy inbound, and from O'Farrell to Otis outbound. Load factors and working leaders influence the zone by making it longer or shorter, but in general, I know I have to make sure people boarding do the right thing by sitting or standing in such a way to prevent fights or arguments at the following stops. Crunch zones also lie in El Corazon de la Mission, between Eighteenth and Thirtieth outbound in the afternoon—or before Twenty-Fourth St. BART inbound in the morning commute. *People listen better before their space is threatened.* This is a golden key to the crunch zone.

I, too, am in a better vibe and tone if I ask someone to move before the crunch zone hits. And when those who have moved see that those I next pick up need the first two seats, the message has hit home in a way that is not threatening or defensive. Score one for the Zen!

Morning Rush

WHILE *GETTING KILLED* ON THE 1 CALIFORNIA LINE ON THE RUN FROM hell, I noticed that Tuesdays were awful. I passed up over two hundred people on my peak inbound trip to get downtown by 9:02 a.m. I never sign on a run that goes downtown without looking at its morning peak arrival time. Think about it. Would you choose to show up at the Ferry Plaza or the Embarcadero at 9:02 a.m. or 8:32 a.m.? If considering the passengers' routines and getting ready for work, and knowing what I know, what time would I like to be driving folks to work? I know that I try to cut it as close as I can and get away with still making it downtown, or wherever I need to be, without wasting any time. The image of efficiency is to take the bus without any waiting time. Making a multi-pass mandatory for riding public transit with a prepaid card helps.

Just like a *Mad* magazine comic strip, if we are all making the same determinations at the same time, we invariably create our own hell. And so what I came to believe from the run from hell was to note what time was the point of no return for folks not able to make it the elevator to work before the clock strikes nine. And I found, down to the minute, that someone walking out their door at 8:22 a.m. in the avenues of Twenty-Two and Twenty-Three could not make it to work in time downtown. The last express just passes by at 8:21 a.m., and my coach would fill to the brim before I even got to Park Presidio, which is around Fourteenth Avenue. If someone walked out the door by 8:15 a.m., they stood a chance to make it to work on time, but they were still risking it. Indeed, the window of vulnerable time was actually about six minutes, which coincidentally was the headway between coaches, and this time window seemed, at first, to be a plausible time to allow for getting downtown. It seems reasonable to make it downtown in forty-two minutes from Twenty-Second Avenue.

Not when the system is challenged to peak capacity, when many are traveling in the same direction at the same time to get to a destination that is within a few blocks of one another. The many new tall buildings downtown have made a mess of trying to catch a bus after 8:20 a.m. from the avenues or from beyond Masonic Avenue. Pass-ups become frequent during this time, as there is simply not enough capacity to bring that large of a swarm of people to work by 9:00 a.m. on the dot.

I started looking at the passenger loads of buses that were to arrive downtown by 9:00 a.m. And sure enough, the passenger load was very telling. A bus arriving downtown at 9:15 a.m. or 9:22 a.m. was much emptier that one scheduled to arrive on or before 9:00 a.m.

Crosstown routes were another matter. Crosstown coaches were less influenced by the peak period flux, but their drop-offs at transfer points were critical for inbound downtown coaches.

My leader, God bless him, was able to escape past the transfer points before those coaches dropped off their passengers trying to transfer to get downtown. And this transfer cost had a lot to do with whether people could make it to work on time or whether they stood waiting for a downtown-bound coach that was already too crowded to take on any new transfer passengers. I also came to believe that it might be impossible for scheduling to try to take all this in account and place extra buses during this witching hour. The bottom line I came to realize is that if individuals found that they could not make the trip in a timely fashion, they would have to move up at least ten or twenty minutes to avoid the bind. The supposed injustice of this model is that at some point after 8 a.m., the time it would take to get where you needed to go was much longer than someone leaving the house at, say, 7:30 a.m. And so, if there was some magic wand I could wave to business leaders to make the perception of Muni doing its job and running on time, it would be to stagger work start times in fifteen-minute increments, so that no one large group of people would be required to clock in at one specific time.

The patterns of going home do seem to support this idea. I noticed that although the start time for people going to work was relatively cut-and-dried, the time people leave work is spread out over a longer time frame, as people may do other tasks before they get on the bus, or they could work a little bit longer than others, and the dramatic impact was slightly lighter than in the morning. Also, because there was no deadline to get home in the afternoon, as there was to get to work in the morning, that more relaxed attitude helped make a better environment for the bus driver in the afternoon rush. Usually.

O grasshopper, the five greens of happiness are a wonder to behold when leaving Embarcadero Building 3 at Davis and Sacramento on the 1 California! I was blessed with a leaving time of 4:58 p.m., and I could make it to Kearny at the foot of Chinatown before the masses descended from the downtown towers at 5:00 p.m. Begin my turn at 4:57 p.m., and I am gaining extra green lights and five more blocks!

My follower turned into a major crybaby about leaving time, believing I was intentionally making his life hell by leaving early. My *escape velocity*, with a leaving time only four minutes ahead of his 5:02 p.m., made a huge difference in passenger load. If I left one minute early, as I can do without getting in trouble, this made the difference in whether I could make the five greens of happiness: green lights at Davis, Front, Battery, Sansome, and Montgomery. If I had less than six people at Montgomery, I could make Kearny just as this light, too, would turn green. Because I reached Montgomery at 5:04 p.m. or as late as 5:06 p.m., the number of intenders would change and thus reduce predictability of a green at Kearny. *Hallelujah, mother of pearl*, this difference was not too fretful because I had passed the area of tall buildings on the flats.

The downtown area is built on the carcasses of old wooden vessels of all types. Boats were sunk, and the bay was filled in to create downtown as it now stands. Montgomery Street was on the old shoreline, and you can detect this subtle difference as the land begins to rise from this point outbound. Chinatown's Portsmouth Square is on the old shoreline. This is where the shot heard round the world was made by US Army General Sheridan, "There's gold in them hills!" The gold rush has been replaced by the daily outbound-transit, peak-period rush—away from work downtown!

All of the small, old, brick, turn-of-the-century buildings above Montgomery are of a different era than the skyscrapers that shoot skyward from Montgomery all the way down to the Ferry Plaza. Commercial Alley is the last reminder of where the dock extended all the way out to where Ferry Plaza now stands. If you stand on Kearny at Commercial and look toward the new shoreline, you will see the first steel-reinforced building of our city and the clock tower atop the Ferry Building. Saving this view was intentional when designing the Embarcadero office complex.

The five Embarcadero buildings architects' genius included an open walkway between the towers, from Chinatown to Justin Herman Plaza, so the historic walkway remains. Designed in the mid to late 1960s, these five buildings proudly display their outlines with white Christmas lights during the holidays. They appear fresh and modern as any other newer building in town. The plaza tile is kept immaculate and looks like it was laid last year, even though this complex is now over forty years old.

Imitating computer chips or boards stacked vertically together in parallel, staggered fashion, they presaged San Francisco's tech importance with a style and design that fits in perfectly today. You can look down Commercial from Chinatown and see the Ferry Building, just as you can see it when you look down Market Street from the Union Square area. Indeed, one of the joys of being a transit operator is the breathtaking beauty that appears in many places on many lines.

On the 1 California, seeing the sunrise from Nob Hill and Jones as the street plunges to the old shoreline energizes a gratitude of living in one of the most beautiful cities in the world. My other favorite vistas on Muni are seeing Alcatraz at Leavenworth on the 45 Union. Alignment of the penitentiary view with Leavenworth Street may be a coincidence hard to ignore from an inmate's view! Cresting Lone Mountain inbound on the 5 Fulton at the University of San Francisco at sunrise is also breathtaking. Saint Ignatius's twin towers stand majestic to be seen for miles around.

The crosstown routes, such as the 24 Divisadero, have many such vistas—between Waller and Duboce as Castro Street becomes Divisadero, at Duncan and Noe, and at Jackson and Pierce. Atop Liberty Hill, the Castro can be seen inbound after crossing Twenty-Second Street. The 22 Fillmore has a great panorama of the downtown skyline crossing 280 Freeway at Pennsylvania and Eighteenth entering Dogpatch from Potrero Hill outbound. The alignment of the Sacred Heart tower on Fell is first glimpsed when passing Jackson and Fillmore after passing Mrs. Doubtfire's house on Steiner at Broadway. There are stunning views everywhere! With forty-three hills over forty-nine square miles, a vista is never too far away.

Choosing a run on the 1 California in the afternoon with the five greens of happiness is a blessing to behold and cemented my mastery of the Presidio Barn runs. For me, choosing the 30 Stockton in the morning and the 1 California in the afternoon was the smart choice. Doing the 1 in the morning and the 30 in the afternoon was not my cup of tea. Pass-ups on the 1 and traffic on Third Street along with the trash trucks blocking a lane in Chinatown after 6:00 p.m. made for a long day.

All the produce refuse is collected on the last day shift trip on the 30 Stockton, and this can be a drag after a long twelve-hour range in the seat. I timed this down to the minute when leaving Cal Train on Townsend. I had to leave on time, not later than forty-one minutes after the hour, if I was to make Sacramento outbound before the first trash truck turned on to Stockton from Grant Street at 6:10 p.m. *I am writing this chapter ten years after I did this run, and I still recall the time down to the minute!* The express service has improved since this publication—and rapid service on the 9 San Bruno and 14 Mission has been added.

Chinatown is reduced to one lane if two opposing trash trucks are nearby, and this can be intense. I quickly learned to put away any stress I may encounter at the beginning of the shift, such that as time wore on in the shift, things would get easier. Finding the five greens of happiness was the final confirmation I found Zen while driving a trolley on the 1 California.

And my tip to those up-and-comers working downtown, or those looking to ask for a raise, show up early and get a lot more work done when the office is quiet. And then relax toward the afternoon when everyone is just playing spider solitaire or surfing the web at their desks anyway. You may find your ride on the bus is much more pleasant when not on the ball and chain schedule of those arriving downtown by 9:00 a.m. I'll bet your productivity would skyrocket if you came in two hours early to get stuff done without constant distractions. Do not do it every day, mind you, but I am surprised at how much easier my commute trip is in the morning and afternoon when you stagger your days by working at home. Tuesday is the new Monday—Thursday the new Friday.

In San Francisco, we do have sort of a split workforce. Many traders in the market or manning the screens for trades are set on East Coast time, and so they arrive early to work and get off around 3:00 p.m. These guys do seem a lot happier than the ball and chain nine-to-fivers. And when they get on the bus in the morning, sometimes with tie in hand, you can't always tell if they have had their coffee. In any event, if your morning commute is not working, try something different.

I have seen the creatures of habit who are just miserable. Those who can work from home and only go downtown a couple times a week have forever changed onboard riding traffic.

Since the publication of this chapter in my first book, *Finding Zen in San Francisco Transit, A Bus Driver's Perspective,* in 2012, the express lines on California do not stop inbound after 8:15 a.m. In fact, a whole new division has been added for primarily express service!

Placing the Doors
(Split Doors Stopping Starting)

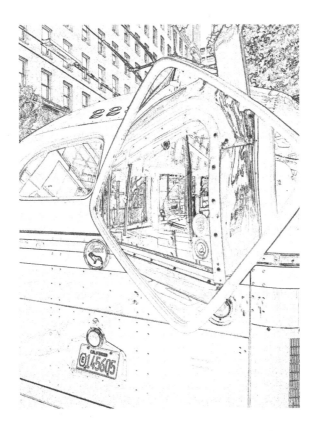

IF PEOPLE KNEW THE DYNAMICS OF OUR PULLING IN AND OUT OF THE BUS
stop zone, they would know where to stand. This would save a lot of
time and cause the bus to run on time more frequently. Aside from
being ready with the fare, where people stand is probably the next
biggest influence on keeping to a timetable. And the best way I, as an

operator, can plus or minus the time I spend in the zone is where I place the door. Safety and door placement over the curb become mandatory when those needing assistance are waiting or getting off.

One of the most challenging aspects that takes its toll on my body is trying to maintain a smooth start and stop, particularly on a hill. All coaches are not equal. To maintain an even stop on a hill, some coaches require 40 to 60 percent more force on the pedal, and then, at 3 mph, where the dynamic brake kicks in, an abrupt off-pedal feather to prevent a lurch. Slack brakes are what cause the abrupt lurch after the air brake disengages right before the full stop. On a heavy day with many hills, this can cause my calf or hamstring muscles to complain. In order to keep hearing "Thank you" when passengers alight, much torque force and muscle tension must be applied in a regular, staccato, repetitive manner. If the time behind the seat is for more than four hours without a break and I am missing a leader, this makes it difficult to walk up the stairs after work! Keeping my body from falling apart as I add on the mileage over the years of driving a bus is definitely a challenge. I want to be able to stay at work and be in the Zen zone!

The secret to knowing where to stand is to *look for the stencil on the red line*. The SFMTA star or the white writing on the curb that says, "Bus stop" are the number one predictors of where the front door will be placed. If you really want to be the first to board, stand by the stencil and wave your hand *when the bus is a block away.* You should increase your chances of being by the door to well over 50 percent. Most people are unaware of this and are also unaware of when we are scanning ahead to decide where to stop. If a shuttle bus, taxi, or ride share car is sharing the zone, then it's important to adjust where to stand *based upon the clearance needed for a bus* to safely pull away and to keep away from the temporary obstacle.

Most people do not understand this adjustment and continue to stand without regard to what other vehicles are loading or unloading nearby. Also, they become moving targets. *A moving target is much harder to hit.* Ha-ha. In this case, I mean people flag us correctly from the curb, and then they move—trying to guess by our reduced velocity where we are going to come to rest.

My coach placement also sends signals about whether I am full or empty or running ahead of schedule or running late. If a bus seems to pull too far forward than usual, look behind the bus to see if there is another one following close behind. This is my signal another bus is coming soon and may be less crowded—no one standing in the aisle and with seats for seniors. Good luck!

I have largely failed in this endeavor. It took me over seven years to get this, and it came from an instructor with much experience. He questioned why I was overthinking where to place the door. He said it was always a no-brainer and implied that it should be the same every day. This jolted me awake from my complacency coma. I never considered that my door placement should be the same every time. When I looked at the bus stop as a never-changing or fixed object, I made the decision to look for where the safest place was to stop irrespective of where the people were standing. *I had always adjusted where I put my door based on where the people were standing, not on where I wanted to place it.*

This information was brought to me after I had an accident and was on a retraining coach. After an operator is charged with an accident, we are assigned to a morning class, then go out with the division instructor who observes and grades our performance (collision avoidance class). I never thought of this as a waste of time and always looked for what new tidbit I would receive that might prevent any future accident. Sure enough, by being consistent in where I thought the best place for the door was, my threats reduced. When stopped in the zone correctly, maximum rear view is obtained, and collision risk goes down significantly.

Sometimes when the bus is very crowded and there are many people waiting on a busy corridor, people get stuck on the front steps. If a group of people are only half on the bus, some in the party go to the back door, but if the front door clears first and the back doors shut, the bus takes off, and those who ran to the back door don't get on. *Many times, our rear mirror visibility is blocked if someone is moving to the rear on the sidewalk just outside of our narrow curb view.* This results in a split group. Usually, the party on the bus near the front door demands to get off immediately, which may not be safe or possible after having pulled into heavy traffic, such as on Van Ness, which is also US Highway 101, from Mission Street to Lombard Street. Under these conditions, it is difficult for me as an operator to determine who is in what party and if I have cut a group in half. Having been familiar with the 30 Stockton in Chinatown, I look for a break in the bodies so I can close the doors without hitting anyone.

One would think that when the bus becomes completely gridlocked on the inside aisle, common sense by simple observation would be enough to ensure that no one intending at the bus zone would consider even getting on the bus. *One would be wrong if one thought this.* In fact, there probably is a correlation coefficient that as the number of people waiting for the bus increases, their willingness to look inside the coach and see if there is room for boarding decreases.

And this pile-on and pile-into effect is something I always hope to avoid. I can, but it means that I must pass up stops to keep from becoming so full I can't see past the yellow line. I get all sorts of help from passengers who want to help out by yelling at the group to move back or to make room for a seat for a senior, but their *help* sometimes creates more problems because of the tone of their voice or the profanity they use. It is at this time that I feel as though I am losing control of the situation; the hard part is to figure out when it is time to stop taking on more people.

This is not as simple as it would first sound, because one must figure on how many people are getting off. It is a simple math equation performed at every stop or transfer. How many did I lose and how many am I picking up? Through intuition and experience, it does become easier to know if I am going to lose more than I gain, but there are some whoops moments—I have room for six, but there are ten waiting. If I know I usually lose four or five, I should be okay and make the stop. *Uh oh, here come five people running, only one person gets off, and now the light goes red, and here comes a walker and a person with shopping bags.*

Should I have passed up the preceding stop to allow for this margin of error? Should I make the announcement that this coach is full? And will they listen to me? And this is where the ninth level of hell begins. What I can do to shut this trend down immediately is passing up the next stop.

The danger is that I don't want people waiting at the stop to see that there is room in the back and that I did not need to pass up. Once again, the equipment cannot maintain full capacity for more than an hour, and the other factor that is hidden from view is the performance of the coach under heavy loads. The idea here is to pass up when the coach is full but in a way the minimizes drama and coach failure. It is this seesaw that makes life interesting. I have to approach this the way I approach spider solitaire—through the difficult moves can come a victory all the sweeter.

The key is to size up the group in approach and to stop the bus and doors proximate to where the intending group is standing. If I have more room in the back, I can stop slightly forward of the mass, encouraging the group to enter in the rear. By clicking open all rear doors, I see those with fast passes flashing me as they board in the rear. The decals on the door to enter in the front do give tourists pause, and they migrate to the front door. Or the person paying the fare decides to come to the front door as the others in their party enter in the rear. I need to accept that those with cash fare in their hands may not come to the front door. I choose to accept the fact that I cannot see everyone's fare and consider the paying of the fare as an honor system. I am emotionally much more relaxed to do a better job and pay attention to safety.

This is why some become displeased when it appears that I am not doing my job collecting the fare. I am paying attention to avoid an accident or mishap, my highest priority, rather than spending the emotional turmoil of taking fare evasion as a personal affront. This is not always avoidable. Sometimes a person who has the cash to pay the fare tries to come to the front door, but they are blocked by people standing on the steps. The rear doors close when I see the sidewalk has cleared, and the fare payer gets left on the curb.

It also gets interesting when the luggage of the tourist, fresh off BART from the airport, gets separated during the split-doors, split-groups situation. The best way to avoid this is to keep together and wait for the next bus. If buses have been passing by completely full, panic or impatience sets in, and bad choices start to rise and contribute to getting lost in the shuffle. Kearny/Geary/Market is such a stop. Tourists need answers to questions about where I go, but this is not the time and place for twenty questions. It is especially not a good idea when other buses are behind me and a new group from the N Judah underground arise now running to my full coach. If I can get past Kearny and Market without a problem, I know I am in the Zen zone of driving Muni.

Cloak of Invisibility

IF YOU WOULD LIKE TO SEE A MAGIC TRICK OR ILLUSION PLAYED OUT DAY after day, look no further than a ride on 14 Mission. The secret of becoming invisible is to sit in a wheelchair, particularly in a large group. The more, the merrier. It matters not where you sit on the sidewalk in the wheelchair. Those intending are only interested in their own self-interest. The thought of waiting for others or considering a need other than self does not compute. We have our blinders on and don't notice the changing conditions around us, such as someone with special needs waiting or approaching the bus stop after we have arrived. In order to be helpful and of service, I need to walk that fine line in allowing those waiting to board first to awaken to see the person in the wheelchair who may be behind them or to the side. I have to be on guard with my tone of voice and how I express myself. *It is important to note that most conflict arises when approaching the front door from behind and to the right from the driver's perspective. The blind spot is larger when the doors are open, as they partially block the side and rear views when open. Hiding behind the open doors causes hurt feelings.*

I have an incredible opportunity to be a guide. Sometimes it is simpler to let those board first if the time between buses is short. If the number of those intending to ride increases beyond four or five, with more boarding in the rear, loading the chair first is best. Those who are allowed up the front steps first usually sit down in the first two chairs under the wheel well and block the aisle. Others sit down in the flip-up seats where the wheelchair needs to secure. Youth with earbuds on and others with children enter through the middle door and sit in the wheelchair area, inattentive to my request to make room. This is when I find it simpler to get up and face them with hand signals to arise. Raising the flip-up seats myself, before the chair lift is used, is the fastest way to get going if the person in the chair is alone and has no help, or if no passenger on board helps to raise the seats. Most of the time, we as operators don't have to get out to raise the seats because someone else offers to help. Other times, help is available, but few know how to pull down and away to unlock the seats to raise them for the wheelchair. This is when I need to convey patience and cheerfulness and demonstrate how to lift the seats. I choose to believe that I am lighting a candle for others—hopefully not starting a wildfire!

I am powerless to control other persons on my bus, but I also have a responsibility to all the others on the bus who need to get where they are going in a timely fashion. The biggest challenge I face today is balancing these needs without going over the top in anger and frustration—but also to keep the coach moving without a fall on board or a security incident. Humor can go a long way in diffusing a tense situation, but there are those who are so broken in spirit or illness they do not want help and are unable to think of anyone other than themselves. Humor here does not work. It is perceived as an affront.

Most riders in wheelchairs have the faculty and support they need to obtain the equipment they need to be mobile. Others are unable to walk without support or need to arrange for a special needs transit yet insist that Muni take them back and forth, unaware of the impact they are having on the line. Others insist I call the police over any small perceived trespass, without regard for the welfare of others needing to get to their destination. Unfortunately, those with aimless purpose sometimes seem to have such a large sense of entitlement. I am aghast at taming this beast. I have to say as little as possible and light the candle for another time, another place. Don't feed the pigeons.

It goes against my Gemini nature to defer and delay a conversation about choosing where to sit, and this is a main reason why I am writing this book. I hope this message gets out to those who are regular riders, so that problems go away.

A recent spate of fights over seating in the front area of the bus has me in thought about how to clear this crunch zone before it develops. As Agent Smith tells Neo in the movie *The Matrix*, "Do you hear that, Neo? It is the sound of inevitability"—not unlike a train approaching in the subway tunnel for a head-on collision! This crunch zone always occurs in the Inner Mission and by Van Ness and Market. This is a great example of where paying a fare slows down running time for public transportation.

The other cloak-of-invisibility problem I find over seating and right of way is the passenger with earbuds on occupying two seats with a coat or bag over another seat. The earbuds act as an invisibility; *you can't talk to me because I can't hear you.* I sat next to this girl who adds to drama because she takes an aisle seat, covers the window seat, and becomes unavailable for talk as the bus fills up to capacity. If someone sits down on her coat, a battle of wills can ensue. It is always a good idea to ask before entering someone's zone of personal space, as is being alert when seats are no longer available. This is a problem if you can't hear us because your earbuds are on. My overcoming the fear of losing aisle space and seats for seniors has been a long and challenging journey as a transit operator in San Francisco. When you board, especially with a bike, or when others are nearby, unhook an earbud by the fare box and keep the Zen going. Thanks!

Islands and Curbs

On Market Street, there are two places on a block to catch or pick up a bus. If you have your *Incredibles* superhero costume tights on, you should know the newer ETI Skoda trolleys weigh about ten tons sans passengers, so be careful you don't pull your back muscles when you catch the approaching bus and lift it above your head. For most of us mortals, however, taking a bus on the curb or on an island is recommended. The curb stops are located midblock, and the island stops are near an intersection by a corner or a cross street. Unbeknownst to most San Franciscans, however, is a method to the madness of these two sets of stops. *Island stops outbound take you south of Golden Gate Park to the Sunset, and curb stops located midblock take you outbound to the Richmond, which is north of Golden Gate Park.* So if you were heading to Cliff House, Lake Street, Land's End, or the Legion of Honor, you would move to a curb stop after exiting a BART station under Market Street. These destinations are north of Golden Gate Park.

The 5, 21, 31, 38, and 38R all go to the residential area (the Richmond) between the Presidio and Golden Gate Park. The 6, 7, 7R, 9, and 9R stop on the outbound islands at an intersection on Market and take you to the Inner Sunset or points south of GG Park.

The 9, 9R services the Bayview, Visitacion Valley area by diverging off of Market just before Van Ness. The point is all these buses eventually leave Market Street, some sooner than others. The 1 California line never actually touches Market and is a good escape from downtown from Embarcadero BART if a special event is taking place on Market, such as a parade or protest. We have tons of them. Because the 38 Geary is being asked to do too much work after line cuts on the 2, 3, 4, 21, 31, 71, and 71L, the 1 California is a safe bet during early twilights and parade events on Market.

The one aspect that puts San Francisco in the number one spot in living up to the phrase *The City That Knows How* is our flexibility in street closures and reroutes for ongoing and recurring special events. I don't believe any other major metropolitan area has as many street fairs, farmer's markets, special events, and parades as we do. The president was here again last week. Our governor would also meet at a downtown hotel. The defense secretary was here to sign off on his Halliburton millions, and the list goes on for motorcade delays: marathons and races, the Bay to Breakers before Memorial Day weekend, the street fairs, Juneteenth, the Cherry Blossom Festival, Chinese New Year, the Dragon Parade, Freedom Parade, Dore Alley, Castro, Folsom, Fillmore Jazz, Union Street, North Beach, art shows, art crawls, bike races, Blue Angels, Fleet Week, and on and on. All with alerts and special reroutes and delays.

The only other thing to talk about are the islands on Market. Look carefully at the Muni bus stop pole; the sign says Weekdays Only for certain buses. Those looking for express service would do well to look at this information at the bus stop.

These flagpoles have information most bus companies don't provide at a stop. Inbound versus outbound is important for express service, as an X bus only works inbound in the a.m. and outbound in the p.m. The exception is the 82X, which can be picked up on Main Street by the Federal Reserve both in the morning and afternoon. This is express is a loop and operates like a crosstown express loop that can take you north and south in both a.m. and p.m. This loop route is the same for morning and evening rush.

Charter and tour buses ferrying workers to the peninsula have filled in this lack of loop service not provided by Muni. A series of loops in the city would reduce the pickup and zone sharing at bus stops made by the shuttles, but this costly change in the past has not been justified in riding numbers. The new density created with all the towers and buildings going up may need a serious revisit on this possibility. Muni could run crosstown loops to connect with peninsula shuttles or Cal Train.

The express signs add a.m. or p.m., and this is as important as the weekdays reminder! Keeping my Zen on, I try to collect these lost puppies, but sometimes it isn't possible to capture everyone. Woe betides the operator on the F line on the weekend! Good luck as an information specialist! This is why I love just driving the locals around on a Potrero Barn coach!

Avenues or Streets

My friends always ask me about what line I am driving. Then they ask about the F streetcar line on Market Street. the railway has several historic streetcars from around the world, and they have been restored and repainted in colors from cities such as Melbourne, Philadelphia, Milan, and Kansas City. It is a wonder to see these multicolored streetcars make their proud way down Market Street. Like most streets in San Francisco, we just use the name of the street when we converse. So we refer to our promenade thoroughfare as Market. We rarely add the word *street*, except when directing those to our numbered avenues or streets. The avenues are out west by Ocean Beach, the Sunset, and the Richmond, and streets are downtown, SOMA, or in the Mission.

Ironically, few visitors or first timers are aware of this. The question "Do you go to Twenty-fifth?" can be answered incorrectly by just saying yes or no. If on a crosstown bus, we must get avenue or street from the visitor, and if leaving downtown, we must also ask, "Do you mean street or avenue?" Twenty-Fifth Avenue is nowhere near Twenty-Fifth Street, so by answering yes, someone can be misled by several miles from their intended destination if only giving the number without street or avenue. This can add over an hour of transit time in getting around. Directions are critical when on the phone or writing information down on a piece of paper. Most of those who miss meeting a friend or getting to a new residence or employer are missing a key piece of information when they get it over the phone.

The next problem is not having the phone number to recall the person who gave the directions. Or not carrying a charged cell phone to make another call while on the bus. If I am driving in a peak direction,

I refer the person asking questions to another person on the bus if it looks like they don't have all the information needed to get where they need to go. After two attempts, I have to disengage. Not being sure of a stop request can be a distraction while I drive, so I have to be careful that I am still friendly at ending the conversation. Sometimes a lack of understanding about safety creates a discourteous impression, and I have to keep my Zen if I am to stay out of trouble.

Make sure you get the cross street when getting directions. Make sure the other party is not giving you a side street as a cross street. A side street is only one or two blocks long. Many of us are unfamiliar with these side streets or alleyways. I would love a driver's test about the streets of San Francisco. I do know certain shuttle companies have this. I would like to see a tourist-question guide added to our training. "Do you go to BART?" "Do you go to Fisherman's Wharf?" "Do you go to the train station?" Inevitably, the time and place these questions are asked are as predictable as the tides. Good idea for my next book!

Keeping the Zen in transit means having the cross street down before boarding a crowded bus. Having the connection point and knowing the interval or headway between bus lines also helps in reducing the lost time between transfers. The transfer cost between modes and agencies is a primary cost for loss of ridership to the automobile.

The Weird Curve

DUBOCE IS NOT EXACTLY IN LINE WITH DIVISION, WHICH IS NOT EXACTLY perpendicular to Divisadero, which zigs to become Castro right where Duboce crosses.

Is Mission one block away from Market? Of course it is, when we don't count Minna or Stevenson.

"Wait, you mean Valencia, don't you?" Valencia is fifteen blocks long and ends at Market on one end at Mission on the other. How could you say Market and Mission are only one block away from each other when Valencia stretches for over a mile between the two?

Perhaps we should say San Jose and Mission are together. San Jose goes from being the major outbound arterial to El Camino in Daly City yet ends without fanfare near Fair Oaks as a dinky residential street at the outskirts of the Inner Mission.

How about the streets named after the planets? They should be together in one neighborhood, right? Neptune is one block from Venus, with Mercury and asteroid Ceres on either side. Halfway across the city off of Seventeenth, we find Mars across from Saturn, both below Uranus Terrace! Oh wait, maybe I do understand this a little better! Perhaps it would be better to keep the gas giants separate from Venus and Mars!

Beach must be by the beach, and Bay by the bay, but wouldn't we rather say Embarcadero travels the piers by the bay and that the Great Highway is the king of La Playa?

And the question asked, "Do you go to Twenty-Fifth?" is loaded with misdirection if asked on Market outbound. Twenty-Fifth Street in the Mission by SF General Hospital is not even close to Twenty-fifth Avenue that can take you to Land's End Beach! Even a simple "I need

Tenth" can have you end up in the Richmond district versus SOMA (South of Market.)

Every paragraph and sentence up to this point have omitted the word *street* or *avenue* but not here. You must use street or avenue when mentioning a numbered byway. Streets are south of downtown and Market, avenues out by the Sunset or the Richmond. Adding to this confusion is the city named Richmond, which also gets interesting in making sure the person is asking for *the* Richmond or Richmond, the suburb in the East Bay.

"Do you go to Union?"

Did you mean Union Square or Union Street?

The 31 Balboa must go to Balboa Park BART, right? Nope. The Balboa bus will take you to the denizens of the deep in the Tenderloin and not out by Geneva or Ocean by the connection to Daly City at the Balboa Park BART station. You'd actually have to get off at Highway 1 to take a 28 Golden Gate outbound to get to BART. But don't get on in the wrong direction, because although this bus ends inbound on the 49 line, which does go to Balboa BART, you would have added over an hour and a half, maybe two hours, to your journey!

The bottom line is the answer to your question can be yes, but it is not the quickest way. This brings us to the next qualifier about questioning a transfer.

"What's the quickest way to get to ..."

Being a native New Yorker, I can't help but be sarcastic in giving the correct answer, "Take a cab. Ride a bike. Text Uber." But of course, they mean what is the fastest way using Muni. This can get interesting. In a city with a population heading toward one million, we have more bus stops per mile than perhaps any other US city, and this slows us down to below 8 mph. What looks like a few minutes on a bus map in the shelter can drag on to an hour when stopping at every light on every corner or getting stuck in traffic with unrestricted permitting of rideshare vehicles.

The weird curve can be found at any valley break or crest of hill. When Union Street heads up Russian Hill at Larkin, if you look at the curb distance, you see that Union does indeed jog a little in alignment as it plunges down to Polk and Van Ness. Another fascinating detail in league with the weird curve is the width of Market Street. Market does not have a uniform width. The building setbacks are not the same either. I dare you to notice where the buildings move back to a wider stance when heading outbound.

Also interesting to note are residential street widths around town. As a street leaves the flats or a valley and heads up a hill, the width narrows.

Look at the buildings along Market Street. They aren't the same distance apart as you move inbound. They get closer together as you move toward the Ferry Plaza.

Indeed, it takes at least five years of living here and taking transit to get to know how the weird curve affects travel directions!

Kitty-Corner

"Is this the way to Powell Station?" intending riders ask as I open the door. I tell them they need to take the bus in the other direction. This question gets asked often at Steiner and Hayes across from the Painted Ladies at Alamo Square. They have arrived at the park from the crosstown 22 Fillmore or 24 Divisadero and are not familiar with where to stand. Just wait over there. I jest, knowing from experience that it won't help.

Pointing to the rear of the coach and telling them to cross to the other side to go inbound only results in a polite smile of thanks, but when I pull away, seven of ten times, they walk in the wrong direction or stand transfixed, looking to ask again.

Most United States–born and raised folks get it when I say, "Kitty-corner." Not so with visitors unfamiliar with our common US phrases. The blank stare I receive means I did not get through. Back to geometry class. The opposite adjacent angles are not only congruent by going the other way but equal distance on the oblique corner. If this doesn't compute, then I need to be willing to pop the brake, step down on the sidewalk, and point like a hound dog's tail right next to them, so there is no doubt. It may not be the patience in stalled traffic that is the hardest trait to master as an operator, but being gentle in answering repetitive questions throughout the day, world without end! Getting my ass out of the seat solves so many problems so fast I would do well to get the concrete out of my britches, for when I do, my legs give thanks, and I am energized to be in service mode.

God bless the Muni lines that still give us time to chat and not shut the door and rush away. At Union Square, however, a large visitor group can throw off the beats to pull away from the curb, and I have to keep it short and simple. My perceived rudeness is not a personal affront. It's because of the beats of the traffic and holding back other trolleys or streetcars behind me in the queue—cyclists moving in a pack from the last light at a speed too fast for lane-change judgment by motorists. The rails, when wet, can become deadly. The front wheel of a bike fits nicely into the groove, and all bike momentum in the front stops, and the rider flies over the handlebars.

The simplest way to convey kitty-corner then is to say, "You must cross both streets behind me and wait on the other side of this street." Choosing Zen to happy destiny means I can remain gentle knowing my work is never done. And shall be done again and again, world without end. Amen.

Twenty Questions

THIS IS A FUN GAME TO PLAY, AS IS CHARADES, IN A LARGE GROUP AT A party. But if that party is a waiting queue on Market Street on Fourth or Fifth, the game becomes no fun really fast as the lights go red again and the buses back up behind the red lane in the middle of the street. I am currently in a dilemma about how to come to the end of the game fast enough to get the party moving!

The quickest solution, as any experienced improvisation comedian will attest, is to agree with anything! The secret to improvisation is to agree with your antagonist in the audience or on stage to keep the train moving, usually with hilarious, inventive add-ons.

The same could be said with giving directions in a crowd of visitors.

"Do you go to the piers?" Yes.

"Do you go the wharf?" Yes.

"Do you go to the bay?" Yes.

"Do you go to Market?" Yes.

All lines end or pass by the water because we are surrounded by it. Almost every line crosses or travels down Market. Saying yes is not a lie.

Should not that be the end of it? Unfortunately, the answer is no. More questions to follow. So here is where I must get the flock moving. Hmm. We know from Animal Planet and the Discovery Channel that huge numbers of birds take flight when a threat is perceived. I need to give them a threat to get them moving! Hmm. Just kidding.

Bike Rack versus the Wiggle

MOST BIKE RIDERS ARE FAST TO LOAD THEIR BIKE ON THE BIKE RACK—which drops down over the front bumper—as they tag in and are gone to the back of the coach. I can guess where they are going to get off, but it is a good idea to let me know where you plan to take the bike from the rack. Many a day when I pull in, I find bikes waiting in the lost and found area. These are bikes left on the rack when the bus pulls in. Most cyclists don't communicate with me when they board. It is not required that I know where the bike is coming off, but it is a good idea, especially if the drop-off is a long way from the where the bike gets put on the rack.

On a warm day, cyclists waiting to board a crosstown run on the 33 Ashbury on Eighteenth Street usually can't put their bike on the rack because it is full. A rider waiting by Mission and Eighteenth can get a place on the rack. By Delores Park, it is too late to get on. The bike rack takes three bikes only, so when a fourth rider is intending, I let them take their bike, if it is a light racer or ten-speed, up the back steps to the rear aisle where there is a large gap in the seats. Most of the time, when a cyclist sees the rack is full, they sigh or shrug and get on their bike to ride around the hill.

We have a bypass that goes crosstown for cyclists called *the wiggle.* This is a bike path that follows streets around the Haight-Ashbury hill. A person new to town does not understand that it is possible to get from the Mission to the Haight without going up any major hill. In San Francisco, we have forty-three hills over forty-seven square miles. This means we have one hill for every 1.1 square miles. Although SF is not one continuous grid pattern, most hills can be avoided by simply jogging over one block.

This is why San Francisco is a much more bike-friendly city than Seattle or San Diego. There is no way to avoid Capitol Hill if trying to ride from Pike Place Market to Lake Washington. It is possible to get to Ballard and Fremont from downtown Seattle without a hill via Myrtle-Edwards or Eastlake, but there is some distance around Queen Anne hill to get there.

So even though Seattle is built on seven hills like Rome and has seven times fewer hills than San Francisco, the escarpment of the Denny regrade and of Queen Anne and/or Magnolia makes for intense climbs on streets that really are not safe for bikes because they are so narrow. True, I love the fact that you can park a car in either direction on either side of a residential street, but trying to ride down a street with an opposing car makes for intense awareness at corners. Hence the imperative red zones by the stop's sign at corners. I see why Seattle is so meticulous about painting its curb clears; there is no other space for a vehicle to wait for an oncoming car. And adding a bike to the mix seems next to scary. Thank God for the Burke-Gilman bike path. Rainier Valley has steep side streets on the south side and has the Renton highlands that act like a barrier to South Center or Long-acres.

San Diego's mesas and valleys are so long and unforgiving one would have to be in professional racing fitness to keep going. The Fashion Valley shopping area makes the climb to Hillcrest look like a training course for running a marathon or Grand Prix race in France! To get from Mission Beach to anywhere else but downtown seems like an uphill battle. Even Banker's Hill and the long upgrade by Balboa Park to Hillcrest seem to make for an unfriendly bike city. Plus, motorists are probably not used to seeing cyclists in traffic. I can see riding a bike in and around Hillcrest for short errands, but I did not see too many cyclists in San Diego or in transit on the buses.

Portland has a bike culture, and I will have to try riding there sometime. I hear the trail near the river to the south is nice, and the gradual upgrade on the Hawthorne side does seem gentle enough. The number of bridges they have seems to make the crossing to downtown not that bad. But boy, can I see flying down the grade inbound, like a zoo bomber, for some close calls! Portland does seem to resemble San Francisco in being the most accommodating for cyclists on the West

Coast. With the transit centers placed around the city, transfers seem to be reliable. I can always tell I have a visitor from Portland when they ask me where the nearest transit center is located!

So let me know when you're getting off. This comment goes unacknowledged from most bike riders as they walk back down the aisle with their helmet still on. Rare is the day that a cyclist actually stops to talk to the bus driver. And hence the collection of bikes I find by the dispatcher as lost and found when I pull in at night! I can also tell when the bus driver is not attentive to the needs of a cyclist. When I see a bus moving around town with the bike rack empty but still down like a people catcher, it's a good bet the cyclist did not talk to the operator!

Bicyclists—Pass on the Left

ONE GREAT BILLBOARD ON THE BACK OF SOME BUSES IS THE ILLUSTRATION showing a bus turned in at a bus stop with a cyclist behind the bus moving to the left to pass the bus. What a great illustration for a cyclist to see traveling behind a stopped city bus! This message has helped countless times, avoiding a sideswipe right from a bike getting caught behind or at our rear door as passengers alight. One of the keys to effective change is to have the message right where it needs to be, and this safety ad is in first place!

Unfortunately, much more needs be done to clarify the dos and don'ts of riding a bike in San Francisco.

First off, dear bike riders, take the parallel street! Usually there is a nice residential, less commercial street just off of a transit artery that is immensely safer for less conflict collision: Scott Street or Baker off Divisadero for starters, Page Street instead of Oak or Haight, Valencia instead of Mission. Howard Street, for example, has marked bike lane sharrows instead of scary Mission Street. Take Polk Street instead of busy Van Ness, which is Highway 101. The list goes on. It just is not safe to be on Van Ness or Divisadero during peak period, what most commuters call rush hour.

Sharrows are the arrow-like bike icons indicated a shared lane with vehicular traffic. They are stenciled in the center of the lane so cars are not in a reduced-width lane because of a separate lane for bikes. All these extra paint marks on the street do make for a confusing first time if you are in a car visiting San Francisco. What with transit islands and taxi and bus lanes, the driving space for regular traffic becomes constricted. This philosophy is extended to discourage automobile use, but with the advent of rideshare vehicles in large numbers, the squeeze play can become not unlike a video game. But unlike on a screen, injury and collision are real.

Second tip: walk the bike. When the space between parked cars and the first traffic lane is not consistently wide enough, walking the bike on the sidewalk is safest. The point is that this bike walk need not be a distance longer than two blocks. Sometimes sidewalks are wide and empty. Taking a driveway becomes the safe in and out. Timing with the car clusters based on the traffic lights also helps smooth the flow in making good time on a bike. If you know you're going to get a red ahead, why not enjoy the eye candy along the way?

Third tip: know the lights. Blazing ahead through a red looks really bad. When I see this happen, I follow behind to see if this violation pays dividends. Does running the light make for a faster trip down the line? In most cases, the answer is no. Violating a red light does not make for a faster trip, due to the following red at the next intersection.

I would lose my cool and scold the cyclist stopped at the next light. They also block autos from being able to make a right on red as they prance on their cranks or violate the crosswalk by being way too close to the traffic lane of the crossing street.

I have a story to tell about why staying near the curb is safe. While stopped on Seventeenth and Mission on my bike on my way home, I pulled clear of the traffic lane and off to the curb. I was partially blocking the sidewalk ramp and felt bad about this, as a pedestrian was trying to cross at the end of the cycle. A driver texting in a sports car behind the pickup was waiting in the number one position, let off on the brake, tapped the pickup not in gear, and knocked it into the crosswalk. The pedestrian I had blocked thanked me for saving him from getting hit. What I am saying to you fixed-gear hot rod bicyclists is it pays to keep the traffic lane clear and not stand too close to the moving cross traffic. The life you save may be your own!

I stopped trying to control them by chiding them at the next light. It wasn't worth the cost to my serenity. I let one girl have it at Van Ness and Golden Gate, and I saw the next day that she took another route. Instead of changing her behavior on one path, she diverted to another. It was the safer route—less traffic on a two-way street. Our stoplights are not timed. The reason for this is to slow traffic and break the pattern of speeding toward the end of the cycle when all the lights go red. Zipping through on a stale red can pay dividends, and most motorists and cyclists get this. The hard part is then to slow down and submit to the next red if it is not timed.

Fourth tip: ride with the pack. This can be dangerous if some in the pack want to pass. Usually, riding just behind the pack is best. Let them blaze the trail for alley car pullouts and car doors. I come behind well lit and at a tracking speed. If they want to rush ahead without lights at dusk, more power to them. At least I will be seen.

Fifth tip: be seen. Now some guys take this to the extreme. Some of these new headlamps look like they could be used to mine gold. The intensity of the beam looks like a close encounter of the fifth kind! But that apparently is not enough. Adding the flash makes for an eye-blinding experience and does not seem to be a way to influence a motorist to be kindly and yielding. Be wary of pushback.

I did have a newly charged light on flash and was using the sidewalk for a block on a narrow residential street where the cars fly by in a single-lane situation. The pedestrian screamed at me as I approached and severely chided me as I dismounted. I did thank him for letting me know the light was bothersome. Even though his response was way over the top, I tried to calm him by seeing his point of view. A trick for calming an argument is to use the comedic improvisation response of always agreeing with what was just said—no matter how shocking or humiliating the point.

I now point my beam downward to the street in front of me a few feet ahead. I also use the dimmer function if I am on a sidewalk. I also slow or dismount if a pup is on a leash or young ones are playing.

I have since noticed that a light on a bike's handlebar is even with the rearview mirrors of a car. I use this to my advantage when coming up from behind a car at a stop sign in inclement weather or when it's really dark outside. Being mindful of other cars and other bicyclists has helped me keep my Zen on the streets and in transit!

Free Ride

FOR THOSE RIDERS WHO ARE READY, A FREE RIDE IS AN OPPORTUNITY TO imagine what Muni would be like with no fare box at all. A smile and thank you is all it takes as a regular breeze by the yellow line to find a seat. The Zen zone is strong, and the crunch zone seems *a long time ago in a galaxy far, far away.* Now is the time it becomes easy to spot those who have not mastered how to ride the bus in San Francisco.

I can put the defect card over the bill meter or Clipper tag-in device with the words *Free ride, Clipper not working.* But this is not enough for those intent on paying a fare without the casual greater awareness of what is going on around them. Their tunnel vision is restricting their ability to learn and adapt to changing conditions around them. This can be fear based or newcomer based. Either way, the free-ride benefit of saving dwell time in the zone is completely lost upon these folks. I must find my Zen to minimize this loss of time and distraction. Usually, hand signals work best. Waving my hand over the fare box and motioning to step past works best. I was able to get my Muni Diaries audience to practice this at my performance as Driver Doug!

They all started to make the waterfall motion as I kept repeating the motion over and over on stage. Ninety-nine percent of intending cash-fare boarders get it, even though they may pause to create brief bumper cars with the person behind them attempting to stick the dollar under the defect card. Or they attempt to tag in repeatedly. Chinese seniors are the number one record holder of consecutive tags on Clipper when the system is not working. When Clipper is off and no sound emits from speaker, I can praise Tibetan monks, Allah, or Prime Creator!

Being spiritual helps when a wardrobe malfunction occurs in lifting up a shirt or jacket with the pass on a lanyard around the neck. Or with a hip check, bumping the person also trying to pay the fare. Creating a fast-track lane and an exact-change lane by motioning with hand signals from my seat at a big stop brings smiles of relief from the crowd. *Step up please! Exact change on the right. Clipper on the left!* And the Zen of knowing *when* to use the two-lane step up!

Those in the shop at the tower or on air at Central Control very rarely contain the empathy of what life is like for hours on end in the cockpit when something not safety significant is not working properly or intermittently. At the end of the day, it's not whether our request is heeded on the defect card but rather how we let such a distraction become an entertainment. The *musts* of demonstrating the patience of a Muni bus driver can come into play even in a free-ride situation, as they're determined to pay a fare no matter what. Maybe they have a strong resentment against those who do not show their fare and cheat the system, and they'll be damned if they board without a beep. Interestingly, this group is just as confounding as those who fumble without fare at the front door, blocking the steps. *If you don't have your card out and need to ask a question, let others at the stop who are ready go first.*

If you are a coach pulling in, it never hurts to ask for a transfer when you get off. Backdoor boarders have this one down. Because the coach is a short line coach, a new transfer with more time is usually given. We cannot waste transfers and may have longer ones already cut. Whether you got on for free or not is not the pressing matter. What is on our mind as an operator is to go home! *I forgot to get a transfer when I got on.* This works great instead of the hostile profanity, going out the back door empty-handed. The next regular coach is usually right behind the short line pull-in coach, and if you are fast at exiting the front door, you can get a new transfer. Being polite and respectful to the operator pays dividends for a free ride, especially if my momma is not involved in your request. Making politicians accountable in riding public transportation for free could make transit more attractive to all city dwellers.

So the free ride should become fun and easy. A smile and a nod is all it takes. If someone continues to dump coins or wedge a faded dollar in the slot, I can become Austin Powers, Church Lady, or Obi-Wan Kenobi. *Oh behave. Could it be Satan? May the force be with you.* Or the English Church version. *Peace be with you.*

Hot Lunch

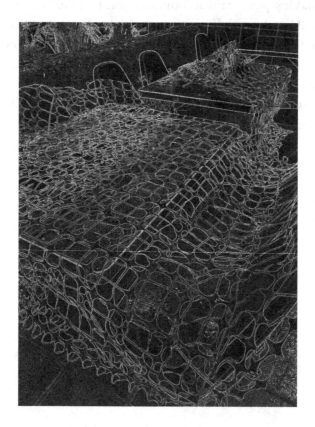

As I walk to my corner coffeeshop at zero dark thirty in the morning, I see another splayed design of ejecta on the sidewalk from someone's drinking spree last night. At least this "hot lunch" occurred outside of the aisle and stairwell of a Muni bus. When someone pukes on the bus, we can pull the coach in with what we call a hot lunch. This means my follower will have a double load and get less time for a break at the next terminal. I believe this is why God invented newspaper and travelers who make nests on and in the bus. Newspapers wedged between the seats or crumpled on the floor make for a quick and convenient remedy for keeping the bus in service and not creating another long wait for patrons waiting to ride in the twilight hours. I usually don't throw newspapers off the bus when it is raining or if I am working weekends or when school is out. I may need the paper to clean rain-soaked floors or mirrors or clean up any other mess of fluids left on the bus. The art becomes using the paper so as to not need gloves to touch any part of the blood, feces, or vomit. And yes, it would be nice if we had bathrooms with hot water at the end of the line! Soap and towels are the luxury of a tour bus operator, I guess.

Teen girls are the number one offender when it comes to puking on the bus. Hopefully, I can spot them before they get on. Usually their girl friend is helping them walk up to the steps. "Hey, why don't you wait a few more minutes and get your balance first?" or "How far are you going?" If they show no sign of listening or no desire to step off and wait for the next wave of heaving, then "Okay, sit near the door and let me know when you have an emergency!" At least this minimizes the damage to the floor of the aisle. Although, if the steps do get hit, it can be dangerous depending on the type of vomit.

You know, you have your clear, almost invisible kind. This dissipates quickly and has no odor. It can provide extra traction as it hardens or dissolves, mostly from stomach acids and esophageal mucus. This is a bonus if she hasn't eaten. Then, of course, are the slippery, half-digested refried beans. The rice can provide traction, and the birds do like this if it makes it to the sidewalk. If she is with guys, they usually dump her and get off the bus early. They laugh and think it's funny. Some friends, indeed. And if with her girlfriend, the point seems to be to get home as fast as possible. So even though she is being helped, am I really doing my duty by not calling for help? Should this be an ambulance call? The possibility of alcohol poisoning and use of a stomach pump may be in order. Perhaps I could let them stay at the stop and call the police. The balance of a major family event stands on the tips of my fingers and a call to Central Control.

Will there be a hospital and ambulance bill? Is this just another weekend learning experience for two friends? Should I intervene or get on with moving my passengers down the road? Being a nighttime driver on the Mission requires making snap judgment calls about emergency treatment or just a quick first-aid remedy. I usually go with first aid: have them step off the rear door before the heaves get too bad, and then use the newspapers to sop up the goo and keep the walking tread dry. Then a scoop up of the papers at the next terminal or by a convenient trash can on the sidewalk by the rear door.

It can be a drag if the person puking doesn't want to exit but continue to heave while sitting on the bus. The other passengers become uncomfortable if I don't do something. I cannot ignore someone sick on the bus unless they are way in the back, the bus is full, and no one comes forward. Fortunately, the empty stomach is what causes the problem in the first place, so there is not too much to clean up. Hopefully. The insanity of getting on the bus to get home is impossible to override if the sick person is with a group of friends. As with everything else, going with the flow keeps us moving.

So, if you are riding or driving the 14 Mission after dark, especially on weekends, make sure you have a copy of the morning edition!

Pudding Pants

HAVING LEFT THE RAUCOUS RECEIVER'S OFFICE AT POTRERO DIVISION FOR the quieter Presidio Division, I thought material for my next book would suffer a drought not unlike the one Northern California had been experiencing for the last several years. As I write this chapter, snowpack is 160 percent of normal, and the folks up at the Truckee Pass are dug in deep in drifts as high as their roofs! The Oroville Dam spillway has had so much water pouring over it that it has needed to be refilled and repaired, lest those downriver be inundated with, well, quite frankly, shit. We all know it rolls downhill! And it certainly isn't pleasant when it hits the fan. However, no tome about Muni would be complete without such scatological reference.

Merriam-Webster has a nice simple definition: 1: interest in or treatment of obscene matters especially in literature 2: the biologically oriented study of excrement (as for taxonomic purposes or for the determination of diet). Wikipedia offers this definition: In literature, "scatological" is a term to denote the literary trope of the grotesque body. It is used to describe works that make reference to excretion or excrement, as well as to toilet humor. In our case, we are affirming this book as a piece of literature, while also probing a taxonomic discovery of foods ingested to create such a mess. Indeed, a trope is a name given to classical rhetoric and deconstruction, the grotesque body, associated with Mardi Gras consumption of mass food ingestion.

So, too, like the Oroville Dam spillway, must our operator's seat be replaced, especially if our pants overflow with self-made pudding. This pudding is hopefully of a texture firmer than brie or muenster cheese, a "better Butterfinger" if like sharp cheddar or lentil soup (left on the burner for a few days). Thus firmer than, say, cottage cheese left in the back of the refrigerator for God only knows how long or day-old pot of refried beans. Let's just say the phrase "Who cut the cheese?" begins to bring meaning to what I am trying to say in vivid detail.

To be sure, passing the gas is a problem in the seat, especially if a hottie or cutie happens to move close in to the fare box at just the right (or wrong) moment, when one prays the wind blows in a favorable light direction. But for whom the bell tolls, when the anus fails to hold back the flood, is that it tolls for thee.

So, too, with stories now emanating from the Gilley Room at Presidio. As I was passing by to pick up my paddle and suggest this new title as a chapter in my book, a group of operators were in deep conversation about the various personal necessity emergencies we find in having to stop the coach and use the restroom. Our code for personal necessity is 702. The story line at our break room was about a difficult situation (saturation) in which a personal necessity was being called at a busy intersection downtown at Montgomery and Market. Personal necessity calls are expected to occur at our terminal break, not in the middle of the line. So it is definitely an item for cause when a bus goes out of service at this location. An inspector rushed to the scene to find out why this operator was holding the bus and blocking a traffic lane.

"I need to change my uniform," stated the operator.

"Did coffee spill on your shirt?" asked the inspector.

"No, I need a new pair of pants. Would you like me to show you?"

Immediately, the look of disdain disappeared on the inspector's face. He got a whiff. "Oh."

The operator got orders to pull the coach in. No disciplinary action taken. There is a rule whereby we have two hours to get a new uniform if it becomes soiled.

The reason we put newspaper down on our cockpit seat is because if we don't, we sometimes feel as though invisible worms are eating the way up our ass as we twitch and squirm in our seat. Our new buses have a seat belt safety feature that sends out a loud noise on our horn, which honks not unlike a car alarm. If our ass leaves the seat, even for a second, the bus will scream out loud, and on some models, if moving, the bus brakes to an immediate stop.

So, dear pedestrian, if you hear a bus honking loudly in the middle of the street, please take heart. It could simply be that we are trying to remove our caked uniform stuck to our butt from hours of steamy driving, or it could be a call for a 702. In any case, the idiot who installed this safety feature did not have experience in driving a bus over a twelve-hour range in a city like San Francisco.

I can just hear the manufacturing representative talking to a purchaser at Muni. "Would you like to add the new seat feature we are offering on our latest model? It sends out an intermittent horn blast while stopping the coach if the seat is unoccupied. No extra cost." Gee, sounds good.

Fortunately, new seats are being installed throughout our ETI Skoda coaches, which are now over twelve years old. To whoever approved the work order or capital improvement item to add new chairs, thank you! Having years' worth of pudding pants episodes cleared by a new chair is very welcome now that I also have a new uniform, to boot (without new boots.)

The road to happy destiny can be found with a new cockpit seat, complete with a headrest and butt rest safety feature!

Litterbugs

I HAD A GROUP OF YOUNGSTERS BRINGING IN FOOD AT THE BACK DOOR after I asked them to take their trash with them when they depart. My comment fell on deaf ears as they went to the back door with their ice-cream sandwich and candy bars. Being a bully and demanding an action has never worked in the past, so I simply make a request in a calm, monotone voice and let my control over any situation die after I take the action of a neutral-toned statement and let the cards (ice cream, soda cans, juice bottles, fried chicken) fall where they may.

Transfer points with fast-food stores are the places where food gets brought on the bus. It isn't too hard to see where the trash comes from. Once I understand this, I can ask intending passengers to take their food or trash with them, and if they board at the front, I get a positive response. I see them take their bags and cups with them when they get off. The 7-Eleven at Thirtieth and Mission and Popeye's at Divisadero and Hayes are the key litterbug stops on the 24 and 21 respectively.

Yesterday, I had an off-duty operator riding my coach inbound on the 21 alert me that the man who just got off at Eighth and Market dropped a full coffee cup on the back seat, and the spill was creeping down the floor to the back steps. Cream and sugar mixed with coffee make for a gross floor and a sticky mess that can be tracked throughout the bus over the following hours of service. I had five more trips to make on this day, so the spill was going to affect all the commuters going home after a long day. No one likes to be forced into a sticky seat or floor when all seats are taken on the peak-period commute home. Litterbugs don't understand the effect they are having on all those who come after them on the bus.

I asked the riding operator to get a newspaper at the news rack on the corner. He gave me some copies at my window, and I popped the brake. I went to the back and laid the papers down on the floor where the streams of goo were moving. They absorbed the coffee from the seats that were affected.

"Let's go!" demanded one of the youths.

"Not until I clean this mess. Look here. There is an ice-cream wrapper on the floor," I responded. "All these seats and aisle are unusable, as this coach will be out of service to wait for the car cleaners, and everyone will have to wait longer for the next bus. I am keeping this coach in service." They begrudgingly got off the bus.

My follower on the 9 San Bruno behind me honked at the delay created by missing a light at this inbound stop. I was holding up the line. Losing a light was a small price to pay to keep my headway intact. I returned to the cockpit and left on the next green. I let the paper absorb all the sticky coffee, and then at the next stop where a trash can is right at the corner, I picked up the wet paper and threw it into the can. The mess was gone.

I do have the ability to call for the car cleaners to come and fix the mess, but the delay in coming to clean the coach means my bus blocks the terminal for my follower, who now has double headway. This one spill, along with the wrappers, dropped off in a second, causes hours of delay in service. The best lesson I can give for change is to set an example by doing a spot cleaning when it happens and when they are on the bus.

It was made obvious to me from the operator who witnessed the spill the old man intentionally dropped his coffee cup and had an attitude. I recall this was not the first time he did this. I filed this away in my brain, to be alert for his boarding next time. Last time, I discovered the mess after a full trip to my second terminal.

Indeed, I do find many interesting articles when I do the rear board walk through at the end of the line, as our rulebook suggests. If a spill has occurred, I may not be able to see the mess when the bus is crowded. It is important to understand a rider can make a difference by letting me know. This was the case on this day, as I couldn't see what happened. At the end of the line, I whipped out my window cleaner pads and got the seats shiny and bright.

It took two minutes to make the final wipe, and I left Ferry Plaza on time. Snap. Can I get an amen in here?

The youth may believe it's cool to ride for free and eat on the bus, without a second thought, but the old man should know better. The skills needed by teachers are helpful in being a transit operator on school trips. I don't like receiving a coach from relief that has had a morning school trip where fast-food wrappers and spilled drink cups litter the floor. I keep in mind the rider on her way to an important job interview and the ice-cream cone that fell in her lap from a young rider who lost control of her ice-cream ball on top of the cone. Other memorable events are the completely full coffee cup that gets knocked out of hand when someone with a backpack passes by. The friendly town drunk who leaves the bottle open by the back seats, and it falls down to spray the odor of alcohol all over the back seats and floor, which is not the best first impression one needs on the way to school or to work.

I always try to do harm reduction in cleaning the coach first chance I get, but sometimes that is a few hours down the road. The best defense is a good offense, but I try not to be offensive in my comments to young people about taking their trash or wrappers or containers with them as they board the coach. But as getting to school is a predictable event with a predictable start time, the saving grace, if one could be so bold, is that you get the same riders at the same time and place every day, and because of this, you can predict when the trash dumpers board. And stopping them from boarding after reminding them the previous day to take their trash shuts down much of the mess later in the week and can have a beneficial effect on keeping the floor clean.

There is nothing like being in the Zen zone with a bunch of students going to school, walking down the aisle after everyone has left at the terminal and finding not one piece of dipping sauce, not one egg sandwich wrapper, and not one coffee cup by the back seats. "You're an awesome bus driver" never hurts either.

Positive action does. I now return you to the trolleybus of happy destiny, complete with clean seats and floor space!

Car Cleaners

I AM SURE THESE COWORKERS HAVE STORIES TO TELL! I CAN ONLY IMAGINE what sorts of things they have had to pick up, wipe up, or mop up in their day. If there is any sequel to this missive, I am sure the experience of a graffiti cleaner, a floor sweeper, or those who pick up the trash have some interesting tales.

Dipping dots and chicken bones are not high on my list of favorites. Neither are the empty cups of mixed iced coffee or smoothies. Open containers of soda or beer are the biggest bummer, especially when not completely empty. They can fall from the small platform next to the rear seats and get kicked around on the floor, sending a trail of sticky fluid halfway up the aisle. We are supposed to do a walk through to the back of the coach at every terminal. This is important to see if anyone has left anything by their seat. I once found a paperback with $500 in an envelope as a bookmark at Fourteenth Avenue and Quintara on the number 6 line. I put the book up on the dash before I left the outbound terminal. Sure enough, when I started back down the hill to Ninth and Judah, two young men rushed into the street in front of the bus and started screaming and waving for me to stop. This was on a dark, moonless night. I opened the door and held the book up in hand.

"Envelope? What envelope?" I couldn't resist. "The money is still there." They were relieved to say the least. It was rent money. Paying rent by cash in San Francisco is common on grandfather long-term leases but can add to drama and problems.

The other big-ticket item was a laptop computer. Fortunately, there was a name and phone number in the case, and I was able to call the owner immediately. They were so happy to get that one back. Cell phones too. I can usually find a recently called number that is a friend of the owner and let them know I have it. In all these cases, I call Central Control as soon as I know I have something, and when the passenger calls information, Central lets them know when my bus will pass back in their direction. They are so happy to see me coming.

This is probably the nicest feedback and recognition I receive at this job. It can come so quickly and simply, and all I have to do is make a sweep of the coach at the end of the line. Not only can this result in the most rewarding gratitude from a passenger, but it can prevent a nasty, sticky mosaic of soda or beer in the aisle from the back seat to the front seats! Ice cream on hot day really creates a sticky hazard on the floor. The cone or stick can become stuck to the floor like crazy glue. Once, a little girl dropped her ice-cream ball atop her cone right on to the lap of a nicely dressed woman going to a job interview. Words to the wise: when going to an interview, take a cab! Or at least bring some detergent wipes, just in case!

And then there is the full cup of joe without a lid. One person tripped up the steps and doused my shirt with coffee. Oh well, at least the color matches the uniform! We are allowed to go out of service for up to two hours to get a new shirt, but I kept on going. Here was the opportunity to state why bringing drinks on the bus was not a good idea, and it stuck!

Newly hired car cleaners have been present on the track and in my coach before I pull out in the morning. I see them applying the finishing touches on the windows and cockpit. The floor is freshly mopped. The bus is spotless. A passenger on my first trip noted the wet floors as a potential hazard. I grinned. Enjoy it while it lasts!

Flu Shot

IT IS UNDERSTANDABLE IN THIS BUSY, BUSTLING CITY WHY WE FORGET to do certain things we need to get done for our own well-being. Some years, I miss getting my free flu shot at the Permanente Medical Group because I never slow down enough to review my day or prioritize deadlines. The good news is that Anyone riding Muni daily may not need to get a flu shot. Riding the bus qualifies!

To be sure, the buses are now signed and posted with a note at the fare box that they have been disinfected—since shelter in place has been in effect. The last time I took out a motor coach from Woods Division, it passed the white glove test. I put my wet wipe around the wheel and on the horn button, and voila! There was no detectible dirt or grime on the wipe. Everything looked and smelled clean. Since this chapter was written in 2015, big improvements have been made to keep the bus clean.

There are enough fluids in the aisle and on the seats to qualify for any quarantine protocols. Airborne cough particles, the de-gasification of body odor, cigarette smoke, methadone leaching, and any number of party inhalants greet our nose upon entry. And the age-old angst against all prayer: why do you have to sit directly behind the cockpit? "Please move back."

"I am handicapped."

No shit, Shirley!

So the one drawback a disciplinary video playback can never show is the olfactory component! A blessed homeless woman gave me her secret tonic to kill all smells. It was in a cologne bottle, but it wasn't glass. It was a unbreakable, Muni-proofed, rounded container with a killer spray nozzle. One spray, when aimed correctly at the seat behind the cockpit, could buy insurance for at least two trips down Mission Street!

I was doing the 22 Fillmore with triple headway on a regular basis when the stinker of all stinkers got on at Eddy headed toward the Marina and Pacific Heights. No way was I going to put up with this shit all the way through sweet upper-class grandmas and seniors going to Jackson or Union. I started to pray. There were two very well-dressed executive types who also boarded at Eddy at the same time this awful-smelling guy got on. This is when my overthinking head really gives me serious emotional pain. I have so much invested in what you think of me and how I look doing my job. My fear of telling off the stinker and how to get rid of him, versus doing nothing, ignoring the smell, as if I didn't care for the welfare of riders new to mass transit, had me in that rock and hard place not unlike Alcatraz Island.

The prayers worked. At Geary, I saw in my rearview courtesy mirror a stirring in his seat behind me that signaled he was getting off! Whew! But my hours of being on edge with extra headway finally exploded. I got up out of my seat as he started down the stairs. Oh, I think you forgot something. I took out my secret weapon and sprayed the back of his coat as he went out the door. Thank God he's gone!

This was one time the video playback worked in my favor. My superintendent and those in the office at the time laughed so hard at what they saw that I didn't get in trouble. The nice-looking executive types had called in on me to complain. I could never figure out how they were unaware of his smell, but my boss couldn't bring herself to write me up over this incident.

I avoided a passenger service review simply by the humor of having another operator as a boss, not someone unfamiliar with what we go through. She got it. Unfortunately, she got promoted, and I had to start all over with a new boss. This starting over is actually one of the most difficult aspects of discipline with Muni. Having to prove myself to someone new almost negates all the stink of past passengers!

It's an old Scottish saying, *what doesn't kill you makes you stronger*. The same could be said of riding the bus in San Francisco!

All Alone

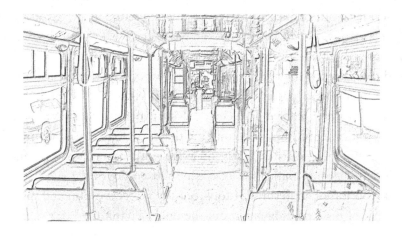

ON MISSION STREET. OLD TIMERS DON'T MIND BEING ALL ALONE ON Mission. As a new operator, I just could not fathom this—no coach visible in front, looking up from Second Street to Tenth Street or looking up from Fourteenth to Twenty-Fourth. If I didn't see my leader in front of me as I left the Ferry Plaza, I would hope for help from the 49 cutting in at South Van Ness and Twelfth Street. The 49 can be a help or a curse. If the 49 has extra headway on Van Ness, then it, too, is full to the aisles and can be a drag down all the way out to Ocean Avenue. This makes for a very slow outbound trip to Geneva.

From the tranquil interior of the superintendent's office, especially when I am in trouble, comes the directive that the skip stop rule does not apply when there are no unusual delays and there is no coach one block behind with the same destination. I have skipped stops during certain runs on a particular sign-up, because of my fears about what happens when the coach gets loaded to capacity. *Interestingly, there is no capacity limit stenciled in on the front of the coach, such as those found on tour buses.* This remains a mystery.

When I get into this fear mode, usually with anxiety creeping into my voice and shutting the door on people, trouble is not too far away. Oddly enough, I love the Mission as opposed to Chinatown. Mission is the width of a four-lane road, although narrower than standard, in San Francisco. It's a blessing because this is still wider than most of our two-lane streets. Mission Street is also flat and has fewer people driving from out of town, so most motorists are cool in that they are familiar with how to get around Muni.

Cars usually stop behind our coach when we are splitting the lane and they can see that the light is red. The question most people ask me about how we drive is "Why do you drive down the middle of the street?" The answer is "We are taught to drive that way!" This got a lot of laughs when I did my Driver Doug as a stand-up routine at Muni Diaries.

Coming in contact with car doors was costing the railway thousands of dollars a month in claims, and so keeping a four-foot right-side clearance became mandatory. This means splitting the lane down Sutter Street between Fillmore and Laguna, Grove between Laguna and Van Ness, and along Divisadero Street, which is too narrow to accommodate a bus in the right lane without putting the right side at risk of doors, skaters, and bikes. Like any experienced San Francisco driving resident, Mission motorists know we will soon be out of their way when the light goes green and we pull off to the curb to pick up at our next stop.

This familiarity makes driving on the Mission, in my opinion, fun. Motorists seldom create problems, and the way is flat and wide enough to pass obstacles. Flat terrain is good because it saves my knees and legs when braking. Especially if the coach is heavy. I have fears about running late and heavy without help in front or behind—because of what begins to happen inside the coach with the passengers.

"Say excuse me."

"How rude."

"Ouch, you stepped on my leg. My leg is broken."

"Front seats are for those with disabilities. Move back."

"I have a disability, bitch."

The list goes on. Fights break out. Pickpockets flourish. The chances of going out of service increase. I guess the wisdom of the many operators before me is to let this happen because it saves emotional energy. Since my job is not that of a carpenter or builder, I cannot see my handiwork as a finished product. I cannot leave a legacy, so to speak, by using superior building materials and putting in four or five nails per shingle instead of skipping nails and laying down faster.

All I can do for self-satisfaction as a bus driver is to avoid fights, avoid going out of service, and not put a burden on the operator in the coach behind me. This is how I define my success. There are no awards or praise forthcoming if I prevent a breakdown or if I skip stops to keep the bus from overcrowding. All I risk is a complaint from those who get passed up, or a complaint or accident report if a fight breaks out. I try to find a middle ground whereby those who get passed up don't call 3-1-1, and those inside my coach have just enough room to not step over one another.

If I pass up those on the corner and there is no bus behind me, then I believe Muni has failed to provide adequate service. Either way, service is lacking, and all I can do is try to let the folks riding know that I am trying to do the best I can. This is where a good interior PA microphone really helps.

If the riders can hear me clearly when I am passing up a stop to exit before the light or between two corners, and I am losing more people than I gain, all is well. Interestingly, there is a God space to do this. I can find a break in the parked cars to open all my doors and let folks exit safely. There is an emergency clause in our rulebook that says we may pull to the nearest safe place to stop. I construe this emergency stop rule to mean that if I am overcrowded, this constitutes a safety violation, and my skip stop and pass up is my highest priority.

With the installation of the drive cams on our front window, something interesting has happened. The training inspectors of my experience level and seniority seem to have also been giving added grace by understanding that when the coach is full, certain flexibilies exist in picking up loads and stopping.

The biggest headache I have is trying to use the kneeler or lift when the coach is full. It does not seem practical or safe to pick up a wheelchair when the aisle is full. The senior riders in the coach protest at having to rise from their seats in the flip-up area to make room for a wheelchair. The wheelchair lift can get stuck if our air is too low. Please be ready to board when the coach arrives, so I can see you. Let me help you by making sure you get on first. Thanks.

Dragging the Line

WHEN A COACH IN FRONT OF ME SEEMS TO BE TAKING LONGER THAN usual to leave the zone ahead of me, I must remember the one-block spacing rule and slow down to keep a healthy space between buses. This is usually an issue on Mission Street, where multiple lines parallel each other for several miles. A 49 and 14 can share a zone because the bus stops can accommodate two coaches. It is okay if two coaches unload and load together. But if there is a third bus nearby, such as a 14R, it is important to keep spacing so that no confusion arises from intending passengers as to where to board when the third coach stops to pick up. Those who need extra time to board need that space in time between coaches to see the line and number on the coach. And if a front door is placed at the top of the zone of the leading bus, there needs to be time to adjust to the spot where the second bus opens the front door.

In order to keep spacing even, sometimes the lead coach operator will come to the back of the bus and pull poles. This will allow the emptier bus a chance to fill up by picking up intending passengers at the next stop and even out the load between the two buses. This can happen in the morning during peak period or in the afternoon before peak period. The newer buses have a poles-down button the operator can push to make it easy for the following coach to get around. Poles should be cradled before any coach moves, so the drama begins with the question of who should drop their poles to pass—and when. *The coach with the load should get priority to keep poles up. An out-of-service coach should be the first to drop poles.*

On the 22 at the outbound terminal by Third Street, a pull-in coach that arrives after its leader may stay awhile for a recovery break. On the 30 Stockton, the same situation used to occur at Beach and Broderick.

72

Same goes for the 41, 45 at Greenwich and Lyon. In trying to get around, delay was solved if I pulled their poles and went around. If I locked up the retrievers in the process and caused a problem by touching their coach, this was not a good idea. I must be the one to go around first by dropping my poles. If the other operator is indisposed at the time and unavailable, I can always find out later what their preferences are. In the meantime, *I got to go.*

I would get so angry when an unattended coach had its poles up at the terminal and I had to go around. I also did not understand why an operator would leave the bus sticking way out in the traffic lane with its poles still on the wires so that a trolley could not pass. "What the hell are you doing?" was not a good way to start communication. "Is there anything I can do to help?" definitely got me out of there a lot faster. Whether a youngster locked up the rear door by letting out the air or a defect with the lift prevented the front door from closing, it was a simple matter to either move the bus or ask to drop the poles. Case closed, and now I am free to move. Except when I am not.

I try not to rush when I am on my pull-in trip going home. I find that if I have an expectation about when I am to check out and that time changes, I have to accept that this is the nature of my job as a driver. The end time is not always exact, and I can't leave my job such as punching out on a time clock. I have learned it does not pay to make plans too close to my off time. Many a drama in the Gilley Room or dispatch office have been started because of an expectation that does not match the needs of the line. I saw how unattractive someone looked in appearing to be a whining baby about not getting their way. Only until I was in the same boat and denied a day off myself. Ouch. Oh well, the nature of the beast.

I tell you one thing. I will never let my vacation time go to zero. Nor will I let any sick time go to zero. I have found out the hard way that when you need that day off and you don't have it, the ability to remain calm and professional becomes difficult. I have been told to never let them see you sweat. And running out of time off seems to be a good example. God made aspirin for a reason!

The Kneeler

"YOU'RE SUPPOSED TO LOWER THE KNEELER FOR SENIORS," OR "THANKS for lowering the steps," sarcastically spoken after departing to the sidewalk, does not help much. A request for the kneeler after ascending or descending, with a condescending tone, as if I am a mind reader, may not reflect where my attention is focused at the time. The rule is request the kneeler *before* alighting or stepping up. I am not in the know if I have not seen you before as to the status of your hip joint, your back, your neck, your legs, and so on. I try to gauge need based upon observing your gait. But in coming from behind the shelter or from the seat after I have opened the doors, I may not be able to see your approach. Yes, there are those for whom a kneeler would be obvious, but asking for a kneeler after using the steps seems ass backwards. Putting a foot on the first step and not moving can work sometimes, especially if used with the glare of disdain. The sense of entitlement I pick up on, however, does tend to make me pause in lowering the stairs sometimes. The quickest verbal command to get the steps to descend is a thank you. Veteran riding seniors know to say thank you as they reach the stairway and, just like magic, the steps go down. Condescension not required for lowering or ascension!

Another secret for getting what you need from the bus driver is to come to the front door if your stop got passed up to get off. The button by the back doors sometimes does not register on our dashboard and does not work as regularly as the chime cord by the windows. Being able to hear the bell is also a plus. Always smart to take at least one earbud off before pulling the string. Even if your volume is low, taking off one bud lets us know you can hear us talking. This courtesy has been lost on most folks.

Screaming or yelling may work, but a quick move to the front, at the first safe place past the zone, and we will lower the steps so you can get out not far from the previous bus stop. We are allowed to do this per safety rule but not out the back door. Late rings with a demand from the back steps do not usually result in an open door, but coming to the front does. We can see if a cyclist or skater is approaching, and we have better control over the doors. The pause or delay in stepping down the back stairs creates extra seconds that could mean a collision upon stepping down, versus a safely lowered kneeler up by the next crosswalk at the front door. We can also move our nose closer to the curb than at the back.

Another trick I make sure my student in line training understands is to use the front door / rear door toggle in front of the door dial. By delaying the front door opening and opening only the rear first, migration of souls sets in, and the slow exiting senior has a chance to make it to the front steps before those on the sidewalk bulldoze up the steps. This also saves on the call to "Move back!"

"Coming out!" is a helpful verbal cue, but if you let us know where you plan to get off when you board, and we can see that you need extra time, we can delay opening the front door so you don't get the bum-rush by those on the sidewalk. I enjoy protecting your right to step down first, but if I don't know when you are getting off, those extra precious seconds are lost upon those bulldozing up the stairs from the curb. Let me help you by requesting your stop, so I can put a request to a face and see where you are going to sit when you board.

Humility and redress with the appellation "Operator" does work better for getting what you need when you have to get off! Two golden words, "Thank you," help keep the Zen when coming to the front door for special requests!

Flat Tire

THE WHEELS ON THE BUS GO ROUND AND ROUND, ALL THROUGH THE town, except for when there is a construction detour or another patch job in the making from the Water Department or P G and E, the utility company! The wheels go round and round, even if the tire tread is not! But you would never know, because the only thing less smooth than the tires are the street surfaces!

Only once did my bus get a flat—an actual flat tire with an air leak where the rubber scrunches down on the street. There was a house under construction, and I ran over a nail—a huge nail. The bus tires cost like $800 apiece and have sixteen ply. I did not believe they would ever spring a leak. I called for the tire man, who came out and fixed the flat.

When we put *flat tire* on our defect card, it doesn't mean we have a tire out of air. Flat tire means our tread has worn unevenly, and when we take our coach up to twenty miles an hour, we hear the drums along the Mohawk. A thump-thump as the worn or flat portion of the tread goes round and round. Only on a newly surfaced street can we tell that we have a flat tire. But there is not too much worry about that! When streets are resurfaced, they are only paved a block at a time and in small sections. This hides the brand-new tire with a sometime defective tread that has been put on a bus.

Perfectly round tires are replaced with new scalloped ones. This is an improvement from tire treads that would separate on a hot day when we turned the front wheel! These were tires probably labeled as new, but it is obvious when recapped tires are used instead. You can see the separation line on the cap, versus a brand-new tire. I will pull in with a perfectly good bus, and the shop man in the tower puts up a chit for new tires. Resistance is futile. If I pull in with flat tire on the defect card, I get a look of disdain like I am doing something wrong. The brand-new tires seem to be inspected only after they are put on a bus, when I pull in and turn the front wheel to inspect the tread at the tower. The fault, dear Brutus, is not with the shop but the quality of the tire shipped to us as "new."

The shop man in the tower makes it very clear what is and is not a safety significant defect in the tire, and any balding tire showing through to the inner nylon mesh is removed, per state and federal law. We cannot have a shallow tread less than 4/32 of an inch on the front wheels. They are rotated to the back, inner rear wheels on the long coaches.

I have been asked by my editor to clarify terms used in this book, such as the term *safety significant*. The October 8, 1999, bulletin of a previous regime is oft cited when describing safety significant defects. We are to report them immediately and take the coach out of service. But, interestingly, the letter never states what they are! And so now, *right here, right now*, just like Jesus Jones, I get to be the unacknowledged legislator of *safety significant* as fresh, untainted eyes read this page!

One definition of safety significant is that for which there are parts available! Seriously, though, I turn to that which is our protocol for using the priority button on our radio. A priority is any threat to life or limb of anyone on or around the bus. A door that opens on a moving trolley or train, therefore, is a safety significant risk. A burned-out trim light or a dirty vent panel is not. A new tire with a blemish in the tread may not be safety significant, if the tread is maintained a 4/32 of an inch. This is where the defect card, to be filled out and turned in at the tower as we pull in, comes in to play about how we operators write up a tire. If I mark *shimmy and hard steering*, the shop responds immediately. If I mark flat tire, nothing may happen, especially if I don't mark which specific tire has the drums along the Mohawk.

The only thing worse than a flat tire on a bus is one on a bike. But the good news is that every bus has a bike rack to take you back to the shop for a new one or just some air. I always give you a free ride if your bike gets a flat on the street. Also, just to let you know, you motorists, or car people, if your car is in the shop, I'll break off a long one for you for taking mass transit for the first time. The first ride is free!

The Squeaky Wheel

GETS THE GREASE, AS THE SAYING GOES. MOST OF US DOUBT WE CAN make a difference. In rare instances, however, one person can effect change on a large scale. In the following four cases, one change is created by one passenger being persistent, and another by using political capital as mayor to meet his own need. The other two examples are rare cases when city supervisors step in to make transit change. Often nothing happens.

Our new trolleys have a redesigned seating area in the front of the bus. Seating bays for wheelchairs appear more prominent, and there is a padded paddle with a drop-down handhold allowing for placing a leg in an outstretched position without blocking the aisle, risking a hit from a passing passenger. A passenger can stand erect without sitting and be protected from getting hit in the aisle. I have asked passengers and operators if they have ever used or seen anyone use this device. No one has.

But I know who got this piece of equipment added. She also did it without any call to engineers, capital equipment procurement, planning or project management! She persistently made a passenger service request over and over and over every time she boarded a crowded 14 Mission bus, usually in the crunch zone at Thirteenth Street, and was unable to rest her leg in an outstretched position by the flip-up seats. Log after log, statistic after statistic, her call volume, over time, made it appear that this was a necessary seat mobility adjustment needed to be made to the flip-up seat area. I was able to contain her anger most of the time, but I had to get her off my bus once by threatening to call the police! She had become so angry she would threaten a wheelchair user in the pop-up area.

78

Placing this leg pad on all new trolleys shows how just one person can affect a multimillion-dollar order for equipment by persistence and perseverance. This pad is used as a seat back when facing the rear of the coach in a walker with seat back, or someone who cannot sit because a leg is immobile, and one woman single-handedly got what she needed on a large, new order of Flyer trolleys from Canada. Wow!

The number 3 Jackson was to be eliminated without a hearing, and the battle cry went out. The riders along Jackson Street made sure SFMTA kept the line. This is a good example where residents along a line can fight city hall and win. All it took was to point out that procedure was sidestepped by making a route change without citizen input. In this extremely rare case, city representation worked to prevent the cut.

The other example is from our esteemed Mayor Willie Brown. Da Mayor would continually get passed up at the Stockton tunnel into Chinatown by the 30 Stockton bus. I almost passed him up, but when I saw he was waiting, I picked him up. After all, he was responsible for me getting hired when he was elected, by having a city job fair at the Moscone Center in 1996! The least I could do was honor his commitment to Muni by picking him up!

Truth be told, in almost every case, even though it does not look like we have enough room to pick up anyone else because our bus is full, the miracle is, somehow, some way, you guys can fit in up the rear steps, and I can roll!

Anyway, to topic. Da Mayor's pass-ups at the tunnel created the impetus to build the Central Subway. (Editor's note: Rosemary Pak was the primary politico to move the tunnel forward.) This is a stellar example of why politicians, such as city supervisors, should ride on the SFMTA; it becomes obvious we need help!

The 24 Divisadero got appropriate overhead utility poles that do not detract from the neighborhood because Supervisor Tom Ammiano rode the 24 on a regular basis and was in the right place politically to get it done. We seldom de-wire or have any overhead problems on this residential stretch because of adequate structure and grace added correctly based on responsive feedback from those living and using the system.

Approaching Zen on a bus line can be affected through political capital and by calling in on a regular basis. The common thread here is that both methods were used by people actually taking mass transit on a regular basis. Decisions were based on users, not by those removed from taking the bus on a daily basis!

Game Boy

OF ALL THE DISTRACTIONS I FACE, NOISE CAN BE THE MOST ANNOYING, particularly if it is emanating from someone directly behind us or in the first seat across from the cockpit. A huge blessing with our new hybrids and articulated trolleybuses is that the first seats have been moved back far enough away to not be so distracting. A large storage bin over the curbside wheel well prevents passengers from sitting too close to us as we drive.

When mom or dad is taking the kids home by sitting down in the last open seats up front, out comes an electronic game device that has a soundtrack that can become somewhat monotonous and annoying, especially when alarms or buzzers sound when scoring points. The first time this happened, I was at a loss as to what to do. My mind kept coming back to an accident when an alarm or bell would ring at the most inopportune time moving down the street.

Leave it alone and ignore it is the simplest solution.

I quietly stated, "I can't continue to operate this coach safely with that noise going on." The dad heard me and repeated it to his son, and the Game Boy problem went away. The boy screamed and did everything he could to protest the takeaway of his game, but I was okay with this noise even though it was ten times louder than the game. I got what I needed by simply stating my problem. All was quiet as they left the coach.

Chock up another victory on the road to happy destiny!

Tagging the Coach

I CAME BACK FROM THE BATHROOM AT CITY COLLEGE AND SAW A YOUNG man running away from the front of my bus. He still had an aerosol paint can in his hand as he ran. I knew I had less than fifteen seconds to capture the image. I ran to the front door, pried it open, and hit the drive cam button. The camera captures up to fifteen seconds, with about eight seconds prior to button push. I nailed him. On the front windscreen, this idiot tagged both windshields and covered them with paint. I was unable to move the coach because my view would be blocked by graffiti.

I found a soda can by the curb that still contained a swallow or two and immediately held the open top to the paint on the windows. Like a deicing blade on a cold winter morning, I let the cola drip out of the pop top and used the lip of the can as a scraper. Because the paint had not dried, the carbonated water was great in cleaning off the mess. Score another victory for staying in service without a call to the car cleaners!

The next week, I pulled in to the Phelan Loop at City College, and I saw a paddy wagon and several cops standing around with radio sets talking to a youth. I heard them say the fine was $10,000 as they put handcuffs on him. The young man freaked out with a scream or a moan of "No!" as he dropped to his knees.

I didn't feel victorious or elated. I felt sad. Could there be another way to instill in this young man the consequences of his thoughtless action? The thought of Ripley in *Aliens* came to mind, when the alien egg opened in the nest one last time to find another victim to grab onto and incubate.

That's the last straw. You went over the line. It's one thing to put some initials on the tail end of a bus as we pull away from Eighteenth and Mission, but it's a whole different ball game to completely block an operator's view on the front window.

My motive to capture his image on screen was consistent with the broken window theory used by the police in New York City: by clearing graffiti in its tracks by (fixing a broken window stat) and stopping the blight immediately as it occurs, the message—this situation is unacceptable—prevents future abuse. By keeping an area or surface clean, people are more hesitant to start a new mess.

I do look at graffiti as an art form and admire the many alleyway walls that contain such aerosol art. Watching the creation process is interesting and informative. California may hold the record for number of wall tags and wall art, but on the windscreen of a bus? I don't think so.

I have event marker buttons to record what happens on the side of the bus, where most tags occur. I also now have nine active cameras covering all interior and exterior sides of the bus. Usually, as I pull away from the zone, I see a tagger hurrying to scribble before the bus moves away. They wear a black hoodie pulled over their head to make facial features hard to detect. I never know if the image gets to an authority able to catch the tagger unless I get a radio call to pull over and wait for a police car to identify the person in the back seat. I usually continue on my way without any confirmation resources used to catch the tagger or taggers.

The passive approach seems to work best. By marking the time and place, resources can be ready the next week and see if the pattern repeats. More often than not, it does. It is these patterns, these beats within the energy flow of the city, that fascinate me and keep my mind active and interested in what is coming next.

When taggers come to the front to talk to me after their buddies go to jail, I know justice has been served. Very few incidents occur once the word is out. Sometimes there is retaliation inside the bus before an exit. They come in huge packs so the police cannot discern who sprayed what as they all wear the same black uniform. When they are all waiting at one bus stop to board, I pass by. This means passing up a stop, and sometimes a passenger must walk back a few blocks, but I try to explain why I didn't stop. They understand; one less bus out of service.

Car Karma

I RECENTLY RENTED A CAR SHARE TO GO DOWNTOWN TO BUY SOME BINS for my storage closet and screens for my windows. When I say I am not a car person, I mean it. This becomes painfully clear when I try to park around downtown in a car. I am much more comfortable in a bus than in a car.

My friends ask in awe about how I can maneuver such a large vehicle in traffic, but being bigger has its advantages. I have much clearer visibility up high with lots of big mirrors. In a car, I am more or less an equal, and I am continually shocked at how close people tailgate and fail to leave a space cushion around me. The lack of using turn signals is perhaps the biggest failure of motorists, and they seem oblivious to how the simple act of signaling your intention can prevent gridlock and reduce conflict and collision.

The reason a turn signal reason a turn signal is not given is because the driver does not know where they are going! Seeing a back seat driver or a passenger with a map open is telling. Large car share stencils over the paint job of an auto alert regular city drivers that a novice is behind the wheel and to give wide berth!

Wide berth, however, is inexcusable with your car's ass sticking out more than eighteen inches from the curb! The thought *I am only going to take a second* is no reason to park more than a foot away from the curb or to double park—especially on two-way streets. The red curb is red for a reason. We need the curb space to clear a turn.

On the bus, I have what I call photon torpedoes. I can mark a spot on the ongoing video in front of my bus to capture a license plate of an offending vehicle blocking the transit lane or bus zone. I feel smugly complacent in generating revenue for the city at the flick of a switch, until I take away the notion of being separate from the people I was photographing. Being in a car share to pick up some office storage bins had me worried about my car karma. I had big stencils on my car and would be tagged as an idiot from the start. Would I end up being the same inconsiderate driver when loading bins into the hatchback?

I parked in the Fifth and Mission garage and decided to carry the bins to the car in the garage. The store wouldn't let me use a dolly to roll to the garage one block away. *No problem*, I thought. *I can carry them.* They were light but bulky. When I got to the garage, the top bin caught on an overhead exit sign, and the whole load tumbled to the floor, cracking the lids on all of them! Perhaps this was payback for all the tickets I issued to folks going Christmas shopping one month earlier!

I have since not seen the bus with the photon torpedo cameras, and I don't take a picture of a vehicle's plates if the car is not hindering any passenger trying to get to my front door. Only in the case of loading a wheelchair or someone on crutches do I make a photo record of the offending vehicle blocking the curb. I allow any car intending to pull out from a parked position space to move into the traffic lane if traffic is creating a solid wall without a gap with which to move into the flow. If someone needs to get into their car, and I am in stopped traffic, I now always give them a car space to open their door and get in. Sure enough, I am let into the passing lane when blocked from a turning car. As I allow others to merge, so am I given that grace.

I can follow the Zen of not identifying anyone as stupid and understand we are all trying to do the best we can with what we have been given.

Surrender

THE MOST CHALLENGING ASPECT OF ANY MOTORIST AND OPERATOR OF large equipment on the road is keeping aware of the *what if*. Such as faced any the cyclist. *What if* that bus in front of me, stopped in the zone, goes out of service? Did I leave enough space between my coach and the stopped coach in front of me if that car breaks down or has a fight on board? A big no-no in the operation of a bus is to never have to back up. In life, of course, if I make a decision that appears to lead to an unforgiving situation, the challenge arises to decide to continue or backtrack. The bigger the decision, the harder it is to surrender to the humility that I need to go back. So, too, with larger vehicles comes the fact that a jam is more difficult to escape once I become boxed-in.

The joy of driving a small Zip car becomes clear in congested situations. The fluidity smaller cars have in traffic is almost a given. That being said, my most embarrassing moments come when my bus is stuck in an intersection, or my tail is blocking the crosswalk after the signal has changed to green for the crosswalk and cross street. Usually, I scan the sidewalk ahead to see who is waiting, and based on previous stops on how the leading coach departs, I make the choice to pull in to the zone behind another coach, with the probability I can usually clear the zone space before the light changes. The contradiction of my error becomes glaring in the form of the horn from cross-traffic cars that cannot turn right behind me. To my horror, I see pedestrians leaving the crosswalk to walk behind my tail into the intersection space needed by a turning car to pass behind me from a turn. This resulting accident is one of the most common to Muni.

In a way, pedestrians become a friend in that their walk space puts an added cushion on my rear. Not knowing the mood or state of the cross traffic when the light does change is a blind spot that can, and often does, lead to trouble. If I am heavy and late, and the bus in front is also heavy, and the intersection is a busy pedestrian and vehicle cross, like Sixteenth and Mission, I have learned that this is not a good time, to stay put nearside on a stale green.

And so too with life, if things are moving fast and I feel light and free, I rarely stop to think about any negative consequences arising from having to know a *what if*. I have come to believe that not to decide is to decide not to move ahead even if the light is green.

Not to decide is to decide. What the hell does that mean? It has always struck me as a cop-out. This is where being behind the wheel of a bus has helped me in my life, in other decisions where I could not guess the outcome. This is a paradox that took me a long time to be able to integrate in all areas of my life: when running late and running heavy, the impulse to move up, or to push the envelope and try to cut down on waiting time, very rarely pays off.

My coworkers and trainers would mention this time and time again as a precursor to an accident, and only when I saw this over a long period of time did I finally get the message. Usually when I am in the lead and another coach moves in too close to me, I immediately must forgive forgive myself because I have done the same thing myself. I can change my stopping distance at the next stop to indicate that I don't want him to follow me. The best thing I can do would be to pull my poles and get out of their way. They usually smile and move on up.

The most frustrating thing about all of this is when my follower wants to tailgate, but they don't want to move out in front. I have to muster all the courage and serenity I have to not let them affect my driving and decision-making. I did learn early on that seeing the rear end of the bus in front of me is not a happy day. Being a free-range chicken is a lot easier than having a train of trolleys in front, or worse, in front and in back.

This becomes the most challenging aspect of not winning the race—when there are too many buses bunched together. The master of this principle will immediately adjust her speed and time in the zone by leaving the door open and pausing before moving forward, keeping the one-block spacing rule in mind. And this rule is the clearest for me to see. The one-block spacing rule is the best rule for avoiding an avoidable accident.

I tend to be too much an all-or-nothing guy, with little headspace for a steady, easy course. Pacing myself in all my comings and goings has been a lifelong challenge. By doing several small steps in a series of activities, such as writing this chapter now, then going to the store for groceries, and then having a stretch and a snack, creates a world that I cannot uncover once I get into the hour-by-hour zone of being stuck doing one thing. I don't work for more than six hours straight through.

I did not see how the idea of surrender was actually what I was doing by pacing myself in doing a term paper, studying for a test, or working out in the gym. My sleepless cramming for a test, a torn rotator or tennis elbow, or pigging out at a breakfast bar—these were all the endgame chargeable *accidents* resulting from a pattern of not surrendering. So surrender can actually mean pacing myself based on what others are also doing.

No better a traffic example is on I-5 between SF and LA. If everyone is doing seventy and there are no obstacles, such as weather or construction, everyone tends to let free-range traffic continue uninterrupted. Like an idiot, when I was new to California from the Midwest, cruising with everyone at seventy-five, I did panic when I saw an oncoming CHP cruiser and braked abruptly to slow to fifty-five. All I did was call attention to myself, and he immediately began braking to look for a safe crossover.

Luckily, there was none, and only later at a big truck stop did I find the unwritten California traffic rule of live and let live; as long as no one is causing problems contrary to the flow, let it go. I guess a correlative of surrendering is to blend in to what the flow or trend is telling you. Having free transit also helps the flow. The use of parking revenue to pay for those riding the bus and keeping the streets clear.

Headway

"When is the next bus coming?"

"Is there another bus behind you?"

"How long before you go?"

All these questions are are about headway. Headway is the time in minutes between buses. People usually ask me what the best line is. And I say to you now that the real question is "What line has the best headway when I am scheduled to work?" Which leads to the important question, "What line has a headway where the loss of a leader still allows for enough time to have a break at the terminal?"—or when I won't "get killed" or "hit" with an impossible passenger load.

Loss of a leader means that the bus in front of me is not in service or not out. A "not out" is a radio term for letting the following operator know that they don't have a leader. I have found that the 24 line and 49 are okay to work without a leader. Some would argue that the 6 line is okay without a leader, but I have not found that to always be the case. A lot depends on who is working the bus in front of me.

The term *working* carries with it a loaded-gun meaning, because not all operators seem to be *working* when they sit behind the seat. Having a *nonworking* leader with a *not out* in front of me can make for a challenging four-hour period without a break. And I have found that if I go more than four hours without a working leader with double headway, I will, at some point, leave the Zen zone.

I need to be aware of the warning signs that I am beginning to break down emotionally. I am now experienced enough where I can outrun or outpace the equipment. A bad bus with low air or slow doors can make matters worse, but I still have enough body energy to overcome most defects. It just is a matter of time before I begin to leave the Zen zone and start to risk angry passengers or unprofessional conduct.

Sometimes the Muni gods step in, and the bus complains and groans to a stop.

Time-out for calling the shop. When I was new, I had trouble, ignoring the defects the coach was signaling to me, and I kept going instead of taking a time-out for myself. This is a subjective call that differs from person to person, and I have had to do a lot of work on myself to see that I cannot make the call about someone else's personal breakdown point or judge whether I thought they should or could keep going in service.

I recently had slow doors and doors that would not close all the time. I was dragging down the line. I was heavy, and too many people were waiting at the next zone. I began to pass up. The key is to know when to start picking up again. Sometimes I overdo the pass-up and get a love letter from the superintendent. I turned the corner on to Otis Street at Twelfth and passed up about eight people. Though I did have room for them, there was another bus behind me. This time, they didn't see it or weren't in the mood to wait. Whoops. I can feel it right away. The rule is to stop and ask them to take the next coach, but my Zen was gone from having made it past busy Van Ness.

I made a mistake, and sure enough, pen went to paper to result in a confer and consult with my union rep and superintendent. But I do find myself more relaxed than in the past. *I am only human.* My coach had defects that took me out of the Zen zone, and those waiting could tell. But minding my own business was all I needed to worry about.

Being a victim never works.

Getting along with my coworkers was perhaps the last feather in my cap. Accepting that I could not make the call on someone else's coach or how they operate was the first step in not getting mad about someone or something outside of my control. It put me in the Zen zone I so admired from senior operators who never seemed fazed by what was going on in the bus in front of them.

When I was asked by another more senior operator about how many buses I was driving, I didn't get it. I get it now. I only have one bus to operate, and minding my own business is all I need to take care of. Trying to do too much usually got me into the superintendent's office or to sign for "love letters" at the dispatch desk from a passenger complaint. I knew I was on a good track when these events stopped happening to me! The only mail I get now is a Christmas card from a past superintendent in December. This is mail I like to get!

So the feeling that I was owed more time gradually became less and less important, and the statement from a senior operator, "*I only have one bus to drive,*" finally came home. And as the years have passed, I see that it matters less and less what others do or don't do. What is important is what I do—more than what I say. *Work the rule and call for help if I need it.*

The guessing game about which run and line has a reasonable headway has become less of a hard homework problem and more about just leaving on time and doing what Central Control always assures us to do when we call in late and heavy: *do the best we can.*

Drive Camera: Horseshoes and Hand Grenades

WHENEVER AN ABRUPT STOP OR IMPACT OF ANY TYPE JOLTS THE COACH, the camera mounted on the windscreen is activated. When my coach skidded on one of those metal plates on the street with loose gravel, my camera went off. I alerted Central Control, and all was well. I wonder how often these cameras are monitored and if they have any influence on our record. A recent incident put me on the radar for a drive cam view, and now I must be extremely aware of the effect I am having on my riders, as I have been tagged to receive any and all PSRs relating to my actions on the bus. But all is well because close encounters do not count against an operator. Just as in horseshoes or with hand grenades, close doesn't usually win the war. Usually.

The last time I came under scrutiny was when I was doing the run from hell, but in this case, I had a sweet run, but I was letting my equipment get the better of me. I had become a crybaby without realizing it. Assigned a small coach on the 14 line, I was becoming resentful of crowding at the back door, which dragged me down on the line. This cannonballed into a heavier load with seniors who need more time to climb the steps, and finding a seat becomes difficult to do. It is now that I need to fetch myself up sharply and pay attention to my interior mirror. I started too soon, and a woman almost fell to the floor because I could not see her in my interior mirror.

Also, seats for seniors become scarce in the crunch zone, and arguments arise over who is more needy of a front seat. This argument never ends well, and I try to do everything I know how to prevent a shutdown and a call for help. To me, this is a failure of the system. Why should all the paying, working people on the bus have to suffer for some ridiculous argument that no one will remember as soon as we get past Sixteenth Street?

If a camera is activated, I call Central Control or put in a miscellaneous to mark the event. In the rain, with wet brakes and on a hill, the odds increase for a camera activation. Like in horseshoes or with hand grenades, close does not an accident make. But in turning into a crosswalk, I do need to leave a much larger space cushion so as to not offend any intending pedestrian. It is not enough that my bus does not cross into the crosswalk when turning with a pedestrian off the curb. The call for scoring in horseshoes, by being the closest to the post and touching the post, is not a score when someone pounds on the door! Close but no cigar.

I have matured my experience without a cell phone complaint just three digits away. I have settled disputes for years, without a camera recording everything I say and do. I am not familiar with getting a call on the radio about something observed on my coach that I may not have seen. All this is an added dimension I must quickly adapt to, or I'll lose my Zen.

Close doesn't count. *The enemy of my enemy is my friend.* This Arabic quotation has become enshrined as an almost reverent proverb. But the prince who said this was decapitated by angry mobs when he got home! Hence this original title, *Keeping Zen!*

Secure the Coach-Pulling Poles

PART OF TESTING A NEW OPERATOR IN BEING QUALIFIED BY A STATE inspector is that of coach securement. As this book is written by a trolley operator, the added requirement of coach securement is in cradling the poles by the hooks near the harp at the back of the coach. Many a day goes by where a coach is taken out of service on the line, and the operator fails to secure the coach in a timely fashion. Of course, there could be a lot of argument about what qualifies as timely fashion, but the bottom line is that no coach can stay on the wires from behind an unsecured trolley with its poles still on the overhead wires.

Hell no!

When my leader goes out of service with a full coach on my time, I am glad I remember the one-block spacing rule and do not get too close. I can drop my poles and go around. There is nothing worse than double headway and a full load. *Hell no* means I am not going to continue for the rest of the trip with angry intending passengers waiting at the curb and a full bus with no room. *Hell no* means I can pass by that coach and continue on to the next stop without missing a beat. My follower can take all of his people, and I can pick up all of my leader's people still waiting at the next bus stops. This causes minimal disruption to the line and keeps buses spaced properly. The rules state pass-ups are only after an unusual delay and another bus with the same destination is one block behind. I will roll past an out-of-service bus as an unusual delay and pass up those passengers so I don't drag down the line and make the gap even bigger. This is a violation of the letter of the law, but the letters don't account for the emotional tension that comes on

94

board when I am full, can't pick up, and people start pushing. I choose the path of least resistance.

Show how it's done.

When there is no bus behind me, I have an obligation to pick up those stranded by the bus that went out of service. It is these times that I get my swerve on and take care of business. As long as I have no one in front of me, I have a clear shot to move up and put an end to the dragging coach that went out of service. Without making anything like a builder, it is harder to get a sense of satisfaction in getting something done. After being ten minutes down, taking on a load of passengers from a breakdown, and getting to the next terminal before leaving time, if I have kept the Zen, the day is a great one. No pats on the back. Just the hope of a thank you from the last passenger getting off at the end of the line!

Post Accident

When a coach becomes disabled after an accident or a security incident, if the operator is occupied with the police or an inspector, it is important that they are not blocking traffic or other trolleys coming up from behind.

It is embarrassing to me when Muni appears to be the problem in causing a traffic delay. Practicing defensive driving a daily basis, almost down to the minute-to-minute decision-making choices we make on the road, can make the difference between smooth, flowing traffic and gridlock.

The experience from the inspector called to a post-accident scene also provides valuable lessons about how to keep my side of the street clear. Since inspectors meet with operators' time and again post-accident. Their directness in getting to the point quickly is an art I have always admired. When their report matches my description, I know I have taken a valuable lesson with me.

If I am coming up from behind, I have learned that being of service not only means keeping my passengers informed, but I can pop the brake and help another operator who is blocked or out of service. Pulling poles is an opportunity to respect boundaries and to check in with the other operator to find out if they need my help.

I see this principle in many situations. If a senior appears to be having difficulty getting up the steps, it is also important to ask them first if they need help. *Sometimes, no help is desired,* and by touching them without permission, bad feelings result. "I want to be left alone" and "I do not need any help because I am able" are two big reasons why seniors don't desire assistance, and it is hard to know this simply by looking at their climb up the steps. Most times, though, if I see a heavy load, all my angst melts away when I offer to help. It is also true if another bus is blocking with the poles up on the wires and not moving. I must first ask, *Do they need my help?* My first question when I am in the swerve is *Where the hell are they?*

Time to go home

If the operator has gone to the store or the bathroom, then I can pull their poles and go around without having to drop mine. The time cuts on the 49 (2009), when severe, make for a tight terminal situation, and getting around can sometimes be a drag. If I arrive on my leaving time and desire another nice trip without overcrowding, I can zip my leader and go. But my attitude really checks what kind of day I have when it comes to pulling poles. Some operators, using the rearview mirrors as directed, see me coming and drop their poles by using the poles-down button or coming to the rear of their coach and cradling them. Others expect to not be bothered, and if I want to avoid stink eye and a nasty vibe, it's up to me to get around, even if I don't have a poles-down button because I have the older bus. If at a terminal with more than one track, such as North Point, I scan across the way to see if the operator is present in the coach. If not, I can stay on the left track and bypass without any hassle. This is the one saving grace at terminals with two sets of wires. Throw in tourists in rental cars and a backlog of 30 Stockton coaches that share the terminal, and all bets are off!

Payback

One of the biggest, nastiest paybacks is when the number one coach is waiting at the terminal when you are the follower and ready to pull in. Add some rain or wind and angry passengers who have been waiting twenty minutes for a bus, and the decision to wait it out and pull in late becomes the better option. Oh well, so much for that meeting or movie or dinner after work.

Even if no payback situation exists, there is nothing worse than seeing on the first day of a new sign-up who your leader is at your final pull-in terminal. This can either be icing on the cake (they pull their poles) or one more straw on the camel's back. Of course, usually by the time you get to your last terminal, you already know what kind of a leader you have! It is another way of saying, *Who is doing the work?*

They say it's a bitch, and it really is. Problem is half the time I never knew I was receiving payback. I was having a bad day without knowing I was the cause. And it took me years to see the cause and effect my actions of pissing off others had when that energy boomeranged back on me.

The first, most obvious payback was one-on-one with other operators. That's when an operator waits the full time at the terminal and then, after waiting past my leaving time, goes out of service. By the time they call Operations, it is too late. The damage has been done. I have double headway and am leaving late. The clincher is when I have no follower, so I can't rely on help from behind. The worst place for payback is at Bay and Fillmore. No way can the three major stops of Chestnut, Lombard, and Union be passed up, and no way can I enjoy an empty or light segment of load before the midway point on the trip. Oh well. Better luck next time.

The famous Daly City 702, where two twilight operators, usually junior to the pull-in coach behind them, take a twenty-minute break so that the pull-in operator has a long headway to pick up passengers from Evergreen, Lowell, and Geneva all the way in to the inner Mission. Instead of shadowing behind two in-service coaches, the operator has to pick up an extra load for the three miles into the pull-in wires. And not just for one day but over and over, day after day.

And when passengers retaliate, it is usually up front and obvious. They pull your poles to disable your forward-power traction motor. Or they release the air from the rear door so that your interlock engages, and you can't move the bus forward at all. Maybe they stand in front of your bus. Perhaps they park their wheelchair in the street. Or throw their bag into the side of your bus. In any event, you are not going anywhere. And I can mark my progress as an operator when this stops happening to me, even at classic corners like Sixteenth and Mission. I am happy to say that by being in the Zen zone, I have not been blockaded by passengers for years.

Getting the respect of my coworkers was one of the hardest and longest lessons I needed to get at work. The traffic, the passengers, and the equipment were no longer a problem. It was in getting right with my coworkers that it took me the longest time to find my Zen.

But if and when we get help and the shop or an inspector is on the scene, there actually is a friendly pat on the back! The shop or inspector taps our rear below the last window to let us know that our poles are placed back on the wires and we are clear to use the power pedal and continue on our way on the wires. Nice day.

Big Mouths and Crybabies

BIG MOUTHS RUN HOT. SO SAYS OUR ELECTED LEADER IN THE RECEIVERS' office before picking up my outfit one morning. Apparently, a common thread running through arguments rebutting a write-up for running ahead of schedule is that of complaining about other persons, places, or things, such as our equipment, as causes for running ahead of schedule. But it doesn't take much to understand the simplicity of why a bus is ahead of schedule: the operator behind the wheel.

I have found myself in big-mouth mode often. In fact, before a suspension hearing, my union rep repeated to me, as he does every time I am in trouble, "You talk too much." Or "You ask too many questions." And he is right. I find myself asking how I got in to this mess, and in retrospect, it becomes clear that I just need to shut up or say that I don't know. Others are trying to help me by giving hints or obvious discrepancies to tip off silence, but my monkey Gemini mind seems incapable of holding back.

Holding back is a valid technique to not run hot. Running hot is running ahead of schedule more than one minute. Most of my friends and riders give a look of disbelief when they hear that we are not allowed to run one minute ahead of schedule. With on-time performance so low, I understand why this rule may seem over the top—and I agree. But like my manager says, the first step to run on time is to leave on time and to not run ahead of schedule. There seems to be less of a concern in running late from management, but as someone in the seat out on the road, running late has many consequences, none that are as comfortable as the seat in the superintendent's office!

Running late in the Mission between Eighteenth and Twenty-Third almost always results in no terminal time at the end of the line.

Use of the kneeler for walkers and use of the lift for laundry carts and wheelchairs can drag down other trolleys. Loss of terminal time may not necessarily take any emotional toll or add to stress. So, although the bus is very crowded in this middle-of-the-line crunch zone, the consequence of complaint or accident is low. Outbound from the Ferry, however, I have found that getting too crowded *does* influence complaints and service disputes. So it is *where we are running late* that influences our trip. Getting into the crunch early on is bad news. The chance of going out of service goes way up.

As passengers, you would do well to look and see if another bus is coming. Use the clock inside the shelter to see if another bus is following in a few minutes. It is this use of technology that can make our railway run more smoothly. Please stop and take a look at this aspect of passenger load on the operator and the drama that ensues when no more seats or aisle spaces are available. Whether it is an operator crying at the barn or a passenger screaming in the aisle, use the next bus clock to your advantage. Good things come to those who wait!

We've Been Waiting an Hour

"WHERE THE HELL HAVE YOU BEEN?"

a) "The pizza delivery boy was late and apologized, so I got a free pizza and ate it all at the terminal. You don't expect me to wolf it all down in five minutes, do you?" I am not allowed to use my phone while I am driving, so I had to call my order in after I got to the end.

b) "The brakes failed, and I had to wait for the shop after filling out an accident report for the three beamers I took out rolling down Russian Hill. The shop wanted me to fill the bus up with as many people as possible to see if the brakes will hold."

c) "I did some shopping at Fisherman's Wharf and don't want you to rain on my parade. Wait here for the next bus right behind me so I can pick up the folks at the next stop. Since you've waited an hour already, another fifteen minutes is nothing."

d) "I'm terribly sorry for this delay. I am in a hurry with a triple load and don't have time for an argument with you. You can get on the next bus right behind me." Shut the door in their face and drive off.

The correct answer is, of course, b). This gains sympathy from the angry mob and also gives an accurate view of the equipment and for providing service. Also, it hints that affluent owners of high-end vehicles will get their due. This unites the angry mob in a can-do attitude. Although this may not be an actual verbatim test question provided during the civil service exam, the insight provided here may improve your skill score. As a transit professional, you are required to handle difficult situations quickly and respond to questions without hesitation. While some books on the subject of driving a bus may provide guidance as to how to remain calm in a dense, congested city such as San Francisco, let's face it—we may not have the patience or time to assume a lotus position and meditate.

When intending passengers become a large mob, it doesn't bode well for my day. If BART is shut down or our Metro tunnel is blocked, a large number of commuters congregate at our trolley and motor coach surface stops. I need the space in my head to answer questions yet pull away in a timely fashion. I also have to maintain space at the front of the aisle so I can see out my mirrors and the front door. I took a cab home the other day, and the cabbie was saying on a talk radio show that the regular caller was complaining that our buses run around empty and that funding should be cut. I laughed and said that the reason our buses are empty is because they are being towed back to the shop! Our trolleys are up to twenty years old and go to sleep, especially in hot weather (2009–2016). This caller obviously was a car person and may have never taken the Muni. I can assure readers that our buses are crowded from morning rush well into the night at 10:00 p.m. Our 22 and 14 lines never really ever get empty. A safety officer, imported from another city, commented on how amazing he thought it was that our buses were still crowded hours after rush hour. So, seriously, then, we need new trolleys, and we need them now!

If I try to use this analogy with the riding public, in paying their *fair* share, they usually become angry. They say I am going to make my money anyway, regardless of what they do or do not put in the fare box, and they are correct. Most riders angry with public transit share this view. I just believe it adds to a lawlessness kind of attitude that seems to not take personal responsibility. Those who are grateful for our transit system pay their fare and are generally courteous and helpful. If there is a way to fund transit and make it free, perhaps the lawless attitudes would be gone. You can't break any laws if they don't exist.

Keeping Zen means keeping my side of the street clean and not worrying about what others do.

Witching Hour

Perhaps this occurs in the five minutes after 5:00 P.M. when all the elevators fill with office workers ready to go home. Perhaps it's senior citizens looking out their windows and seeing that the rain has stopped and the sun is out. Perhaps it is the classroom bell ringing at Marina Middle School, signaling the end of the school day. Or the end of a baseball game, a Niners game, or the last fireworks grand finale. All these things have a different time of day or night but fall under the phrase *witching hour*. This hour is the time, just like out of *Mad* magazine's panorama cartoon collage, with everyone from every part of the city saying the same thing at once, "Let's go before the mob starts!"

Leaving time from the terminal never had more importance. Many times, I never know exactly when the clock has struck or the shot was fired. All I know, with a sinking feeling as my bus fills up before I even get to the second transfer point along our run, is that I am going to get beat up on this trip.

Lest I forget the skip-stop rule, when our bus gets loaded to capacity, I no longer have room and can't take on any new passengers. The fault, dear Brutus, is how the hell I do it and avoid the ninth level of Muni hell!

Stop Request

ONE DEFECT THAT DOES NOT USUALLY APPEAR ON THE DEFECT CARD IS
that of stop request. Most of the time, we as operators become so
familiar with our routine on our run that we almost don't need the stop
request lights or bell to know where and when people are getting off the
bus. Likewise, I know where I must stop and open the doors, even if it
first appears that no one is intending in the zone. Hospital stops are a
no-brainer for coming to a stop and lowering the kneeler automatically.
Certain stops around corners and with limited sight distance are also a
good place to stop even if I hear no ring. Hermann is such a stop on the
22. Also Kansas before turning toward Seventeenth. Recent changes
to our operating rules, through voter initiatives and with technology,
have given a strong voice to our riding public and given managers tools
to enforce the rules and make those of us who operate the buses more
accountable for our actions.

It used to be you guys were just as tired and fed up (as I was) when you were on your ride home. No way were you going to find the Muni number and dial on your landline to an office that was now closed about being passed up by a Muni bus. Today, with cell phone in hand and a simple 311 on speed dial, a call can be placed immediately and a written record and ID number generated on the spot.

When I was being observed, I received a call within five minutes from Central Control about someone I had passed up three stops back. Wow! That is a big change from the first ten years I spent behind the wheel, with only the landline 673-MUNI! So even if I put in a miscellaneous form, no way was I getting out of a hearing or discipline on pass-ups on the 49.

The bottom line I learned from all this is that not observing the one-block spacing rule can get me in trouble when my leader is close in front and another bus—such as the 14 line bus—is behind me. I must realize that new riders are not hip on how to signal a bus at a multiple-line stop. Not being ready is not a valid excuse as a pass-up. The only one who needed to be taught a lesson was me!

Twelfth and Otis is one of those around-the-corner stops that need be made, even if we don't see anybody waiting as we turn the corner from the 49 or cross over 101 on to Otis Street. A coworker recently commented on a PSR he got as a pass-up at this stop. No one was waiting at the stop, and he kept on going. I, too, have done this many times but have been written up for accumulating too many of these no-stop, bus stop actions. Coaches send digital information from their onboard motherboard about how many times we open the doors and for how long and at what stop. Every action on the bus is recorded, including PA-announced stops.

With the simplicity in calling a three-digit number, 311, and a digital camera file in cloud storage, not on a seventy-two-hour loop (that erases and rerecords), those of us who have been around for ten plus years must adapt to this change and realize that pass-ups we make to manage our passenger load or headway must be made, even if this causes delay. Coming to the curb and opening the door may no longer be enough to satisfy the requirement of making a stop. Moving away from the curb can only be done if there is no bill boarding from other large vehicles.

This change is hard to make to override a habit I developed over a period of time. I have been so obsessed with continuing to make the schedule at all costs that I have reduced dwell time in the zone at certain stops. I am overcoming this by trying to stay in one place and keep my doors open longer. Even still, there are some late runners who don't make it in time, and I have to let go of the outcome. I must be clear of fear as to whether the latecomer will call 311 and complain that I passed them up. There appears to be an invisible ledger of karma that can keep trouble at bay if I wait for runners. Same is true for right of way with other cars. God usually gives me a signal that my grace is about ready to expire! If close calls start occurring with an unusual increasing frequency, I immediately pray toward a larger space cushion in space between vehicles and in waiting for passengers to board and sit.

There seems to be an increased perception from those who miss my bus that I am not doing my job when I do not stop. I accumulate too many pass-up notices within a three-month time frame. Once again, our mirrors only capture a small zone alongside our bus, and we may not see someone running from across the street or perpendicular to where our coach is standing.

As a passenger, just yesterday, I saw this happen several times while I was sitting in the last seat at the back of the bus. People would run from the BART station steps on the side of the bus, and I could see them running, but the operator could not see them and pulled away. This makes us look bad, but we aren't intentionally passing them up.

This hasn't been easy. Especially with new riders. I have to do what has been suggested: slow down and do not worry about a full bus. These are the two biggest demons I have had to fight on the job with headway changes, and if I can cross the retirement ribbon finish line with my operator status in good standing, I will have crossed victoriously! Keeping Zen is all the challenge I will ever need. It is a basic as this topic and the action in a stop request.

Late Ring

I APPROACH A STOP THAT I SOMETIMES PASS UP WITHOUT A RING OR without anyone standing on the curb. Still no chime, no dash light. I coast without accelerating. I make the decision to stay in the traffic lane and pass the point of pulling to the right to bring the door to the curb. I pass the bus stop. *Wait, wait! I pulled the cord!* Most times, I can flag stop the coach and let them off. But at other times, I must continue forward to the next safe space. This does not always go over very well. Anger arises because I pass by a stop. And I have come to use my intuition to know when this is likely to happen. Sure enough, I can stop without a ring at a baby stop and see someone get off the back door without a ring. Indeed, operators with years of experience do develop extrasensory perception.

And after trial and error of being told about our mother or our birthright, we adapt our sixth sense as to when and where we will need to stop without a request. Greenwich on Van Ness, Kansas or Hermann on the 22 line. Twenty-Ninth Street on the 49. The list goes on.

I have come to believe there are glitches within the DVAS and GPS that cause just enough of a delay in ringing a stop. I have learned where these are, slowed accordingly, and called out a stop, just to make sure. And even then, I still must find the closest safe place to come to rest and let someone out. I have learned it is easier to just let them off as soon as possible, rather than go to the next stop. As a line trainer, I let my student know where these places and stops are so they don't have to go through a painful learning curve from the passengers. As with many things, the devil is in the detail!

So as a passenger, when the doors close and the bus begins moving, this is an okay time to pull the cord for the next stop. Or at least a block and a half away from the next zone. If we are making a turn, you have to understand that our eyes are focusing on pedestrian threats and traffic, not on the overhead stop request display. If no chime sounds, please be aware of this. Most conflict arises from the assumption that the chime sounded when it did not. We as operators note where this happens frequently and stop and open the door automatically. If we don't, then sure enough, the battle cry comes forth from the back door! This is how you, the passengers, can train us, the bus drivers.

I, too, can *train* you to ring at the correct moment, or else you get dinged by having to walk back to the previous stop! Ringing late for Broadway and Steiner means you are going to Vallejo! Those reading these words on a flat sheet, such as a map, may not realize the hill involved between these two stops. If, for example, you want Nob Hill on the 1 line inbound, and you don't get off at Taylor, you are in for a rude awakening for the Fairmont on Mason. The uphill grade is the maximum allowed before a street becomes a staircase!

Truck drivers unfamiliar with the streets of San Francisco find out about our grade changes the hard way. As do tour bus drivers. A large tow truck must be employed to get the vehicle clear from a cross street scrapping, whereby the long, seven-ton vehicle or trailer must be removed from the wedge created by a flat street crossing on a steep grade. I hope the Union 76 Truck Stop outside of Sacramento has a grade map near the break room for drivers heading into town from the Midwest!

New riders can always be found out by the way they depart. They are the culprits of the late ring—or of no ring at all. *I rang the bell!* Sitting on the back bench, they wait until the bus has come to a complete stop before they get up from their seat. They try to make their way through the aisle to the back door. By then, the regulars have stepped down to activate the doors and are long gone. As the doors begin to shut, they step down after the doors are shut, and I am ready to leave the zone. I know where these late bloomers lie, so I have learned to look at the back door one last time to see if someone or a group is holding us up.

Sure enough, the late-ring crowd finally make it down the steps. When I am training a new operator, my extra set of eyes can help the student be alert to when and where this happens. This always comes at the worst times, when we are late and without a leader. Many times, we get behind the wheel to move up our coach into a better headway. God, please help this book find its way into the hands of a late ringer! Keep the Zen!

Open Run

It took me several years to learn this term. I found out about this term after overhearing Central Control responding to a Street Operations inspector inquiring about a run number. "That run is a not out," came the response to a blank space in the headway between buses. The rules are as clear as the black-and-white numbers of a railway timetable about our leaving times, minutes between coaches, and checkpoints along the way. Only thing is we have no printed timetables, and the 22 Fillmore has no more timed checkpoints on our paddle issued with our outfit! Now, I have to admit I put that last sentence in here to make it sound more dramatic. Truth is it really doesn't matter that we have no published timetable. And as the street inspectors have been removed from Chestnut and Fillmore, Sutter and Fillmore, Sixteenth and Bryant—Third and Twentieth—and other places, such as Potrero and Sixteenth and Kansas and Seventeenth, it makes little difference anyway. Just like the prelude to an elimination of a line, cutting service reduces ridership and creates less attraction for riding a bus in the first place. At some point, cost reduction becomes self-fulfilling, and we, as a class of operators, become adjusted to new realities, such as having a bus, or buses, missing in front of us. This adds to pass-ups due to full coaches. It leads to the missive to "throw out the schedule" when operating a coach on the line. I heard this a lot four and five years ago. Now I hear a sarcastic and condescending tone about making up a schedule and making up stops. With an on-time performance of around 60 percent, I just laugh at this comment. If we had a level of punctuality over 85 percent, then I could see the point in running on time. But as it is, a difference of 62 versus 63 percent makes no visible change.

The hard part of all of this is guessing how to adjust headway and speed, not knowing what kind of a day we are going to have. The standard response is to make all stops until the coach fills up and then begin skipping stops. I object to this sometimes, because the folks in the middle of the line get passed up more frequently and get lousy service. This is very apparent during special events when large crowds wait along avenues, such as by Golden Gate Park after Bay to Breakers or Barely Bluegrass.

Some coworkers disagree that I should let the passengers know that there is a bus missing in front of or behind me. I believe knowledge is power, and most of my riders are glad to be informed. But I do get the drift that many of my coworkers abide by an ignorance is bliss mode. In any event, knowing that I don't have a leader by an open run helps me in knowing what to expect. I am not one to be a crybaby to the dispatcher or the union about how bad I have it with an open run. I have seen others attempt this drama for little effect. I love it when I am away for a week and hear complaints from my regulars or the operator doing my run. What was once a quiet and uncomplaining operator on a run becomes an "oh my god" when I am away. Interestingly, when I come back from vacation, the open run in front of me magically gets filled! There may be a reward in heaven for me working without a leader, but I do get a taste of this when I come back from being away for a while!

Thank you for riding Muni!

Move Up Four

WHEN A COACH GOES OUT OF SERVICE IN FRONT OF ME, IT MEANS MY headway has doubled. So in order to minimize the impact of no leader, I am allowed to split the headway and move up. Most move-ups are made over the radio and are usually two, three, or four minutes. Sometimes we know we have lost our leader before Central Control knows.

Other times, we are in the dark and rely on the contact from the operator who goes out of service, hoping we are given timely information to move up before we find out the hard way. It wasn't till I talked to an inspector about headway that I understood the science of move-ups as a standard operating order based on the headways between buses on the various lines during the various four-hour headway windows. It had never occurred to me that headway move-ups were standardized and that I could learn a lot by knowing what supervisors were trained to know when they were trained.

In fact, a lot of what I am writing here is based upon my experience and observations that may contain gaps in knowledge that are known by my superiors. And much of my knowledge was less complete than I first admitted, and those in charge are actually a lot more knowledgeable about what was going on than I was from my point of view. Most conflict arises out of misplaced desire. My desire to run on time was misplaced because I was not aware, for example, that I did not have a bus running behind me, and I should not move up because I would be creating a hole behind me.

On rare occasions, I am informed that I have triple headway, and oddly enough, I find myself less anxious and more grateful than if I am just missing one bus in front of me.

This is because of what I call the seven-minute rule: in seven minutes, many waiting for the bus start to make other choices—get on another bus, or take a cab, or walk to another bus line.

When push comes to shove, there is a magic moment when the ability to make the schedule is so impossible that there is no longer the need to try to make it work. And as the coach fills up early, it becomes obvious that there is no way to try to pick everyone up. The hard part is when there is a move up of four, when it may or may not be possible to pick everyone up. The point at which to pass up may not be so clear. Can I pick up those five people, or will this create havoc at the next stop? Should I keep it crowded for the next two blocks, or should I start reducing my load now?

There are very clear rules about when to stop passing up. When the bus is full, one must pass up stops. Sometimes the number of people in the aisle can be a variable. Is the crowd mostly young, or are there people with canes and walkers on board? The demographics of who is on board is also a factor to consider a pass-up. Sure, I may have some room for a few youngsters in the back, but if a large group of seniors with grocery carts is waiting at the next stop, and there is no room in the aisle in the front, the stop is not going to go well.

When in doubt, make the stop, following my general orders, but do so in a way that adjusts the load. If I pull forward in the zone, intending passengers can see if there is a coach behind me that is usually emptier, and also those with a valid fare can enter and tag in on the rear doors. This skill really helps avoid the "Please move back," which very rarely works. *Actions speak louder than words* is a principle that works well here. It isn't what I say but what I do that makes the Zen of driving Muni much easier.

The Fulton 500

NASCAR IS HAVING TROUBLE FILLING SEATS AT ITS RACETRACKS. ENTIRE rows of bleachers are being removed so the remaining seats look filled. Attendance is down. My suggestion is move the bleachers to Fulton Street by Golden Gate Park during morning inbound peak period!

Stand by the curb on Market Street inbound and feel the magic: the swoosh of air as the Fulton 500 trolleybus passes by, late for the Transbay Terminal. Our statistics match up with this reality: the buses are only running at 60 percent on time. And yet nothing changes. All the big bosses are told is that we are all running hot. Hot as in ahead of schedule. How can this be? How can we all be running ahead of schedule if we are late?

There are no street inspectors at our checkpoints. Leaving time from the terminal is not observed. All trolleybus movements are seen on a laptop, color coded by shades of red depending on how much ahead of schedule we are. If a bus goes out of service and we move up, this shows up red. We need to get permission to do so.

The delay in putting in a request to TMC (Transit Management Control) on our radio takes away the benefit of leaving early. Our follower may not be able to see us when we leave and not know we have moved up. TMC may not be aware of a coach out of service in the few moments needed to make a headway adjustment. Taking the matter in our own hands by leaving immediately after seeing our leader go out of service is against the rule.

Having an inspector on the line, such as by the terminal, could make a big difference. In the sixties and seventies, this was the case, as a rapport would develop between the operators and the inspector at the end of the line. Such accountability is gone.

115

With the Fulton 500 racetrack, under the current model, no rapport is built between operators barely able to rush to the bathroom. No third-party observer, like an inspector on the line, is able to broker a response in buffering headway about what orders were given to both the leader and follower. Cutting recovery time and running time creates a lack of communication and the drama of game playing when, in fact, an operator may simply be trying to keep headway safe.

As in quantum particle theory, observation changes the behavior of the atoms! So, too, with observation on the line by an inspector! The particles, the bus drivers, change their behavior when being observed. This makes for even headway and a reasonable passenger load. The delay in not knowing and being unskilled in a switchback for adjustment creates rushing to be late. The art of the switchback seems lost on TMC.

When two coaches are late, the third coach is given a short line switch to pick up the extra intending passengers waiting for a double headway because of the gap in service. Bus one goes to the end of the line, full of passengers, and gets a break. Bus three *waits a few extra minutes* at the switchback and picks up those missed by bus one. Bus two should move up at the end of the line and leave early, before bus one, after a short break, because bus one did most of the work. Bus one gets a short line switch on the next trip, so they get to be on time on their next outbound without being overloaded. Bus two gets a short line switch like bus one, so they get the break they were denied at the first terminal because bus one was late. Bus three gets to pick up at the next terminal and carries extra passengers to the switch one and two got in the other direction. All operators get a break, and the headway is corrected in one trip.

Certainly upper management must wonder why on-time performance is always in failure mode. I do not believe they have an answer. They have never given an explanation in the news media. No one ever asks why. Taking away more running time as a penalty for running ahead of schedule only leads to less on-time performance, not more.

Indeed, without terminal time to build rapport and no margin of error for delay, I usually do leave early, with two minutes in my pocket to protect myself from kneeler or wheelchair delays or traffic snarls.

It can easily be seen on the screen that buses are leaving early from the terminal. The increase of ten to twenty thousand extra ride share vehicles per day on our streets only leads to bigger delays and a shortage of recovery time. No relief is in sight.

So let the games begin! Install some bleachers on Market Street to watch the Fulton 500 in action! Watch death-defying maneuvers and racetrack switching from lane two to lane one on the inbound!

Without turn-back wires at Thirty-Third Avenue or Twenty-Sixth Avenue, or inspectors at La Playa or Transbay, expect huge clusters of long trolleys, followed by breaks of fifteen minutes or more. Use of Larkin and Golden Gate could help in the afternoon at Van Ness and create less congestion on Howard when a coach fails due to overheating and needs assistance.

Restoring the Zen on the Fulton 500 comes into play with added short line wires and the running time to leave on time. Arriving late to our terminal does not make a joyous day.

Knowing the Lights

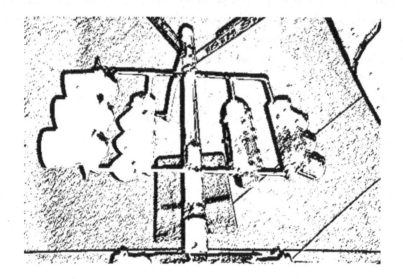

Looking at this chapter heading, it sounds spiritual. Indeed, the effect of using knowledge and experience about when traffic lights turn green feels spiritual. It feels like going with the flow. When I time the lights and bring the coach slowly up to the stop line, and the light goes green, it saves wear and tear on my knees and on the coach brakes. But very few motorists take advantage of this idea. Time after time, cars whizz by my coach, only to be stopped at the next block, waiting for the light to turn.

Here I come, lumbering up to the intersection, only to roll past them, with my momentum coasting me to the other side before they put the pedal to the metal. The amount of money and energy that could be saved if even 20 percent more motorists approached stale reds at an even pace is probably a huge number when the multiplier effect is considered. Because I, as a transit operator, go through intersections up to eight times a day, at least five days a week, I know when I can make a light or when speeding up pays no dividends. Motorists, who may be randomly taking a trip choice that isn't done on a regular basis, don't necessarily know the lights. And this does cause delay, particularly when turns are involved.

The lights are not the same throughout the day. In the morning, greens I can make become impossible in the afternoon. Once the timing is figured out, all the guesswork is removed, and the job becomes relaxing and easy. I had so much anxiety when I was new, because I didn't know the lights. I could not tell if it was safe to cross over the line as the light turned red. It is impossible for vehicles to cross our intersections here in San Francisco with three-second yellows. No way can a sixty-foot coach clear an intersection with only a three-second amber. In knowing the lights, all this becomes academic.

It is also important to see how the intersection flows with the cross traffic. Is the street one way? Does the direction of cross-traffic travel enhance crossing late, or does it hinder? Is cross traffic turning or is it mostly flowing straight? Every intersection is different due to pedestrian and car volume. Motorist and pedestrian conflict as a vehicle tries to turn on a green when occupied by a walk sign. Pedestrian scrambles solve this problem—isolate the pedestrian crossing time.

When I already know if I can or cannot clear an intersection, my day becomes easy. Simply by counting the number of people waiting at a stop, I already know before I pick up whether or not I can make the light before it turns red. I can also know the point of no return when it comes to approaching traffic coming up from the rear. If I can pull away from the curb before the next group of cars arrives, I am good to go. The hardest part for me to accept is that of surrender. I don't have to win. When I stay in win mode, I am actually in loser mode. If a car is approaching faster than other vehicles, I must immediately surrender to that vehicle.

When I lumber up behind them as they are stopped at the next red, I always leave extra space. I always try to let them have complete visibility. I stop back so they can see if it is safe to turn or if someone is stepping from the curb late. Plus, they have a hard time fingering me or seeing who I am!

Limited sight distance is one of the biggest hazards of living in a dense city where the buildings come up close to the sidewalk. When I stop back behind the line, most of my problems go away. Knowing the lights reduces hard braking and trespassing upon the crosswalk. Knowing the lights is a good metaphor for life in general. If we are new to a task or assignment, it helps to get feedback by watching those with more experience and learning from our observations of their actions. So, for me, knowing the lights is actually a form of surrender of not being first.

The final aspect of surrender that took me longest to accept is when a car passes on the right when I am preparing to make a right turn. If a car tries to squeeze in on the right, I have to adjust my stopping point. So the biggest offense is the best defense. And this keeps me in the Zen zone.

Buttonhook

Four-foot right-side clearance is a must at all times when driving a bus, especially for a right turn. Double parked vehicles, pedestrians standing off the curb, and cyclists standing on their cranks past the stop line are all hazards that make the buttonhook right turn necessary. The first question a motorist or pedestrian would do well to understand is, *Am I blocking transit by stopping here?* Use of the mirrors and scanning every five to eight seconds becomes very clear, very fast, in what makes for a professional driver or an unskilled motorist. Likewise, cyclists who are new to riding a bike in the city become very apparent at a red light or bus zone.

When a new curb clear is installed on a corner, and a new ramp is cut at the crosswalk, I make the call to Central to create a record about a corner that has not yet been painted red. Motorists begin parking on a curb clear that is not marked in red, and this creates problems for clearance in turning.

A buttonhook turn is one in which we make a wide sweep to the left before making a right turn so our wheels have enough clearance as we finish the turn. Many of my friends seem dubious about driving such a large vehicle in a city, but when turns are made wide enough and set up before the corner, things get much easier. I feel more comfortable driving a bus than a car in the city because I have more mirrors. My mirrors are bigger, and my vehicle is larger and with more lights. What gets me is when cars double park or are left unattended on a curb clear where we need the space to make a turn without de-wiring. Getting the red paint on a new curb clear may not stop a vehicle from parking, but it does make most people move when we come from behind. Anything I can do to improve the odds of having a clear turn helps me keep the Zen.

The Noodle

One of the nicest tricks to leaving the zone safely at a nearside bus stop is what my line trainer called the noodle. If done correctly, it reduces squeeze play merging, and the setup for this maneuver helps prevent sideswipes caused by lack of visibility from the rear as a car approaches, particularly if that car is turning right to pass the coach. I had trouble in spelling maneuver, so I looked it up in my dictionary. My *Webster's Ninth New Collegiate Dictionary* has several definitions that fit this move. I have found it nice to have a dictionary handy when I write, because it clarifies what meaning I am trying to convey, and I take interest in all the other words I come across in trying to search for the correct spelling.

I recall when I was in grade school, one of the best exercises I enjoyed the most was to use a dictionary for correct spelling. The teacher suggested, and I have never forgotten this, to just open a dictionary and browse. I encourage any students reading this manual to spend time poring over a dictionary. This is such a helpful, creative endeavor that helps us clarify how to communicate and increase our vocabulary. Our perceived fitness to communicate aids in directness and should not be an intimidator. Finding the simpler word is best for reaching the most, but I am amazed at how few people really know the definitions of the words they use, and how much learning is skipped when definitions are misapplied or not understood. This becomes apparent when listening to someone reading aloud. I was shocked to see how many people stunt their learning by glossing over mispronounced words, as they don't have a clear meaning of what they are reading.

So the definitions of *maneuver* that apply to this technique are as follows: 1b—to make a series of changes in direction and position for a specific purpose; 2—to manage into or out of a position or condition: manipulate; a—to guide with adroitness and design; b—to bring about or secure as a result of skillful management—*maneuverability, maneuverable, maneuverer.*

The setup for the noodle is important. When coming to a stop nearside, the bus is as close to a straight line parallel to the traffic lane as possible so that visibility in the driver-side rear mirror is maximized. This is in the rule book, so that the front door is close to the curb, within six inches, and the rear door or doors are also within one foot of the curb. Many times, this is very hard to do due to lack of room created by double-parked vehicles or cars standing in the zone. But the good thing about nearside stops is that they are usually clear, and if any car is at the nearside corner, odds are they can easily move away, and the car is almost always attended, and when they see the bus coming up behind them, they move. So when the nearside zone is clear, pulling the bus up parallel to the curb helps those passengers departing and gives maximum rear visibility.

After boarding and alighting and when the light turns green, or at a stop sign, the problem is being let in to traffic to proceed through the intersection. Keeping good car karma helps, by always allowing a turning, oncoming car or a car trying to pull out into traffic the space to move and not to block them. Even in construction squeeze play, I have found that *best man wins* or *me first* usually adds more delay than spacing, which allows for a smoother merge. So having good car karma helps with the noodle. When beginning to move from the zone, the noodle involves not using the turn signal and abruptly turning left into the traffic lane but rather slowly moving forward, straight ahead in the curb lane. So if an accident report should ever result, I would not have to check the box *turning left* or *using the left turn signal.* Any operator soon finds that activation of the turn signal when merging left almost always has the unintended consequence of vehicles speeding up to pass left and block the merge. The thought of getting ahead of a big, billboarding vehicle outweighs the smoothness created in allowing us to move ahead without stopping. So by moving straight ahead, all cars can see that the bus is moving and clearing the zone and intersection. This also signals that the bus is finished with boarding, and no more delays will result in more people running to the door and stopping again.

If a car wants to race, that vehicle can easily pass the bus on the left, as there is no conflict in the traffic lane. And this also helps because now the bus is clearly in the lead in crossing the intersection for any secondary car, and the size of the bus usually stops any additional threats on the left. Because we are still parallel to traffic, we can see in our mirror any threat coming up from the rear. And as we get close to the far-side crosswalk, we then move to the left, free and clear of any threat.

When I began to call the shots for when I could pull away, with clear visibility to my rear and no threat on the intersection far side, I knew I had found the Zen of the noodle.

The Late Ring

NOTHING CAN GET A PASSENGER ANGRIER THAN PASSING UP A STOP. I CAN tell a lot about their day by how they respond when I pass by where they wanted to get off. Intuition does come into play when I am in the beat of the flow, and I know to stop and open the doors even if there was no ring or verbal request. I joke I don't have eyes in the back of my head or possess supernatural powers to mind-read the desires of our passengers. Actually, I do have these extraordinary skills or abilities! With the experience that comes from years of driving, I kick in to an automatic pilot mode that remembers where and when to stop and how many people will be getting off and on. I never let on to this because ignorance (although not an excuse during a disciplinary hearing) is bliss. Contrary to the blissful ignorance I master through the years is the expectation of need from our riders, without any verbal communication at all. This is the Zen of driving Muni.

As soon as I see something out of the ordinary, I immediately file it away in my head as a possible yellow flag. This ability to flag an abnormality to our flow, such as a distracted passenger, or the time it takes for someone to sit down and where they sit when they first board, is a way to prepare for a possible mind-read situation when the person is ready to get off.

And if the boarding passenger goes into the black hole, the seat behind the cockpit, where I cannot see or hear them, the risk of a pass-up or late ring goes way up.

If they are in a large party and are talking among themselves, particularly tourists, then the late-ring pass-up increases dramatically. How a person passes by me at the fare box is a key to understanding the drama of how they leave the coach. No eye contact or acknowledgment of our existence increases the intensity of anger they may express when they attempt to leave. No courtesy or recognition of us doing our job, and fare evasion, go hand in hand with nasty name-calling at the end of this boarding event.

The attention to detail when a person boards is the secret to having the magic of mind reading or eyes in the back of my head.

Some operators never use the interior center or aisle mirror located in front of us above the windscreen, but by scanning this mirror as I am directed to scan left-right-left on my exterior mirrors, passenger problems can go to near zero. Also, the small mirror in the corner by the front door is perfect for aiming at the black hole. Thus, I can see everyone in the seats toward the back door and the two seats directly behind the cockpit, should someone shift their body position in anticipation of the stop. I get the heads-up if someone is falling asleep or inattentive to where the bus is headed. When I stand up and let a sleeper know, before they fall asleep, that this is their stop, it helps prevent a lost cause at my next terminal or pull in, trying to get them off my bus.

If a chime cord is not working or the dash light indicating a stop request is not lighting up, the mirrors come to the rescue of what can be a Zen breaker, usually resulting in name-calling and verbal abuse.

But the danger I have in appearing unconcerned with someone who wants to get off is that I get so complacent in knowing the rhythm of my day I don't allow for differences in my passenger requests. If I have passed up a baby stop at a certain time week after week, my automatic pilot fails me if I haven't been scanning my rear interior mirror. And hence my Zen is broken by an angry stop request.

"Back door!" is a friendly reminder of my remiss, but nasty name-calling has me usually proceeding to the next stop. The more anger someone directs at me, the longer the next stop may be. I have to fight the demons of resentment within me to stop when someone is very angry. Anger doesn't usually work with me. I like to strike back with indifference to meet their expectation. Hey, if I am a blind idiot or a moron, then it fits that I continue on to the next stop, as any faithful moron would!

But if that God-given break in parked cars is available, I stop when safe to do so. It is when there is no place to safely stop that drama crescendos in a late ring. But I do recover from such name-calling a lot faster now than when I was new.

And if the late ring is from someone who needs the curb, I do feel bad when I can't find that safe spot a short distance from the regular bus stop. Even though other passengers may come to my rescue by agreeing that there was no ring, it does little to comfort the angry passenger. All I can do is file the incident away and recall where the offending passenger boarded, so as to prevent the late ring from happening again in the future.

Stopping next time around at the same stop, even though I have no request, helps to make the problem go away. Interestingly, someone from the back will come forward to the front door and request the next stop. This is a nice check from the universe that this problem has been put to bed because I have not resisted the late ring. *I have to be willing to make the stop.* And when I am, all is well, and the Zen of driving Muni returns.

Sleepers

THE BEST OFFENSE IS A GOOD DEFENSE. THE BEST WAY TO PREVENT someone from being asleep is to spot the candidates when they board. And even then, there will always be those who come in the back door or appear alert when they enter. But at forty-five minutes a trip, there is plenty of time to fall asleep. Many wonder why the heat is not on when it's cold outside. The answer is we don't want people falling asleep. The heat makes us drowsy, especially if we are already tired to begin with. If I anticipate someone falling asleep, I ask them where they are going. If they are going into a deep trance, they won't even look at me or answer the question. I either pop the brake then and there to get them off, which usually doesn't work, or, as a gentle reminder that I am being of service, let them get the rest they need. Half of the time, they sleep for one terminal only and get off when I am back in the other direction. And 98 percent of the time, two trips as an unwritten rule, and they get off. It is the 2 percent where I have to call Central for an inspector or the police.

All I can do is tell my truth the best I know how and see where the cards fall. But better these cards fall than the drunk who started drinking at happy hour, and now it is last call! Note to bouncers: have a friend ride with the drunk, so at least we know where to open the door to let our friend off! Don't push your problem onto my bus. If you bring a sober friend who knows where the man of the sauce is going, fine. At least I have a destination.

We are not a shelter. *We are a transportation company.* If I know where you are going and you have a destination, I am okay with that. If you can't answer a simple question about where you want to go, then we have a problem. I have learned that popping the brake and getting the destination first when a drunk or potential sleeper boards is best to get an answer. Otherwise, it is time to call the cops—hopefully not when I am trying to pull in and go home.

Once I called the fire department. Twenty-Sixth and Mission is the collection depot on Sunday morning for the ne'er-do-wells coming down from their latest binge. And nowhere else is the metaphor "dropping like a rock" more apt. This man was the only one waiting at the stop, and I took in a deep breath and sighed. "Here we go." He was seething with anger just under the eyes but was really tired. I guess I just felt sorry for him and thought that his being tired was greater than his anger, so I let it go.

I know from experience that this is the key to avoiding trouble. But when I tried to rouse him at the end of the line, he wouldn't budge. I asked him to get up, and he cursed at me and called me names. He then smugly went back to sleep. So I could ignore him and let him sleep or get him off. There had been theft of personal items at this terminal, and I needed to use the bathroom. I would have to exit the coach. Because he had fluid dropping from his lower lip, I decided to play the medical emergency card. I called the fire department. He tried the same bull on the firefighters when they tried to get him up, but he was outnumbered and outgunned. Three big guys in full battle array got him up and out, and all I did was dial. Whew. But at what cost to the city? And this is where homelessness and drug use really tax our city. The cost of these services really adds to the taxpayer bill. But would an assault upon me from an angry passenger also have a cost?

Staying in my chair and calling Central Control for help is the solution for keeping my job and staying in the Zen of driving Muni.

Next Bus

MUNI TIME IS NOT LIKE REAL TIME. THE DIGITAL NEXT-BUS TIME IS displayed on most bus zone shelters, with the estimated time of arrival for the next two buses. But anyone who has spent any time in the bus zone knows that the arrival time displayed by next bus is not a given. Sometimes the countdown stops, Sometimes the countdown to arrival actually increases in minutes. Sometimes the sign states that the bus is arriving when no bus is in sight. Then it shows a bus departing, and there is no bus. What causes these invisible arriving and departing buses?

The interesting point here is that Muni time is not constant. As transit operators, we are continually making adjustments in our minds, followed by actions at the light or bus stop to continually readjust our headway, depending upon whether we are ahead or behind our regularly scheduled arrival or departure time at the various checkpoints along our line. Sometimes leaving late is a means to an end to arrive early at our next terminal. Other times, leaving early is a huge mistake and actually causes us to arrive late at our next terminal. But how could this be?

If I leave Daly City early, I may have a large group waiting for me at the Evergreen stop, which is the major transfer point from points south in San Mateo County from our sister transit agency, SamTrans. My time spent in the zone here and in subsequent stops to Geneva, the first major transfer point in the city limits, costs an extra five to seven minutes. Picking up seniors and those without fast passes takes extra time at the fare box, which is our biggest factor in our average miles per hour, or rate at which we move through our trip to our next terminal. Very few folks have a fast pass at Evergreen. If the 14 Rapid coach is late or missing its leader, the local coach, the one I am driving, can become heavy with standees and run late. If the other helper coach, the Rapid, arrives first to Geneva, this can help when I arrive there, as fewer people are waiting. I would then lose more people getting off to go to Balboa Park BART than would be waiting to board and go downtown.

This difference in passenger load affects comfort levels and number of seats for seniors. I have to make the decision to leave a little earlier to compensate for the heavy load and delay at the fare box, but this increases the chance that I will arrive first at Geneva, the first major transfer point in the city. This would keep me heavy inbound to Ocean and delay my arrival to my inbound terminal. If I hold back and leave Daly City later, I might get help from the Rapid and might not be as full, as this other coach would arrive at Lowell first and also maybe at Geneva, so I would start to become lighter and have fewer passenger congestion problems. It is these considerations that can lead to a game of *you go first* that delays the line and creates bigger gaps between buses. And so those waiting at Daly City are in the constant state of struggle and flux, asking the timeworn phrase, "Are you the first coach to leave?"

Let the games begin ... and why lines get eliminated. The number 7 Haight would wait at the Golden Gate Park terminal across from the Golden Arches until the 71 Noriega would come and barrel around the corner to pick up at Stanyan and Haight. Waiting for the 71 would cause the 71 to become even heavier and run later, because the 7 wouldn't leave on time from the park terminal. And by holding back three minutes, the 7 could shadow behind the 71. *The 71 became the number 7, and the old 7 to Golden Gate Park got eliminated.* By looking at the numbers of passengers on the 7, management decided to eliminate the 7. In doing so, they eventually had to make the 71 an articulated bus on weekends. In the meantime, on the sign-up before they added the sixty-footers to the Haight, the crowds waiting at Fifth and Market became so large that it was unsafe to stand on the island because it was so crowded. By giving up an extra line, the duel is now at Masonic, where the 6 Parnassus gets the extra burden from a 7 driver who holds back. This is where the games make for a long weekend of work. All this holding back on another coworker just takes away a bus line.

So why would these games not have a referee, such as an inspector monitoring leaving times? Good question. Now that all coaches have cameras, and all coaches can be monitored by GPS on laptops, many such delays have been avoided. When the Rapid coaches run in packs on the Mission, the regularity of space between coaches becomes somewhat disrupted. When I kept getting asked, "When is the Rapid coming?" it is a safe bet that they are leaving late from the Ferry so as to not run hot.

If they would just leave on time and pace properly, this question would never be asked. When a sign-up becomes stale and the games get heavy, everyone starts hoping for a new schedule. I noticed that my headway and load factors improved dramatically a few weeks before the end of a sign-up. It was because checkpoints were being observed by inspectors. How I wish I did not have to wait for the end of the sign-up for paperwork to be served. The difference to job quality by running on time is astonishing.

Another wait and see was at South Van Ness and Mission, where the 47 could wait at the light by Goodwill and allow the 49 Van Ness to go first to pick up the waiting hordes at Market. If the 49 in front of these following two coaches is shadowing behind the 14 line on Mission and holding back to do less work from Ocean, it becomes clearer as to why these gaps in buses occur and why wait time increases. This only causes operators to avoid this blob and hold back, hoping that the coach from the other barn has to be first to do the work.

This gives management the incentive to eliminate runs where the following bus is usually empty. The famous example is to take anyone complaining about the schedule to the big board at Central Control. Coaches running ahead of schedule show pink to red the hotter they are (ahead of schedule). Buses running late turn from white on time to yellow as slow. When the schedule works and everyone leaves on time, no one has the need to run ahead of schedule, and we can be late or show up yellow on the board. If things get busy, we don't have enough time left in our recovery time at the terminal to leave on time, as we arrive after our leaving time, so we hedge and stay ahead of schedule. Running hot is not because we have too much time; it is because we fear our loss of time will have us run late, and arguments and fights will break out because there are not enough seats. By being "efficient" in reducing buses that our usually empty, all hope of keeping the schedule goes away, and the gaps between late buses become more frequent.

So the key becomes not to allow a long enough recovery time at the terminal so an operator can leave early.*

The content herein does not necessarily reflect the views of the SFMTA or its policies and rules.

The Overhead

One of the differences our corridor streets have that most cities have lost are the sets of wires over the center of the lanes. Only nine US cities still have overhead from the fifties. Newer trams recently built may be increasing this number. In SF, we have numerous utility poles alongside the sidewalk that have support wires holding the power. These traveling wires are for our trolleys to be powered by electricity from our hydroelectric grid. Our O'Shaunessy Dam is one valley north of the Yosemite Valley and provides not only drinking water but power for our trolleys.

I love the fact that our city uses this carbon-free source of power for our extensive trolley lines. We have more miles of trolley wire than any other city in the world. I am proud to work for a railway that has so many different modes of equipment—and that I can call myself a bus driver but not use any fossil fuels when picking up passengers. I feel like an active agent helping our Earth stay as clean as possible.

Our overhead requires routine maintenance, and it is common to see our big yellow trucks working on the wires over the street. Now all of our trolleys are equipped with battery power or APU, auxiliary power unit, or EPU, emergency power unit, to go around a crew working on the wires overhead. There are sets of trays of batteries that power this mode. This is another technology change that makes life much easier than in the day when we had to roll around an obstacle or get pushed by another trolley. Gone are the days when passengers would be asked to step outside and help push the bus through an intersection or dead area at a breaker crossing. Before bicycle racks were mounted on the front bumper, we could push a dead-in-the-water trolley from behind with another trolley.

I try to learn about the parts and pieces of the overhead whenever I see the crew taking a break or just having finished doing a repair. I like to know their terms for things, so if I have to call in a repair, I can at least give Central Control an idea about what I am talking about.

The biggest reason nothing gets done is that the wrong switch or converge is being described on the radio. It is difficult to call in a specific problem in detail when of a driving mind—being in an alert, problem-solving state of mind. This is a different part of the brain than that which answers a question about how many stops away until a destination, or a part location in a complex intersection of lots of special work. Without knowing the standard name for a part, any report for damage is left open for misunderstanding about where the maintenance is needed. Try as I might, I haven't been able to convince those outside of training to add this to our syllabus. Line trainers become the key.

Crossovers

If you ever look up in the middle of an intersection where two trolley lines meet, you will see crossovers. Below these are the fiberglass slots along the traveling wires and jump-over wire bridging the gap, so to speak, over the dead area where the wires cross. This insulates the positive and negative wires from touching each other. We must power off our coach as we coast through this dead area. That is what those yellow dots are that are marked on the street. They mark the dead area where depressing the power pedal has no effect on forward traction. So if you see dots in the middle of the crosswalk, it means we have no power at this point.

Should not the breakers be placed in such a way that there are no dead areas at critical pedestrian and car crossings? Thank you! Now you are beginning to see things from a trolleyman's point of view. The dead area placement is affected by where the power poles are positioned, which has much to do with trees, buildings, and numerous other obstacles. Take time to study an intersection and notice what decisions went into why things are where they are. Eventually, you could graduate to an intersection like Church and Duboce! Or S. Van Ness and Mission! It isn't as simple as it first might seem, especially if streets come together at odd angles, due to SF's topography.

Surge Suppressors

On the leading edge of all crossovers is a thing that looks like an Oreo cookie, perpendicular to the wires. This suppresses a spark from a depressed power pedal, should an operator have power on when crossing a breaker. If you have ever been on an electric bus that shudders suddenly, this is because the operator has the power pedal depressed over a breaker. This occurs when trying to move in stopped traffic, especially on an uphill near a stoplight.

If the dot on the street isn't measured correctly, or worn away, or unmarked, a jolt can be felt. The surge suppressor reduces this jolt. It is a pair of insulated disks that try to suppress the flash from power attempting to short between the crossing wires. Sometimes these become detached from the wires due to frequent jolts, and this causes trolleys to de-wire near intersections and turns. It took me six months to get the surge suppressor fixed at the Townsend CalTrain crossover for the 45 Union. The glaze in the gaze of an inspector trying to guess what I had described over the radio told me nothing was going to get done. No one in street ops or as a trolley operator knew what a surge suppressor was. This compartmentalization between departments (it's not my job) in the city is a hassle any small business person understands in trying to get a permit or pay a fee with the city. Can't we all get along?

Breakers

Of all crossovers and switches, where opposing poles of electricity cross, is the universal term *breaker*. This is all we are required to know as an operator of electric buses. A previous manager of the Overhead Division was asked to create a class plan to instruct new operators on the various parts of the overhead, but he retired before this was put into play. I try to get the names of the various parts of the overhead when I see the crew on break by a repair area, but this is not easy to do.

Different guys on different crews may call a part by a different name. If I am moving through an area on a bus, or if at a terminal and the crew is busy, it isn't all that common to get answers to questions about crossover parts and switches. Their general response is "Did you call it in?" Rats. Okay, next time I have a problem in an area, I'll call it in. But not knowing the name of the part I see in need of repair makes it a challenge to use this part of my brain while driving. And hence, most operators don't make the call.

Nothing happens until more than two operators call in a de-wirement problem. So I have to get my leader and follower to also make the call. This is not as easy as it sounds because we no longer see one another at the terminals because recovery time has been cut. Being on a racetrack means that if I want to communicate with my leader or follower, I have to be familiar with where our paths cross. I then have to get their attention and make sure they can hear me.

One of the first questions asked about inter-bus communication is the necessity to go through the OCC. We can't contact another bus directly. The best we can do is get the cell phone number of our relief and make a call at a terminal before relief time to let them know of a delay. Calling Central is the simplest and best way to make contact and should be the primary method of inter-bus contact. I have seen that making deals with another broken-down operator is usually too self-serving and not in the public's interest. Many times, a coach's overload in going over a breaker occurs after the bus is hot and has been in service for several hours. A bus's performance changes as the day progresses, and power surges in the breakers have a lot to do with where a bus breaks down.

Dog Bone

In the middle of a converge or diverge is a set of opposing toggles that guide the collectors through a switch to make a smooth transition from one set of wires to another. Their pattern resembles the classic cartoon dog bone—two wide flanges at either end with a narrow middle. If they stick, due to changing weather conditions, such as morning dew and fog, I ask for special sauce to be applied to reduce sticking.

Sometimes the toggles refuse to change or only go halfway. This causes de-wirements at switches. The problem is the toggles may only act up intermittently. This can cause a resource drain if an inspector is required to monitor a switch until a de-wirement is observed. As more coaches go through the area and it warms up, a switch may be okay. Or how a previous coach hit the dog bone can make a difference. Sometimes the de-wirement only occurs after one coach makes a right turn preceding a straight-on coach. Or if a coach has worn shoes, bent collector, or a twisted pole.

If my leader caused the problem the way he or she went through, my follower may have no problem. This creates an awful cat-and-mouse waste of time. Inevitably, the switch needs to be fixed. I say sooner than later, but it isn't up to me. Only inspectors can make the call. I have learned that even if nothing gets observed or fixed right away, I can relax knowing I did the right thing. Leaving up to God's time is a big resentment I needed to get over as a bus driver. In the meantime, 3 to 5 mph when crossing through special work!

Pan

Above most inductive switches is a sheet metal piece referred to as a pan. This shields the transmitter ball located at the end of the right pole from sending its signal to other switches in the area. When new switches were installed, they were without a pan of metal over them to shield the signal. I went through a two-year battle to get pans installed over the inductive ring, which is wired to turn the toggles in the switch. Especially at North Point and Van Ness. After countless de-wirements, pans were installed. It is this poverty consciousness that pervades most government agencies, transportation notwithstanding. Waiting for failure is the watchword for trolley repair and overhead repair, and it is another battle in my head that I have to let go of if I am to stay safe. People ask me why I am writing this book, and this could be my number one reason. I can't change the system, but I can change myself. And this changes the impression I am creating when behind the wheel of that large automobile. How did I get here? Sounds like Talking Heads, no? The new doughnuts are white and are not necessarily installed with a pan on top. Only after months or years of calls do they get a pan that shields the signal from another trolley. Cue Bob Dylan's "Blowin' in the Wind" as to when the switch will be installed properly.

Truth be told, some switches activate for no apparent reason. No matter how meticulous a pan is installed to shield a nearby trolley coach from inadvertent trigger, some switches activate on their own. I have looked at my switch control dial in the normal position, only to see that the semaphore has changed, or I hear the click of the switch changing even before I am over the doughnut. As a line trainer, this is a mandatory lesson about what makes a trolley operator different from a motor coach operator: we must listen to what the overhead is telling us, especially when we need to turn on a switch.

Fortunately, I am always aware of what position the switch is in before I cross the intersection. I have not brought down any overhead due to a falsely triggered switch. As a line trainer, I tell my student where these ghosts are in the system. A study of the natural earth energy lines does make for a compelling reason as to why these electrical mysteries keep happening.

Doughnut

Underneath the pan is the doughnut. This is the electromagnetic loop that sends the turn signal message from our foot pedal button on the floor to the switch. In certain areas, such as Main and Mission, Mission and Thirtieth, and Market and Eighth, a following trolley must not activate a turn signal until the lead coach has passed the frog of the switch. By reactivating the toggles before the lead coach passes, this causes the lead coach to switch incorrectly.

I am good at spotting this, and because my follower is in a rush, he has to then reset his poles because now the switch is set in the wrong direction because he passed the doughnut, and the lead coach took the switch. The distance between the doughnut and switch is too far away, and more than one trolley can pause between the transmitter and the diverge. Anyway, I haven't heard of anyone getting in trouble for this, but I think they should. Call me Mister Overhead. If following the one-block spacing rule, these de-wirements would not occur.

The newer trolleys have a smaller footprint on the wires. The brasserie is smaller, and the carbons are thinner. The poles are two feet longer. Less metal is used, and parts are more flexible. To be fair, these improvements have helped tremendously. New switches seem to have fewer problems, and all trolleys can get around a repair area using battery power. These changes have made for a nicer day behind the wheel.

Selectric Switch

If you look up near an intersection of two trolley lines, you may see two staggered, parallel gray boxes before the converge of two sets of wires. These are selectric switches. They are triggered by the angle of the dangle. When a coach begins a turn, the poles begin to skew on track and are no longer parallel on the wires. The angle of the bus, with the poles askew, triggers the switch because the gray boxes are hit simultaneously by the angled poles. If you stand by such a corner, you can hear the click as a trolley makes a turn on to another line. Being in a Zen state means being able to hear the click!

The Complaint Department

Is closed. Or so I was told every time I entered the tower at Potrero by the lead shop man whenever I had to pass by. Perhaps this message stemmed from the incident with the dirty filter I had on my bus when I pulled in one night.

The clasp holding the grille that protects the filter inside dropped to the floor, and I gasped at seeing filthy dust bunnies on both sides of the fiberglass tray. Babies were crying, and seniors were coughing all day long on my bus. I kept my cockpit window open and was blessed by the Pacific breeze, which can remain continuous throughout the day, so I didn't notice how dirty the air was streaming into the coach. This was my first realization why operators don't turn on the heat in the coach. On my crosstown ride home on the 22 Fillmore, I finally got the lesson from an operator about the dos and don'ts of when to use the fan on a bus.

Do turn on the blower to high before pulling out to warm up the cold metal terrarium inside before sitting down inside the cockpit to set the controls. Sure enough, after the first five minutes, the blower motor warms up and quiets down. All the collected dust and carbon settled in the tubes gets pushed out from the first burst of air, and air quality improves. Once warm, the blowers can be turned off before picking up at the first bus stop. Don't leave the fan on for extended time during a trip.

Do use terminal breaks as a good time to reuse the fans to reheat the coach, again while standing outside the coach or using the bathroom. I also learned the valuable lesson about the other drawback to a warm coach: sleepers. It is usually a matter of fifteen minutes of warm interior air to bring dozers off into la-la land. Making a coach a hospitable interior climate is not helpful when pulling in on a twilight run! Our twilight trips last up to an hour, so it is key to spot potential sleepers when they board, especially during the first few minutes of departing the terminal.

Do keep mental track of who is boarding, especially when the aisle becomes crowded and the rear interior view is blocked, so you can't see who is lying down on the back seats.

Don't allow persons with blankets to board rear if I cannot see where they sit. Do pop the brake and stop a sleeper in their tracks when they first board by asking where they are going. If they cannot answer, politely and keeping their dignity intact, state that Muni is not a shelter, and my job is to get you where you need to go. This usually helps in getting an answer. If they are just shining me on, I tell them I am pulling in. I don't want you to get stuck far away from where you need to be. If they do answer, I can wake them up at their requested stop. If they are really dead in the water, I have to wake them up a few blocks early.

This may seem like a call above and beyond duty, but the only way to get them off is by going to their seat and letting them know we are at the stop. This saves a call for an inspector, the police, or the fire department later on when I desire to go home.

I do provide wake-up service. It saves downtime so my follower doesn't lose me as a leader when I am waiting for the inspector or police to rouse a deep sleeper. On late nights, it is sometimes easier to let sleepers go for a trip or two to catch up on sleep, but there are limits.

So back to my pull in at the tower and my tirade upon pull in. I held up the fiberglass baffles and shook the nasty dust on the floor. "This is unacceptable! Seniors are coughing, and babies are crying!" Silence. My mind conveniently goes blank on what I said next, but I was full of rage. The tower was full of other shopworkers and the yard starter, and other operators waiting on equipment.

My compassion for safety and doing my job backfires at times in inappropriate ways if I do not express myself at the right time. This time I nailed it. I finally showed an inadvertent omission on an item not considered safety significant. I got angry at the right time and never looked back. And there was nothing anyone could say about it from the shop because I was right. And I bore witness in front of all my peers. This was one of those classic moments.

My *out to get me* conspiracy theory thinking has not served me, but I never knew it because I never stopped to see the effect I was having on others when I passed anger on to someone else at another time and place. And so the transference of frustration at hearing, "The complaint department is closed," thereafter by the lead shop man at the Potrero tower, smiling. It is not all about me.

I now feel the relief of this realization as I sit here and type this in on my netbook. This is why I write. This is why I write. If I were a normal nonwriter, I may have never needed to do a personal moral inventory. A secret of why emerges. It helps get out the crazy. In this case, the nasty dust bunnies trapped in the filter of my brain and behavior!

I just had my jacket snatched down at Townsend on the 45! I left it on the operator's seat back and stepped off to talk to my leader. I got my uniform jacket back, but my diaries book was taken. So much for the record from January to June! Hmm. I wonder if the Muniverse is trying to tell me something: secure the coach when leaving, if only for a moment. Now I have to tie my bag to the back seat. I hate having to worry about security when I am just trying to take a break. This job keeps me on my toes; as soon as I slack off in one area, such as security or defects, the complaint department responds in kind!

When I am rested and mindful, I am in the Zen to do the right action and keep the complaints at bay—at bay with the barking sea walrus and seals.

The White Lie

Because San Francisco is such a small, compact city with water on three sides, our crosstown bus routes intersect with every line that goes downtown inbound, or out to a beach on the ocean, or by the bay in the opposite direction. Since we also have a large visitor population, we get asked about directions at the front door when we pull up to a stop. In order to maintain a relaxed, Zen-like posture and relaxed state of mind, I have finally learned what the visitors are really asking, based upon what stop they are standing at. The white lie saves time and confusion even though what I am saying to them is not literally true.

On the crosstown 33 Stanyan, I head inbound on Haight Street for four blocks before I turn off on Ashbury to go over the Twin Peaks, Clarendon hill, on my way to the Castro, the Mission, and Potrero, which are all nondowntown neighborhoods. But my direction is outbound, even though I am heading inbound on Haight. The question asked continuously by at least one party of visitors on Stanyan and Clayton at Haight is, "Do you go to Market Street?" The honest answer is yes. The helpful, not literally true answer is no. After coming down the Clarendon hill, the 33 turns on to Market at its uppermost point, when it becomes renamed as Portola, at what I like to call Dead Man's Curve. I turn almost 180 degrees on a hairpin turn with a vista of downtown and the East Bay. It is a dramatic turn with a very scenic twist. But there are no major destinations or points of interest at this hairpin turn, save for the lovely view. I then travel down upper Market for about two blocks and then head for Castro village, which does place us one block from the Market and Castro underground line, or the Castro Station, which does connect easily to all downtown areas and eventually to BART. So if my riders don't appear rushed and are

145

in sightseeing mode, I say yes, to take them to the hairpin vista. If it is afternoon rush and they have shopping bags, I say no. The question they are asking, *Do you go to Market?* really means *Do you go downtown?* They aren't specifying where on Market they want to go. After asking time and time again where on Market they want to go, I have come to the conclusion that they mean somewhere along Fourth or Fifth and Market and Powell Station. So I have learned just to say no and ask them to wait for the 7. Or walk down to Masonic for the 6 if a 7 has just passed. If I am without a leader and I am running heavy and late, I always say no. This is how we can control our load when carrying passengers who would normally have boarded the coach in front of me.

The same is true on Potrero Boulevard, which is like the old business loop highway that used to be the main road before the freeway was built. People ask along the thoroughfare if I go to Market. Once again, after much experience, I have found that the simplest way to move along is to say no. Wait for the number 9. Which really means that I don't go downtown to the Union Square area.

So I find myself having learned what people need by their questions, to answer no, and save time by not going through other questions that add to a delay. Experience with the time of day, how they are dressed, and the regularity of the same question over and over keeps me talking less and in a mode to help those who have a destination along my crosstown route.

I default to the nearest stop when they ask the open question of a specific business, such as the golden arches. I pass by two golden arches, three Safeway grocery stores, and three hospitals. I can answer yes and call out the first one I pass by. Usually, most people recognize where they are when they get to the stop they need. Describing the landmarks is usually unnecessary. I don't need to use sarcastic humor because it can backfire and lead to a bad experience. I learned early on that there will never be an end to the same questions being asked over and over, so conserving my response is the easiest way to staying in the Zen zone.

Service Dogs

Or should I say, service animals. All creatures great and small do we see on a day as an operator of trolleys. As a new operator, it takes a getting used to of all the various creatures that qualify as a service animal. I would like to see the permit of that pit bull or that boa constrictor, but we are trained by the blowback from the owner not to question their integrity, lest we violate the rules of the Americans with Disability Act. And so we learn to continue with a nod and a smile—until another passenger complains about safety being violated.

We are only allowed one nonservice dog per coach. If a small dog can be contained in the arms of a passenger, this is usually okay. But if another large dog enters, if it is a service dog, this dog has priority. Trained service dogs are expected to behave in a respectful manner. Some passengers are calling their dogs *service* dogs, but they do not behave as I would expect a service dog to behave. Any number of service dogs are permitted on one coach, but I would expect their owners to be mindful of where they sit, especially if another dog comes on board. If you bring a puppy on board, I would expect you to carry newspaper for an accident. Hopping off the bus after a tinkle does not seem responsible, and I resent those who seem unaware of their effect on others remaining on board. Car cleaning is not in my job description, but I have learned how to keep in service with extra newspapers!

Faux Pas Number 117

FOR TREKKERS READING THESE ENTRIES, A SIMILARITY TO THE FERENGI text, "The Rules of Acquisition," may become apparent. Containing over two hundred laws of conduct with respect to financial decisions and actions, it is a sort of Bible for this alien species. It is quoted often as a form of wisdom for maximizing profit in any encounter where a clear-cut answer may be difficult. So, too, do we have an unwritten (until now) code of conduct of how to ride a bus in San Francisco. Perhaps, at your curiosity and genuine interest in such matters, I may produce this sacred list for public view in a book or on my Facebook wall: Douglas Meriwether, www.daoofdoug.com.

As you can see, the number 117 implies there are many such faux pas on board or around a coach that lead to a less than profitable outcome of reaching your destination in a timely fashion. Oddly enough, it never ceases to amaze me that almost no one is familiar with Muni faux pas. It may take a holy pilgrim to find a new law or rule of parts acquisition for the railway.

In Gene Roddenberry's world of *Star Trek*, the entire culture seems to be familiar with the rules of acquisition of an alien species within the federation. Here on present-day Earth, in San Francisco, I have yet to encounter a single person versed on *The Dao of Doug: The Art of Driving a Bus*. There seems to be a complete cluelessness on Muni faux pas that prevent transit from running on time. Certainly the thousands of riders of Muni must wonder why this is so. Although I don't have Picard's clarity to make it so, I hope this helps.

Indeed, as voters are again be asked to fund another proposition for bringing money into our transit system, it is clear that many in this organization do not understand the Ferengi Rules of

Acquisition. I don't recall what number this rule is, but if you want to buy new buses for a riding public, or provide timely parts replacement for its fleet, you do need to pay your bills on time if you want to continue to be able to buy new buses or order fresh parts, including tires.

This would include brushes and bushings for traction motors and doors and parts for airbags and wheelchair lifts to pick up those with mobility problems. If, in a voter pamphlet, you ask the public to fund the bus system with more parking meter money to "have a clean, safe and reliable transit system our world-class city deserves," one would expect that the extra money would go to the bus transportation department. (See the *Examiner*, p. 4, April 14, 2013.) Work orders to other departments have given rise to a new nickname for the MTA's initials: ATM! Muni is a cash machine for other department budgets, especially if you keep promising the same thing over and over, year after year, with different propositions. Perhaps this groundbreaking dialogue can begin here with the mention of faux pas 117.

Faux pas 117 is demanding to board a coach in a wheelchair, even after I suggest taking a following bus. As a bus driver, I am always concerned for your comfort. My suggestion to wait for the next coach is based on the experience of the condition of the equipment, the passenger load, the headway, the weather and traffic. (These last two conditions are on the civil service test!) All these have their corresponding number on the faux pas list, but none seems as simple as 117: simply wait for the next bus if your boarding requires use of the accessory power and secondary use of the AC inverter. Having to wait for a tow truck or for the shop can take up to forty minutes. If the shop arrives in twenty minutes and can't unstick your wheelchair from the lift or from inside the coach, another delay of up to three hours may exist in waiting for the tow truck guy to build air back up in the coach.

As a bus becomes warmed up and heavy, the dynamics change, and many times the simplest solution is to simply wait for the next bus. Listening to an operator's suggestion, even though it sounds contrary, may be the best course of action. We are all trying to do the best we can with what we have been given. Parts are replaced on an emergency or crisis-management basis. Good news is no news, except for spare parts.

If a report appears in the paper about a door staying open, it is a good bet the brushes and rollers are on their way.

Sure enough, after a highlight of an open train door in the news, I have never had to call the shop for slow doors or doors that won't close, or had to pull in with doors that stop working! In this case, bad news is good news. The money will be found to fix the problem. In the meantime, keeping Zen is a best friend.

Thank You for Riding Muni

Or so went the announcement that we could cue up with our DVAS (digital voice activated system). But under new management, with the service cuts to our riders, this manually activated announcement was removed. Does this mean that the thanks are no longer needed? Ha. Just kidding. Sometimes I do get in trouble for ad-libbing on the PA or microphone. Very few coaches have clean and clear PAs, and when I have a good one, it helps when the coach is crowded.

When I have been a passenger on a crowded coach, standing in the aisle, it's very hard to see where the coach is, especially at night. I have learned from riding Muni, calling out the stops helps people get ready to get to the door. Timing is everything, as they say. If there is construction ahead or a bus zone is blocked by a big truck, it is nice to open the doors nearside and let them know they can get off here—and to make sure it is safe; no bikes or skaters are coming up from the rear.

The microphone really comes in handy when I am pulling in or going out of service. I sometimes don't have to repeat myself when everyone is in the know. I have also found that if I am willing to pop the brake and step out of the cockpit and face the audience, I get a much more positive response in clearing the coach. I always have to be mindful of my tone of voice. If I end the sentence on an upbeat note and not an annoyed or aggravated tone, this does wonders. I am always amazed at how quickly I forget the impression I am making by how I sound. My overhead voice can go south real quick if I am impatient or feel entitled about why I think they should know that my bus is going out of service. A smile and a transfer at the box is usually all it takes.

But adding some messages under the safety queue might help, such as in the rain: "Thanks for shaking the water off your umbrella before boarding!" Some of these newer umbrellas are huge and carry lots of water! The extra water on board makes for a slippery step and creates a jungle-like humidity in the bus, which fogs up the windows.

The key to keeping the windows clear, especially the front windscreen, is to hold the doors open as long as possible. This lets in the fresh air and prevents the humidity from going up to high. When I am standing at a long red light, I keep the rear doors open, and this keeps the fresh air circulating. No one likes a puddle on their seat, so all of the side windows are closed. Also, the ceiling vents have been known to create a puddle on the floor if they are left open the night before or while in service. I always try to secure the hatches and windows if I am pulling out in the rain. Holding the doors open as long as possible keeps the air fresh and keeps my mirrors from fogging up.

There is nothing worse than closed windows and high humidity from all the umbrellas and jackets that are wet. Keeping visibility at a max is mastered when the rear doors are held open and the baby heat settings are set for both the coach climate and the driver climate.

I recently did a coach trade in the monsoon season and had fog everywhere. By holding open the doors and adjusting the heat down, after just a few stops, the windows cleared. I have never had to get out some newspaper and wipe the windows since. Nice. We now return you to your Zen zone, already in progress!

The Zen Zone

THE BEST TIME TO WORK MUNI IS WHEN THE BUS HAS AN EMPTY AISLE and half the seats are open. This occurs in the morning on most major holidays and on Sunday mornings. The pulse and rhythm, the ebb and flow of passengers is steady state, and harmony abounds. During the week midday, usually from 10:00 a.m. to 2:00 p.m., with leader in sight, is also a wonderful time. Good job, good pay, and no threats on the horizon. It is the wish and hope of every transit operator to select a run where the Zen time is maximized. Everyone is relaxed and happy, and the schedule flows perfectly.

Every time I do my homework before a sign-up, I try to find this zone in a run, and I try to guess where this zone is and how it can be sustained for four or more hours per day. And it is truly a complex matrix. One false move, one error in judgment, can be a costly mistake that results in trips to the superintendent's office and love letters from the dispatcher. A love letter is, at best, a piece of mail containing a caution and reinstruct, or if close to the danger zone, a *warning* in boldface, which means you are off the hook for disciplinary action, but if this happens again within a short time frame, your goose is cooked—time off without pay. Imagine coming to work in the morning, and the first thing you see is that your paddle is missing from the row. *Go see the dispatcher; you've got mail.* What happened this time?

There is a pecking order I have discovered when people go to work. Early is better. At least when judging by faces I see boarding the bus. First, we have the humble Latino working class off to Fisherman's Wharf. The bus boys, the dishwashers, the true working-class backbone of the city. Then we have drones. The white middle-class working stiffs who work downtown for something, something, and something, whether it be an architectural firm, or a law firm, or an advertising agency. I see the fresh, young up-and-comers first. They are going places and have probably moved here from somewhere else for their first big break in the big city. They have the smile behind their eyes, which is full of promise of a great new job with a résumé that probably says, *I am new and trainable and not bogged down by a dysfunctional family past from having grown up in California.* They say, in their eyes, *I got away from my one-horse town with the single blinker light.*

Then come those who have been here awhile. What, forgot to shave this morning? Painted the town last night? Tie one on, did you? Or they come rushing out of a doorway without their tie on, to finish the Windsor once they get it on in the aisle, now crowded, as the inbound arriving time approaches nine o'clock. And after the clock strikes nine come the midlevel managers. Lattes in hand, they head for the corner office. The echelons who eschew the time clock for a supervisor role or particular grade or rank in an organization downtown. The school trip: youngsters are much quieter in the morning than in the afternoon. Students are quietly and purposefully podded in to their music or contemplating their day ahead. Then come the moms and their babies— off to the day care or to do the daily tasks of running a family. And then come the ancient ones—the seniors off to do some food shopping or their appointment to see the doctor.

And then the Zen.

The midday time when everyone is at work or at lunch. And this is when rush hour is over and when most morning runs pull in, where we transit operators can lie down to chat in the Gilley room or go to the gym to work out. Maybe it's a trip to the post office or the store. For those lucky enough to live in the city, we can go home to do chores. But for those straight-through runs, this is the Zen time, when things are steady and even and usually not full of much drama.

So staying in the Zen zone is the sweet spot that makes living in a big city with a good job with good pay a wonder to behold, with everything right in the world. But heaven forbid that the run in front of me happens to be an open run with no regular operator. Or a run with days off of Tuesday Wednesday, which usually doesn't get filled on a regular basis. This hit-or-miss wild card, not knowing who is ahead of you or whether or not you have a leader, creates possible destruction of the Zen zone.

Should I adjust up or down in my running time? Will I be running hot if my leader cuts in late with a last-minute detail from dispatch? Did I piss off the dispatcher the other day by questioning how they do their job? Am in a payback situation? Payback is a bitch, a phrase or term I will never forget. Especially when Central Control has me on ignore. And this is when the Zen zone can become Muni's ninth level of hell.

I will never forget run 84 on the 1 California during the sign-up from hell—with no end in sight. I was warned by the executive board at a union meeting that this was to be a long sign-up. I remember making my choices for my choice slip before the sign-up at the Presidio. My hero, my union representative, was standing right beside me as I saw the run with big pay and weekends off still available on the range sheets minutes before my choice slip bid window.

Wow, I thought. *Here is a big run with weekends off still available. How could this be?* And my steward said, "There are times when the runs pick me, rather than me picking them." *Interesting*, I thought. This must be a sign from the Muni gods that I had arrived in my seniority level. I finally was able to get a four-hundred-plus run with weekends off during a good time frame, between 7:00 a.m. and 7:00 p.m., with some standby time for lunch.

Little did I know there was a reason why the run was open. It was the icon for the ninth level of hell. It did the 1 line from Thirty-Third Avenue and Geary leaving just after 8:00 a.m., with an arrival downtown just after 9:00 a.m. It passed the avenues just after the last express downtown. It meant that panicked office workers, who just missed the last express, would ask me at the door if another express was coming. No problem. I can do this. After a couple of weeks, they would realize that by 8:22 a.m., if they hadn't gone out their door, they would miss the express. It would just be a small matter of weeks, and the questions would stop. But they never did. Week after week, different workers would be late, and a bad dream turned into a nightmare.

Recycling Day on the Bus

"EXCUSE ME, EXCUSE ME." THE ANCIENT ASIAN ONE STARTS CARRYING her bags of cans up the steps by the back door. The crash and tinkle of a number of bottles and cans cry out when the bags hit the floor on the aisle. Tip number one: be seen and not heard. Smashing cans and draining bottles on the coach does not a welcome make.

Working hard to recycle is an admiral effort. Closing down recycling centers forces every broken soul still clinging to welfare to take a longer journey on the crosstown 24 to Bayshore and Industrial. Every Chinese grandma recycling in the Clement/Geary corridor now takes a 38 to the 24 and Divisadero and Geary, where they are not a welcome sight with wheelchairs on board from Kaiser or UC Mount Zion. Muni is a transportation company for people, not garbage, and repeating this affirmation may be a spiritual step in the right direction. One man's garbage, however, is another man's or woman's income. The golden rule is bringing any oversize load is not a given but a permission.

Enter the Mission regulars, the best of the best for getting hard work done. Against all odds, their used pickup trucks' handmade plywood or box modifications have recycling income down. Next are the stalwart heroes seen pushing shopping carts down Potrero, walking the two miles down the road to make it to our single remaining recycling center. Their bags are draped over the cart on all sides and can carry more than five bags of glass and can.

Years of welfare entitlement for some has led to youth crime and broken car windows, because it is mistakenly believed to be easier than the waste of money learning stale facts with outdated textbooks. Ignored is the fact that our city leaders have given us the free education choice with City College. Spending more money has never led to the success that occurs when the desire to excel comes from the within—an inside job.

The Asian empire industriousness, the envy and hate of some chronic homeless complainers, still gets the recycling job done three times faster if, and only if, Muni is used with correct attitude and humility. Because of right-sized respect for all, they don't contaminate Muni buses with recycling odors and leaking bags. Get a clue, guys.

Muni's policy is to leave the discretion at the front door, or back door in my case. We operators may allow boarding of cans and bottles. Safety is our highest priority. If aisles and stairs by the back door are blocked, and if a senior or wheelchair cannot use their area by the flip-up seats, we have a problem. During nonpeak periods, with plenty of empty seats and low traffic, as long as everyone has a seat who needs one, all is well.

My take, after the long haul of cans being taken from Geary to Industrial on a school trip, is to repeat, "Take the next bus."

Dump and Run

AT FIRST BLUSH, IT WOULD SEEM THAT THIS IS A RUDE ACTION AND THAT this chapter may contain inappropriate material not suited for young audiences. But happily, this is not the case. In fact, dump and run, when practiced flawlessly, is a thing of beauty that has me in the grateful, creative mode that places me firmly in the Zen zone.

When an intending passenger runs diagonally across several lanes of moving traffic, smiles and waves at me, and madly dashes to the front door just as the traffic breaks or the light turns green, they have the distinct honor of being the passenger of the day. A quick flash of the fast pass—already in hand—or a perfect swipe of the tag-in card—has passenger of the day in the bag. Someone with quarters counted, already in hand, with the perfect waterfall method of slipping them down the slot, also wins first place.

And this was a trip to get over. I was getting angry and in a scold mold to tell them their actions were not safe. What I resist persists. I learned to calmly state, "Hey, that wasn't safe. I couldn't see you when you came from behind and in my blind spot. You may not be picked up because unsafe behavior is not rewarded with a ride." So as soon as I got over myself as being Mister Safety, all these late rushes stopped coming—such as the bum-rush—to the front door before arriving at the curb. I can always delay opening the front door and let those who migrate in the aisle see that they can depart faster if they go out the back door. Once again, what I do and not what I say has a beneficial effect. Controlling the load inside my coach by delaying the opening of the front door has helped.

So here in the city, we have an unwritten rule of conduct about crossing the street to catch a Muni bus. If the sign says don't walk, and the red hand starts flashing, do what the sign say—run like hell! If the white icon is solid, pay it no never mind. In fact, you can look anywhere but in the oncoming lane of traffic and be content in realizing that the cars must yield to you. Hah!

The haughtiness and entitlement that pedestrians have when crossing the street is second to none in San Francisco. But I don't advise this sentiment when crossing near an off-ramp from the freeway, especially on weekends. Out-of-town drivers, unfamiliar with our provincial attitudes, may have not yet been trained on how to drive in our city.

Indeed, looking at the license plates, especially with the name of the dealer or city on the trim ring around the plate, speaks volumes about where the car and its driver are coming from. If you see an SUV with a Dublin or Pleasanton tag, give wide berth!

Perfect timing with no delay. Now that is definitely the Zen of driving Muni.

Back Door!

THE GREEN LIGHT HAS BEEN ON OVER THE BACK DOOR FOR AT LEAST twenty seconds. A large number of passengers have departed through the back door and entered in the front. The kneeler was used for the nice grandma, and bikes were loaded on the front rack. *Or someone takes a bike from the front rack that does not belong to them!* It is at these times that the cry comes from within the masses at the back of the bus, "Back door!"

And if I am in the Zen of the moment, I have anticipated this delay and can turn on the green light and look in my rear mirror to see if I can see the rear doors opening from someone stepping down. But sometimes the battle cry comes too late, or I can't hear the call from the back because of the crush of humanity absorbing any sound from that far away. Or the blowers are on, and the acoustics are poor, and I have already started moving on to the next stop. But I have also found that to continue on to the next stop without letting the doors reopen results in bad blood that does not have to be. If I can turn on the green light for the back door and relieve the tension, all the better.

There is nothing worse than an angry passenger pushing to the front to confront me on why I turned off the back door switch and prevented disembarking. So the key, when crowded, is to pause, turn off the light, and see if I hear a "Back door!" The contradiction is that just when I desire to pull away to keep my headway from getting longer is exactly when this back door problem arises. I have just one last word: when packed, stacked, and racked, try moving to the back door a block in advance. Granted, you don't have to stand right by the door, but at least get ready to find the flow that starts when people start stepping down. I also find fewer problems with the doors when I keep the rear doors standing open for those one or two second beats that prevent the doors from being forced or damaged.

"The middle step is the abracadabra mechanism when the green light is on." Or "Step down for open sesame when the green light is on." If the PA is not working or is turned up too loud, or not with any sound at all, I can always hit the toggle to open the doors anyway. Tourists or those first-timers don't understand how to activate the rear door mechanism, and sometimes they find themselves on to the next stop if I can't see them when the coach is crowded. But the simple cry of "Back door!" is the quickest way to see the green light come on or have the doors opened manually. Pushing on the doors or staring at them does not usually make them open.

When youngsters are loaded from after school and I have a good PA, I remind them to stay clear of the rear doors. True, the doors are strong in and of themselves, but the hinge mechanism and the brushes and air-delivery system that powers them is very fragile and weak. Toggling the rear door to stand open at every stop does signal to the youth that leaning on the door with a backpack is not a good idea, and they stop leaning. Once again, what I do rather than what I say seems to work best.

New riders can always be found out by the way they depart. They are the culprits of the late ring—or of no ring at all. *I rang the bell!* Sitting on the back bench, they wait until the bus has come to a complete stop before they get up from their seat. They try to make their way through the aisle to the back door. By then, the regulars have stepped down to activate the doors and are long gone. As the doors begin to shut, they step down after the doors are shut, and I am ready to leave the zone. I know where these late bloomers lie, so I have learned to look at the back door one last time to see if someone or a group is holding us up.

Screaming or yelling at the operator may not work as an abracadabra mechanism. Seeing green and not putting off or putting out red is a sure sign I am in the Zen zone behind the wheel!

Seniors Come Out

AND THEN THE RAINS CAME. AND NO ONE HAD AN UMBRELLA. AND NO one was dressed for the cold downpour. And socks got wet. And shoes got ruined. And it rained for forty days and forty nights. Actually, was it in 2006 when we had forty-four days of rain? From the Fourth of July to sometime before the Blue Angels in October, the sun never came out. Not even like in Seattle, where at least you get an hour or two of sunlight in the afternoon. Then the weather breaks, and it's beautiful. Here comes everyone and his brother to do errands, get the pantry caught up, go to the doctor's office or the post office, or a million and one other things that make taking the bus a must. Not for those who can bike, walk, or run but those with mobility problems or strollers or humongous shopping carts from hell. The kneeler is needed at every stop, and you had better wait till I sit down, blah, blah, blah. Everyone comes out at once, and you may as well throw the schedule out the window.

Truth told, the weather effect only holds for about three days. Once people find their umbrella, or galoshes, or their rain jacket after the first storm of the year, everyone adapts quickly, and the weather no longer becomes a threat or an excuse to not take the bus.

But if there are two nasty days of weather, which in San Francisco means biting-cold fog or heavy, monsoon-like rain, you can bet that the pent-up demand to go out and get things done builds, so that by day three, if the weather turns, as it usually does, out come the ancient ones and the rule of law, the rule of God. Respect your elders and give them the time they need to board and find a seat. If a lift request is needed, be sure to wait until they have found a place for their cart or are clicked in by the flip-down seat. I have been in trouble for making the light before they are seated or locked.

I am very gently starting and don't push past walking the dog until they are sitting down. The most problems I have with angry passengers are those who don't seem to be able to tell that my starts are smooth and slow. Of course, there are those times, too, when the points of power are set higher than most, and I am turning the wheel to the left, and I hear the apples and bananas ripping through paper bags and thuds and duds falling and rolling around in the aisle—or the sound of a cane dropping to the floor as gasps go up throughout the coach. And I dread to turn and ask, "Is everyone okay back there?"

Most falls on board do seem to be random and unexpected. I have learned about the no-man's-land from about six chairs back to the front of the middle or rear doors, where there are no handholds or stanchions for the longest stretch along the aisle. If a senior disappears from sight, and that's not hard to do when crowded, as they are usually shorter or smaller, they enter into the purgatory area before the rear door. If they are carrying something in their hand, such as bags or a cart, it makes for an unstable and unsafe situation.

Being in the Zen zone means I am using my interior center mirror to make sure everyone is settled before I move the coach.

Reroute in Effect

IN THE *STAR TREK* MOVIE *THE SEARCH FOR SPOCK*, THE FAMOUS LINE "The needs of the many outweigh the needs of the one" is no more self-evident than in the Muni schedule, especially during special events. Some regular bus stops have a rider alert bulletin posted on the bus shelter or on a utility pole. One of the failures about rerouting buses seems to be that the needs of the many are dismissed for the needs of the few or the one. It makes no sense to send a bus around an area that is congested from a special event, thereby throwing off the schedule and creating irregular headway between busses. When the Castro neighborhood streets are blocked off for Halloween or New Year's Eve, the 33 line is sent over one block to Nineteenth Street, which is up a steep hill with lots of parked cars and is gridlocked due to traffic blocked from driving through, forced onto the same nearby streets like Sanchez and Eureka. The bus, and everyone else, gets stalled as the bus tries to make turns that are stressful and difficult to make without violating the four-foot space cushion around the bus.

Any delay of two or three coaches puts a black hole in headway that creates more work for inspectors, and it sometime takes up to two hours to fully correct at the following terminals for that line. There seems to be no clear communication procedure to learn from the mistakes of the past. Hence this missive.

Fires and the blocked streets from the service vehicles also create havoc, with instructions for reroute that are either impossible or not safe. Coaches become sequestered along the blocked-off street, and the schedule fails. But if I had faith that reroutes were done from the point of view of keeping buses running and free of congestion, I might be able to make a big difference.

Muni is really good in getting diesel shuttles to an area where trolleys are blocked, but I would hope that standard reroutes were in place and understood by all, so that I would be given the standing orders to make a decision to steer clear of the congestion point and report conditions immediately. I am not able to suggest reroutes. The minutes of delay become magnified into hours if the reroute comes after trolleys are already blocked. During these times, my eyes on the road can be helpful by calling Central Control. This is when having a professional attitude when using the radio can be a make-or-break perception of good relations with those who have a challenging job to keep Muni rolling without being able to see what is happening.

Special Events

<small>FINDING THE ZEN ZONE DURING SPECIAL EVENTS CAN BE A CHALLENGE,</small> such as doing the 21 line by Golden Gate Park on the weekend of a major concert or running event that ends or lets out near the Polo Fields in the park.

I made a wise choice to work the 21 line on weekends in the summer because I vowed never again to do the number 5 Fulton line on summer weekends, ever. And so while I was waiting to leave my terminal by the park, I saw a number 5 packed with people pull up beside me. The operator was hollering that she was not going to Market and to get on my bus. Truth was she was going to Market, just not to Powell Station. All the concertgoers could just as easily have walked to Civic Center station or to Powell from her short terminal at Jones and Mc Allister, but she wasn't having it. No one was listening, and no one was getting off her bus. She was experiencing that part of packed, stacked, and racked where no one moves or listens because they were lucky enough to get on a bus and will be damned if they got off their lucky ticket to ride.

I had a completely empty bus, but no one would get off. Here is where past experience about being passed up by full buses puts lead in the feet of all passengers, and no amount of verbal instruction helps. These folks were able to cheat death and fit on her bus, beating out who knows how many unlucky souls. Perhaps the fear of being made to pay a fare was stopping them from moving. They would be damned if they were going to be suckered from a coach they had so victoriously boarded. No, in this case, no one was falling for it. They knew they were going downtown, and that was the end of it!

In hindsight, I could have asked everyone to board my coach. That would have given her breathing room to start picking up with an empty bus, and I could have continued with my shorter distance, full but not in an agitated state of mind. I have always sought to give a break to an operator who is overwhelmed because I know there are times when I am in that predicament, and nothing good comes from it. Learning how to give and gain the respect of my coworkers is perhaps the most and last challenging aspect of staying in the Zen of driving Muni.

New Year's Eve

HALLOWEEN IS ONLY THREE DAYS AWAY AS I WRITE THIS CHAPTER, AND it's a Saturday, and already I saw costumes last night and even earlier in the week. But the holiday season vibe is picking up, and everyone is in the change of gears of the season. The air is crisp and clear. The trees and grasses are making themselves known in the warm, still afternoon air by the scent they let out as we walk by. I don't know about you, but when I recall working on All Hallows Eve and driving through the Castro on the 24 or the 33, my brain jumps ahead to the next disaster, New Year's Eve. For some reason, especially on New Year's Eve, there is the prevalent thought to let it all go. But now, not having had a drink in sixteen years and not really missing it at all, I begin to see a false promise about New Year's Eve. What the heck is the deal for a calendar click, and why does that call for a drink?

But of course, to celebrate the new year. Oh, yeah. You might have a different idea about working on New Year's Eve! Perhaps this title should read *You Get What You Pay For.* If Muni is free from 8:00 p.m. on, what do we know from experience about things that are free? Such as the futon frames we see scattered on our sidewalks, or Christmas trees on the corner on January 7? Worthless. The conflict in the premise of free public transportation becomes painfully obvious on New Year's Eve—or should I say New Year's Day at about 1:30 a.m.

Those riding home at 9:00 p.m., great deal. But as 10:30 p.m. approaches, folks are headed out to party, and the buses become not unlike the 8x in Chinatown—packed. And so on to two most memorable stories I have about New Year's Eve, or should I say, New Year's morning, at about 2:00 a.m.

There—on the island on Duboce Street at Church, just outside of the tunnel—stood over one hundred people taking every square inch of the island. This is a two-car island, with the overflow of intending passengers waiting on the curbside sidewalk. But trains leaving downtown and the Ferry Plaza fireworks were exiting the tunnel and going out of service to return to the barn at Balboa Park. The streetcars (LRVs, light rail vehicles) were full and dumping off more people to wait to go out to the avenues and the Sunset. Muni's free service ended at midnight that year, 2009, and only the regular motor coach N Judah service remained after midnight—one standard diesel bus every half hour.

I was pulling in on the 22 line and gasped at the huge crowd waiting at Duboce and Church. And to my horror of horrors, I looked left at Market and saw a young lady driving an outbound N Judah motor coach on Market, ready to make the turn to Church and then left to Duboce. If ever there was a ninth level of hell, this was it. She had a relatively empty bus, as those downtown were taking the underground to head away.

If I could relive this moment, I would have run to her coach at the light before she turned to Church and warned her about what lay ahead on Duboce. Take Haight Street, and don't look to the left! Put on your Muni face and pray you can make it through the stop sign! I never knew what happened, but suffice it to say it was not pretty. This operator, whoever she is, should win some kind of hero's medal of honor for having to make her next stop. I read in the paper the next Monday about complaints about owl service, but nothing, *nothing*, in writing the day after could do justice for the battle cry that must have gone up when she made the turn to the island. All I can say is, girl, you deserve a vacation to Hawaii or some other fantastic place. Whew! It was really cold that night, and I wonder how her next trip went. Peace be with you!

The next story was on my last time I chose to work New Year's Eve. I pulled in from the 22 Fillmore out at the Woods Division in Dogpatch and had to travel back downtown to catch a 38 Geary outbound to Japantown. I caught a 90 owl shuttle pulling out along Third Street to take me to Ferry Plaza. Fantastic—I just cut off at least a half hour to get to Market Street, and now the easy part would be taking a 38 Geary home.

When I looked at the Next Bus clock on the bus shelter at Montgomery, I saw there was a twenty-one-minute wait time. Instead of waiting half an hour, I immediately changed plans and started walking to Union Square and walked along Geary for twenty-one blocks to see how far I could get on my own. I figured the bus would catch up to me by Van Ness, and I could get a ride over Cathedral Hill to my stop on Fillmore.

When I got halfway up Geary at Leavenworth, I began to see unreal city unfold. The 38, which was twenty-one minutes in arriving back on Market in the Financial District, where I started my walk, was finally arriving to the middle of the Tenderloin, and as I looked into the coach, I saw it was packed. The operator opened the rear door light, and two people got off.

The light turned green, and the bus started to slowly move forward around the taxis that also wanted to pass by the area full of partiers trickling out of the clubs on the corners.

People on the street started fingering the operator and were attempting to enter the coach by prying and kicking down the doors. Fortunately, the bus pulled away with only some cracked glass. I now knew I'd have to walk all the way home—but this was a lot safer than being on the bus!

Since then, I don't work on New Year's Eve. Being free doesn't work during peak period demand. Some cities have tried allowing the bus to be free during nonpeak hours.

The Bigger They Are ...

THE BIGGER THEY ARE, THE HARDER THEY FALL SEEMS TO BE COMPLETELY unrelated to this, but after filling out the number of accident reports I have over the years, I think somehow this does seem to matter. Every occurrence relates to what I was first told in my final interview upon hiring, as well as in my classroom training during the discussion on accidents and writing the accident report. It is the only class that has stood out in my mind over the years. It was a very clear take on what this job meant as a part of our larger economy and was so right to the core that even through challenging contract negotiations over the years with our union and management, and even with public comment in the news, these words still ring true.

This was during the mid to late nineties when Netscape was the godsend and Yahoo was unstoppable. *Yes, they have great stock options and a creative workspace, but what they don't have is your longevity at one job.* Other senior operators in various classes at the training department, and even in the Gilley room, have echoed this sentiment in a slightly different way with the simple encouragement to *stick around and see how it goes.* My favorite is *sit back and watch the show!*

I identified with this on a deep level, and I am glad I did. No matter how hard this job was to be, no matter how awful I thought it was, I was to persevere and keep at it. And sure enough, just like any other job, I started to see the repeats. The patterns of the same thing happening over and over, and how to deal with whatever became a natural working part of my mind. This one trait I have learned from my grandfather, who was up early every day to commute into New York City to work for Con Edison, from my dad behind his desk in the study to prepare another grant request to the National Institute of Health, and from

Wilton, who got up at five to work in the shipyards at Newport News: keep on trudging. All these men had something in common: they never received any accolades or promotion for their steadily paced work, but they kept at the same job for all of their life.

And that steady paycheck was something I never really had, with like eight W-2s during I think it was 1978, or the five I had in 1987! My heart goes out to any young person struggling in their teens or twenties who doesn't see the benefit and simplicity of keeping to the grindstone for a period of time, like years instead of months. The fallacy of cut and run, that I quickly grasp a job description and need to move on, was not the real truth. Learning how to overcome a challenge and see it through to the other side is actually more important for long-range skills in developing intimacy with others. To be sure, I also envy the youth aspect of trying different things, but at some point, I realized my life could be simpler if I just kept to one thing at a time and gave it more time than I thought I should. Walking off a job in forty minutes or after one day seemed to be more of my modus operandi than to wade through difficulty and ask for help. If I could have just waited it out to get a few suggestions on how to break down a task into smaller, easier parts, I may have gotten the chance earlier in life to see the other side of failure. If any sidebar to this chapter exists, it would have to be to put young brashness aside to get feedback about what has worked in the past for others. And the cost of this simple action, to ask for help, which is to say, to not ask for help, has probably been the largest missed opportunity cost in my life that could have saved me lots of grief.

To get back to the training class, I vividly remember our instructor's first question to our group of cadets, if you will, freshly being minted by the city to become a transit operator. The instructor asked, "What is the first thing I have read time and time again on accident reports, or heard from an operator in a conversation about an accident?" And what confuses me and has left me completely confounded year after year, even though I piped up with the correct answer as soon as he asked it, was the lack of simplicity and clarity I possessed in writing out my reports. I always wondered why it took so long for the division trainer to grade my report. Now I get my answer about an accident within a day or two from the accident. And I could not see why other operators knew why this was happening and why they got their verdicts so much quicker than I did. And I have been teased and mocked to almost no end about the *War and Peace* or *Gone With the Wind,* lengthy essays on my reports. I talk too long, and I write too much, and my only surmise is because I am too much a thinker and spend too much time in my head. I guess it's why I am enjoying this book so much.

Most of my prose in the accident report was always assuming what the other driver, pedestrian, or cyclist was thinking or why they did what they did. In true Joe Friday Dragnet form, did I need to hear, "Just the facts, just the facts." Because that is where a disconnect comes from. To keep it simple and just report what happened, not what I think happened. I loved the dispatcher's reaction to my reports: rolling their eyes and handing it back to me, or their frustration at having no room to sign the report because my words bled over into their section. This was helpful in seeing that I needed to cut down the verbiage, and at one point, I realized I should do a rough draft of just the accident description part of the form, and then, after feedback from the dispatcher, rewrite it shorter and simpler, what actually happened, without all the guesswork about why people did what they did. So even though I got the answer right away in my first accident class with our instructor, I did appear clueless many years later in reducing the report to the simple actions leading to sideswipe, T-bone, squeeze play, or fixed object. If I could have read other reports, or known the simple food groups of how accidents are classified, I would hopefully have done better, but I am not counting on it!

So have you guessed what the simple answer was and is? Cue Richard Dawson in *Family Feud* to say we polled a recent transit operator class and got their best response. What does a person say after having a collision or accident? The answer is "I didn't see you!"

The car just came out of nowhere. Blah, blah, blah. So I make sure that I am checking side to side, left-right-left, so there is no guesswork about who is encroaching on my lane, my territory. And tracking rate of speed is the best way to guess when a motorist is going to make a foolish move that isn't safe. Impatience can usually be seen a mile away when sight lines are clear. But in congested, built-up San Francisco, we usually have limited sight distance. Buildings come right up to the corner, or there is almost always a beer truck, bakery truck, or parcel-delivery truck parked on the curb or double parked, right up against a crosswalk or corner. And this is where considering *the bigger you are, the harder they fall* really becomes important. The transit professional has a word for this when this happens; it is called billboarding. You can't see the forest for the trees, and there is little reaction space to avert a threat that comes from behind the obstacle. The friendly toot or light flash can be useful, but the bottom line is to adjust by slowing down.

Alpha Dog

PEOPLE WATCHING IS THE GREATEST JOB BENEFIT OF BEING A TRANSIT operator in the Baghdad-by- the-bay. Friends and family always ask about the great benefits a civil service worker must have, being a government employee. I usually mention the post office as having the best defined contribution plan or pension. But in the day-to-day flow of ants moving to and from the anthill that are the skyscrapers built on the bones of boats in the bay downtown, it isn't a column of numbers in the year-to-date tab on a paycheck that is a job perk in being a bus driver over and in the arteries flowing from the heart of San Francisco that make for daily job benefits behind the wheel. The benefit is not being stuck inside an office. It is feeling as though you are on the outside. And yet when the fog is freezing the bones, the wind is whipping through your layers, the bus is like a shelter from the elements. To comfort those at the mercy of the weather, it becomes important to stop close to the alpha dog in the queue on the sidewalk, so all can enter the bus as soon possible, without blockage at the gate.

Visitors are easy to spot, as the alpha dog always holds all the transit passports in their hand for all of the group. They usually follow at the end of the queue. When a large family passes the fare box without paying, the alpha comes up the steps at the end with the fares. Sometimes, a large group passes, and there is no alpha with no fare! To keep my ambassadorial role as a representative of the city, I don't say anything. When I do, they usually have their fare buried in the back of their backpack. This is another example of how we fail the city. No one assumes responsibility to inform visitors on how to ride, where to stand, or how to validate their pass.

A fare only becomes valid once the month and the day or days are scratched off on the passport sheet, which is not unlike a lottery scratcher ticket. Many times the person asking the questions is in front, and the ticket holder is at the rear. I can usually tell who they are. If they are asking a question I don't understand, I ask them where they are going. If they can't answer this, I then switch over to intuitive mode and say yes and ask them to step up. When this fails, I beckon them with my hand.

When this fails, it's because I have put too much expectation and hesitation in my voice, and I have to let it go. A simple nod is all I need. Then, if it turns out they are going the wrong way, there is usually a better transfer point down the line that will get them on the right bus with less confusion. I need to remember when I was new to the city and did not know inbound from outbound, because tall hills or the fog make it impossible to know which way is downtown or east versus west.

Talking to just one person, the alpha dog as Zen master, is best to keep the herd in line!

Alamo Square

NAMED BY MAYOR JAMES VAN NESS IN 1856, THIS 12.7-ACRE PARK IN the middle of Victorian mansions built during the 1870s to the 1920s was noted as a watering hole in between the commandant's quarters in the Presidio, to the Mission Delores Basilica, both occupied and controlled by the Spanish, who were the first inhabitants of San Francisco. A lone alamo, or cottonwood tree, marked the watering hole for both Spanish Army soldiers and, later, San Francisco residents. If you look at Hayes Street between Pierce and Scott, and the southern edge of the park's sidewalk, you can still see water weeping from the ground, marking where this lone cottonwood tree stood, marking the tiny oasis. This natural spring is more evident after a heavy rainfall. The steep grade running through the middle of the park is part of an unlisted fault line running through the city from the Presidio by the Lake District to the Bayview and the Hunter's Point shipyard area.

Alamo Square has become a tourist must-see spot to view the Painted Ladies, San Francisco's first tract housing—houses built with no owner in mind. Most of the mansions built in the neighborhood followed the pattern of most home building at the turn of the century: houses were built by the owner-to-be and contracted out by a carpenter and builder known to the would-be owner. This district is second only to Pacific Heights in density of 10,000-square-foot mansions, some still undivided after all these years.

Another architectural fact is to notice which Queen Anne style windows still remain curved, not replaced with square window frames. There are four basic architectural styles in San Francisco's residential neighborhoods: Eastlake Stick, Italianate, Queen Anne, and Edwardian. The Painted Ladies, the picture postcard row of houses with the city skyline backdrop, are Italianate: gingerbread-type scrollwork around the windows and eves, and ornate woodwork design, such as the dowel found at the roof ridge top.

Eastlake Stick, named after the designer, Sir Eastlake, were available from the Sears and Roebuck catalog and could be assembled from a kit delivered to you by boat or train in the days when weed and dune were fast vanishing to streets and wood frame houses.

On the west side of the park, you can find the Italianate William Westerfield house, complete with widow's walk and intense lightning rods on the roof and eves. This National Historic Landmark (no. 135) is worth seeing, as are the Seattle Block on Golden Gate and Steiner, and the Tivoli theaters' bed-and-breakfast hotel on the corner from the Seattle Block of houses. These latter buildings are more toward Queen Anne than Italianate, as they are marked with cupolas and curved windows. The final style is of Edwardian, usually the simplest in lines and complexity and marked by huge rectangular windows.

The west side of Alamo Square has Edwardian houses, and you can see this by the huge windows on the front of the houses over the driveways. Proceeding west on Hayes, past Divisadero on the right side, you will find Eastlake Stick Sear's specials, with only two stories remaining. The bottom floor was taken away after these houses collapsed in the 1906 earthquake!

Divisadero Street is a great street for a bite or a drink or dessert; the Bi-Rite store has ice cream rated the best by many. My favorite sandwich shop is the Bean Bag Cafe. A neighbor of mine actually got married here, as loyal customers develop friendships that can lead to vows!

Also along "Divis," as we nickname the street, is pizza, Greek sandwich, and Louisiana Fried Chicken! If you are cycling through the area, there is Mojo Cafe, designed with you in mind. You can get the best bike ride routes from other patrons here. The Harding Theatre, dormant for years, is ready to open with a fresh marketplace interior.

The Alamo Square, for "Lone Cottonwood," is accessible on the 21 Hayes line, which can take you from Ferry Plaza and the SF Railway Museum all the way to Golden Gate Park. There you can transfer to the 5R Fulton and traverse the entire 3.5-mile journey along the park to Ocean Beach for a view of Cliff House and Seal Rock.

In any event, the 21 Hayes can easily qualify as the *trolleybus to happy destiny*—as it slices through the heart of San Francisco.

SF Railway Museum and Gift Shop

AT THE END OF THE LINE IS A COZY LITTLE MUSEUM RICH WITH THE history of transit in San Francisco. Its name is the Railway Museum, and it is midblock on Steuart Street at the foot of Market by Ferry Plaza and the Embarcadero. Admission is free. The museum is closed on Mondays.

Inside you'll find lots of interesting history books, children's books, videos, and historic memorabilia about the history of our equipment and lines used in San Francisco. Also in the back is a full-sized replica of a 1911 streetcar with a bell that works. Young ones can stand at the motorman controls, while parents browse the artifacts and audiovisual displays. In the fall during Muni Heritage Weekend, Muni brings out historic vehicles for picture taking and a select short-line ride down Market or Mission Streets.

I have had the pleasure to operate the 1950's Marmon-Herrington trolleybus and the 1976 Flyer, in use, brand-new, when I graduated high school. Also in the loop for a short-line ride is the 1969 General Motors motor coach. Several GMs also show up for the show. You can watch a trip on YouTube by searching "Driver Doug 1969 GM Muni Heritage." The cover design of this book uses photos taken from the Muni Heritage Weekend in 2014 when I had the opportunity to drive the Marmon-Herrington trolleybus. This bus is the icon for the Trolleybus of Happy Destiny.

If you are a patch collector and like posters, the museum has several classics. Sign up for membership, and you'll receive a 10 percent discount. The photos on the calendar are fantastic! Visit: *https://streetcar. z2systems.com/np/clients/streetcar/membershipJoin.jsp.*

Even if you aren't a member, admission is free, and the items found inside are unique San Francisco collectibles or gifts to give in memory of the visit. The Baccari Worm, Muni's logo of the late sixties, is also available on T-shirts and handbags. This is one of the world's classic logos, worn by all who believe San Francisco has the best transit system in the world for frequency in surface transportation.

Find out how a cable car works and see the wheels of the world. My favorite livery color scheme is the 1960's cream and green livery of the San Francisco Municipal Railway on car no. 1006. I also love seeing car 1056, Kansas City, Missouri-Kansas built in 1948 and San Diego's visit the zoo in green with gold on car 1078.

The Railway Museum is a great place to capture these beauties as they turn to and from Ferry Plaza or as they turn on and off Market. If you are good with shutter exposure, nighttime shots can feature our beautiful light show on the Bay Bridge span behind the turn from the museum to the Ferry Plaza. Late afternoon or early morning also captures the gossamer web made famous in *Charlotte's Web* of the Bay Bridge suspension cables reflecting the sun's light, especially after a rain. You may also get a rainbow as a backdrop!

Today, for example, the SFMTA currently operates cable cars, historic streetcars, light rail vehicles, our new tram for the central subway, motor coaches, trolleybuses, and articulated motor coaches and trolleys. We have one of the most unique and diversified fleet of transit in the country, in the world. Our city is still accessed by ferry boats— Blue and Gold, Red and White, Golden Gate—and BART trains from the Oakland Railway system. Let's not forget CalTrain from the south and our new high-speed link from Anaheim.

The SFMTA also connects with Sam Trans to the south and Golden Gate Transit to the north. AC Transit transverses the Old Key Lines from the East Bay, connects to Muni, our short name for the San Francisco Municipal Transit Agency, the SFMTA, at the Trans Bay Terminal. Electric, diesel, and hybrid electric equipment makeup our land-based transit, and for those lucky enough to sip a latte over the bay on the way to work, get fresh salt sea breeze passing Angel Island, Alcatraz, and reach Alameda, Vallejo, Tiburon, Larkspur, and Sausalito. Smart transit rail connects central San Rafael to points north and will eventually create a seamless transit web along the 101 corridor.

Pedestrians are still king on the walkways, as our city never left the streetcar mentality, as our rails never totally disappeared in moving people daily. Much to the shock and awe of most transit operators and visitors, less than 20 percent of intending street crossers ever look to see if a car is coming. You can always tell a newcomer driver by their *compulsive honking syndrome* in trying to change pedestrians in San Francisco. I tried it my first five years behind the wheel and only gave myself a headache.

No, the key to happy destiny is a visit to the Railway Museum, Golden Gate Park, or a date with the gate—Golden Gate Bridge. You can actually feel like you're flying above the bay in the air, overlooking the cityscape to the east or the big blue of the Pacific, with seven thousand miles of uninterrupted ocean, save for the Devil's Teeth of the Farallone Islands and the Sandwich Islands, the most isolated land mass on Gaia. At least for now. But times they are a changing …

Ferry Plaza

VISIBLE FROM ATOP THE TWIN PEAKS OVERLOOK AND ALL ALONG MARKET Street is the tower of the first steel-reinforced building in the city. The clock tower above Ferry Plaza survived the big quake of 1906. Back in the day, all four tracks of rail on Market Street looped around in front of the clock tower as pedestrian bridges carried folks to the extensive ferry system in existence before the Bay Bridge was completed in 1937 before the World's Fair, then called the International Golden Gate Exposition, on Treasure Island.

The second-most often asked question after "Do you go to Fisherman's Wharf?" is the less specific, "Do you go to the piers?" All other variations on this theme are "Do you go to the bay? The ocean?" and "The waterfront?" Except for the specific Fisherman's Wharf, the answer is always yes!

San Francisco is on a peninsula and is surrounded by water on three sides: to the north, the east, and the west. Any crosstown bus goes to water. All downtown buses go to water. The few exceptions are the mainline outbound terminal of buses that end near the county line, such as the 9, 14R, and 43. Even so, if you ask any of these questions, it is believed you want to go to the inbound terminal, as these lines end near water inbound.

To be fair, very few cities have such a geographic uniqueness. The east coast of Florida is perhaps the most obvious in its urban footprint: barrier island, Indian River, tall buildings on the shore, flat and straight roads leading inland to tidal flats and swamp forest.

West Texas and the grasslands of the breadbasket all mark the county seat in the center of a rectangular or square county with range line roads more or less following perfect grid patterns, interrupted only by streams, lakes, or rivers. Rangeline Road is a common name for streets bordering county lines. Cities along Old Mo or the Mighty Mississippi have interesting boundary configurations due to stream meanders, but basically, most urban areas are not unlike a hub and spoke system radiating from a central city core, founded on a relatively flat, buildable plain near a water source. Indeed, San Francisco was started on a beach where the bay indented into a nice quay, protected from a direct line to the ocean at the Golden Gate.

Sir Francis Drake passed by the gate because he thought Angel Island was a continuous land bridge preventing an entry. It wasn't until two hundred years later when the Spanish Army tread upon the Sweeney Ridge—near where Sharp Park Boulevard now lies in Pacifica—was it discovered that indeed there was an inlet for a large interior bay.

The Ferry Plaza is a great ground zero for our address system and for the pier numbering system. Odd-numbered addresses are always on the south and west side of any street; evens are on the north and east. This could be considered our town square, although it is configured as rays leaving a sun. Everything like tree branches splits off and divides the farther you get away from Market Street, the main promenade.

Reading on Muni

BEING ABLE TO READ ON MUNI IS PROBABLY AN ART FORM. MAYBE IT will be a new X game or reality show. A built-in announcement on our digital voice activation system (DVAS) states, as soon as we close the door, "Please hold on." On to *what* has been open to conjecture. "Dear life" may be the number one response to a recently polled riding audience. But just as we operators appear to master the incomprehensible act of driving a bus in San Francisco with plenty of bozos, so too can our riders master feats of derring-do just like any superhero. Reading on Muni can actually be mastered. As can texting or typing on a computer. My hat is off to you stalwart heroes who can multitask while riding an electric trolleybus.

I read newspapers when I take the bus in the morning. No problem. The coach is quiet and relatively empty. But trying to read in the afternoon is much more difficult because of the noise and limited space. If two passengers are engaged in a heated debate, or someone is on their cell phone with attitude about their mate or friend not behaving in a way that is suitable to them, this all becomes public knowledge! Trying to ignore these heated conversation blasts is next to impossible.

Most of my friends have told me that this is why they don't ride Muni anymore. "If you could just get rid of these boundary-crossing crazies, I might give the bus a second chance." Most riders, no matter how rude or loud they act toward other passengers, are usually kind and gracious to the operator. So how we deal with the battle of wills between two passengers becomes not unlike a UN Council of Nations, or such as in an envoy sent from the embassy! Restating the needs of each party helps, as does the person who was first in disrespect and why. But it is hard to come up with any hard and fast rules on paper.

Only with the months turning into the years, with a repeat of a similar situation, can matters be dissolved quickly. Just when I think I have it, another twist occurs and reveals more.

Keeping Zen means not taking things personally and starting fresh every day.

The Argument You Cannot Win

A GOOD MUNI BUS DRIVER SHOULD BE SEEN AND NOT HEARD. WELL, I certainly don't fall into that category, no way. Most operators follow the golden rule of *information gladly given, but safety requires avoiding unnecessary conversation.* When a passenger wants to be right, the best advice is to let them win so that I can once again reduce the distraction and move on. If I have asked to see their transfer, and they show it in such a way that I cannot see the time or the day, I ask for the regular fare. If they become angry when they hold the transfer in my face, I say thank you, and that usually ends the drama.

But there are those who must enjoy confrontation and being right. "I am sorry, but I did not see your transfer when you first showed it to me." By this time, I am wondering why I asked for the fare in the first place, but I always check my inflection and voice to make sure I am being neutral in my tone. Even still, this sometimes has no effect, and some question me as to why I am being so rude. This brings me to the argument you cannot win. I don't see why they are calling me rude. I am just doing my job. And even when another passenger comes to my aid by saying that I am just doing my job, this has little effect on the drama.

Whenever there is a problem on the bus, I have to ask myself, how important is this really? Would I rather be calm or would I rather be right? And giving the space to wait until someone comes forward to complain keeps incidents few and far between. Only when someone has a complaint am I to act. And how I handle the situation either makes it go away or get worse. The first thing to do when a fight looks ready is to open the rear doors and pop the brake. The sound of the brake let's everyone know that we aren't moving. The rear door open gives an out to one of the people in the argument. Since impatience is usually the prevailing mood, one of the party leaves. If they don't, then I can ask one of the folks to come up to sit by me. Or state that there is another coach in a few minutes, and you might find that more comfortable a ride.

All in all, I have to check my mental state and ask myself, am I being of service to those in the coach or do I have an agenda based on some sort of fear about what I think may or may not happen? But a word of advice: don't feed the pigeons. That is, don't feed into a senseless argument. Do not respond to the Borg. Resistance is futile.

As time has given me insight, I do have an intuition about how far people are traveling on the coach. I can spot the problem child before they board. And I can guess where they will most likely get off. Their destination on the Mission is Sixteenth Street. A rush to the door usually results when they see their dealer on a nearby street. "Is this an emergency?" I ask. When they shout, "Yes!" I can use the rules to my advantage and get rid of them, being careful that there is no threat of an oncoming skater or cyclist.

This impatient energy is one full of mishap and accident. By asking them to come to the front door, I interrupt that energy and make it safer. But only if getting them off the coach will improve the mood of everyone else riding. It is when the request for a back door is out of sync with the lights and the traffic that I move the coach forward a little bit, to bring the doors to a safe place while signaling to traffic behind me that I am not moving away.

Usually people get loudest before they depart. If they are arguing when they get on, I have to let it settle right then and there or prevent them from getting on in the first place. I have learned that when the music or the voices get the loudest, it is either a cry for help or a deep need to be heard. Or a revolutionary protest and rage against the machine, in this case, the Municipal Railway, for which gratitude has been lost.

If someone has a "helpful" suggestion on how to get to a destination, and they already have my answer, fine. I have learned that I don't need to argue the point. Everyone has a different pattern that works for them on how to get from point A to point B. Since Muni has so many different lines, when a question is asked about how to get somewhere, different answers come every time another person is asked. It is not that anyone is lying. It is just that there are so many ways to get to where you want to go.

We don't have eyes in the back of our head, and we are not mind readers. If riders cannot show me their fare before they cross the yellow line, all I am required to do is state the fare. Usually they don't acknowledge me at all. And I have found that this is actually a good thing. It is not on me to be the policeman for the fare. We have fare inspectors for that. When I let go of judging them and trust that it is not up to me to determine if they are being honest or not, my day goes much better. I am a bus driver and not a stage performer on Broadway. Though I have been on Broadway for one block between Fillmore and Steiner when I am on a run on the 22 line, I usually am not on stage! Keep me in the Zen, and oh by the way, if you look over to your left, you will see Mrs. Doubtfire's house!

We now return you to the Zen of driving Muni, already in progress!

Compulsive Honking Syndrome

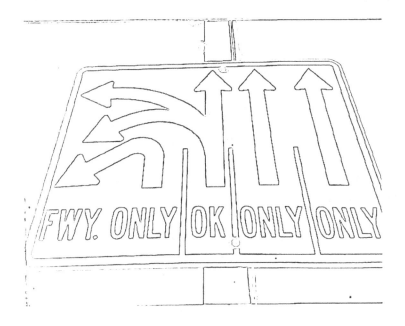

Some of the treats of classroom training at Muni are the vintage videos with footage of San Francisco in the 1970s. They show equipment smoothly flowing down Market Street with virtually no traffic and no delay. Screech forward to today's reality—the sound of spinning tires, radical acceleration on the pedal, and long horn blasts, which are heard daily.

Before a meeting with a friend, he inspired me with a title for this chapter, and he had already come up with an acronym for this common occurrence heard trip after trip in his cab and on my bus—CHS, compulsive honking syndrome, or as I jokingly added, a part of a person's compulsive horn disorder, CHD! A person with CHD may develop CHS if they do not catch the infection early on in their

191

behavior pattern. For once set in the firing pattern of neurons, only through a meditation routine not unlike followed by a Master Jedi, such as Yoda, can the disease be remitted. Or, perhaps, by now reading the *Dao of Doug*.

The good news, just in, is each one of us can change our habits by awareness of staying true to who we really are and not reacting to a perceived slight by an effing moron or douchebag. In slowing down my body movement by quiet time each evening, I get answers. Find your time. Can you do it in the morning, or is before bed better? In this case, I am an evening person. My to-do list check off is an up and atom energy best suited to the morning hours.

I never would have known this had I not stopped to question and analyze why I was jumping to conclusions or rushing to judgment about a person, place, or thing that at first appeared to be in conflict with my path. Just like an automobile butting out from the curb, double parked, and giving me the horn. In fact, there are several common flow patterns that lead to compulsive horn syndrome, and once understood and quantified, they can provide the Dao (the manner of living) of nonreaction to breaking compulsive horn disorder. Below are the situations that can trigger CHS and lead to permanent disability with CHD. CHPs usually cannot cure this disease, even though with a ticket or reminder, they can stop an infection

Double-Park Backup

This occurs when looking for parking and just missing the space because you pass by a car getting ready to leave. It also can occur if car number two sees car number one attended, and the brake lights are on as the motorist is starting the engine. Car two, the perceived offender, seen first by car three, or me in the bus, can't stand to be blocked in the time it takes car one to pull away and for double-parked number two to take the space. If car two cannot make the curb on the first pass, beware of compulsive honking syndrome. Also, if car two makes the mistake of waiting for one to pull away, but the driver is just getting something out of the car, with no intention of leaving, car two gets the horn blast for blocking and waiting too long.

I hear the long, hard blasts all the time, and it is disheartening. Sure, the plan is to make SF for the *Lifestyles of the Rich and Infamous* the tech dream of tomorrow, but the density toll on wealth providing everyone with a car really disrupts the peaceful energy of yore, especially with unrestricted ride share vehicles entering the city from out of county.

Hide-and-Seek Parking

This gets a honk when cars are just waiting, double parked, for a pickup or space to come their way. The agony is not easy to recognize when cars are simply going around the block over and over to find parking. This wasted time of a vehicle trip being spent causing congestion but of no use of conveyance is perhaps the biggest drawback to having a car in San Francisco. The simple act of going to one parking garage and keeping the vehicle put would save this syndrome from infecting others. In San Francisco, *three rights do not make a left* because all streets are not two-way or go through. It is impossible to just go around the block in many cases, and this adds to car clutter on the streets of San Francisco.

The idea that parking should be free is ridiculous. Why should this real estate be free? The baby boomer's biggest negative impact is the cars we bring to the city. This city, along with Manhattan, has older buildings with no parking. That's how cities became functional. Flooding our city with more cars and demanding more free parking is ridiculous and unsupportable. This makes a good case for having motorists pay for public transportation, so we can ride for free.

Open Curb Construction Sign

This one got me last week. I let them have it with the tradition of Foghorn Leghorn, because my PA exterior loud speaker wasn't working that day. But all my sarcastic skill over the bullhorn would have been moot, as the car was unattended. The car was in a bus stop marked with construction sawhorses, the owner finally returning with takeout after a few minutes of waiting. Truth be told, his flashers were on, and I knew it wouldn't be too long a delay for him to return. I got him with photon torpedoes, my dash camera, as I took a picture of his plate and bumper up against the temporary bus stop sign.

This is part of a class war between civilian city residents and city government. I must use my power as a civil servant wisely and consider the conflict I may be bringing to the table. I continually have friends come to me protesting unfair parking tickets and asking how to proceed. These incidents seem to occur with alarming frequency when I take a picture of other vehicles to send them a ticket. Is my issuance of a fine really impacting my passengers' safety? If driving defensively and leaving myself a space cushion of at least four feet, can I avoid a line delay?

Corner Fire Hydrant

This is such the cool place to hang out, no Muni bus driver or motorist should honk if someone stands here. We have our special hydrant at Fillmore and Geary and another by Peet's at Sacramento and Fillmore. This red zone, usually open, is actually perfect for a quick stop and pickup, and most pedestrians are cool with this space. It is scary, however, if an intending pedestrian is pausing to cross on the light, and a car swoops in fast and furious to stand and drop off. It's a major cause for sidewalk or street rage, the city version of road rage on the freeway.

Curb Clear Muni

In my first five years as a bus driver, these short red zones, by corners where we turn our bus onto another street, had me angry and depressed every time a car was parked on the corner at a curb clear. On the 24 Divisadero, there are many turns that become dangerous if we can't allow for proper traveling space on our overhead wires. Our poles need to have a wide arc outside the shadow of our driver-side window so we can make the turn without de-wiring. Castro to Twenty-Sixth, Noe to Thirtieth, Divisadero to Jackson, Washington to Webster are but a few turns where we need to have no car parked.

Now that we have cameras, I feel empowered. With help from the planning department at our monthly safety meetings, we can provide information to get these turns, or curb clears, freshly painted so motorists can see the red. Better them than me in seeing red!

My hope is for the addition of small No Parking signs handcrafted with the SFMTA star that state that the red zone is a trolleybus curb clear. (And could we make them in neon colors with a red alert tone, like on a Klingon Bird of Prey?)

Bus Zone Special

These are the guys who never check their rearview mirrors. Did you ride share drivers know a professional driver checks the rearview mirrors every five to eight seconds? This simple action would prevent those standing or stopping in the middle of a bus zone. We cannot come to the curb to drop off wheelchairs, walkers, or seniors needing the curb!

This would be a justifiable and morally responsible ticketed offense. It is an expensive mistake and could simply be avoided if you check your rear views to see if a bus is coming. Thank you!

Far Side Crosswalk

If a motorist is looking at their smartphone or GPS screen in hand or mounted on the dash, their view ahead is compromised, especially when turning. Using peripheral eyesight is dangerous. This is a prime cause for pedestrian injury and death in our city.

Transit professionals certified annually with a VTT card, verified transit training, have the knowledge to scan ahead one to one and a half blocks ahead to see the scene developing. We are scanning ahead to see any threat developing. It helps that we have large mirrors and are sitting higher up on the road.

The compulsive horn disorder manifests daily at this crosswalk. A following car, not able to see a crossing pedestrian on the cross street or side street, honks loudly and clearly because they can't see why the car in front of them is not moving. It's because the far side crosswalk is occupied. Please, dear motorist, accept the path experienced city drivers follow; a space of five to seven seconds is needed before the vehicle in front of you moves. This precious pause saves lives. Crosswalk lives matter.

Stale Green

Did you see the light turn green? If you didn't, it is a stale green. Slowing down approaching a stale green is transit safe. Speeding up is not indicated and can result in finding out what your insurance deductible is for body damage to your car and liability damage to those injured or sent to the hospital. Leaving the scene does not make it any cheaper for your bank account or spiritual awareness account.

Jumping the Gun

This can result in a serious side-on collision and is dangerous to the person jumping the gun. A fatality at Octavia and Oak resulted in major trauma and the death of a doctor sitting in the back of a shuttle as the shuttle driver jumped the gun on a fresh green. A trucker heading down the hill at a high speed decided to go through the opposing stale green. The result was death. South of Market streets suffer this same fate.

This broadside collision made the news and is sad because it occurred at a newly opened parkway that replaced an ugly overhead freeway canopy. Of all the scenarios of using the horn, this one is okay. *This is an example of appropriate use of the horn.* The usual outcome of compulsive honking syndrome telegraphs one message: I am an idiot, and my few seconds of impatience are being broadcast in my horn, as I cannot see why you aren't moving. The result is retaliation in that the vehicle you want to move will stay longer in your path.

5150

This is the police code for a crazy person. Muni's code is 800. Blaring a horn at a mentally disabled person walking in the middle of the street can result in a line delay. The horn does not work to your advantage but only adds to the delay as they stand and block your vehicle. Broken glass in the front door, a pulled windshield wiper, or kicks and dents in your fender are a high risk from using the horn in this situation. Stopping and waiting is best. A smile never hurts either.

Change of Direction

This is dangerous, and use of the horn may be okay. The signal of a horn is, *Please make up your mind.* Granted, the person in the driver's seat is probably being distracted by a back seat driver or a map being held by another person in the car. This almost always occurs when there is more than one person in the car. A single toot is best.

Limited Sight Distance

Use of the horn does not help the car in front see any better. Waiting in a queue of vehicles at a traffic circle or four-way stop is when CHD manifests. Allow the person in front to go when they feel it is safe. You are not driving their car and cannot see what they see.

One thing we bus drivers learn early on is we are not the arbiters of determining another motorist's skill on what they think is safe or how knowledgeable or skillful they are in experienced driving. We can get clues by the way they are driving before a limited sight distance event occurs.

My most common expression to be aware I may compulsively use the horn is, "What are you waiting for, an engraved invitation?"

Merge and Feed

The horn will not be needed if you change lanes when spacing and pace are even. Cranking the wheel hard in stopped traffic only blocks two lanes instead of one. If you want to avoid being honked at, make your lane change early or when the gap in cars is created when traffic starts moving and an inattentive motorist hasn't looked up from their phone.

Indeed, texting by others has its advantages when they delay in moving when the light turns green. You can use this advantage to change lanes safely and become a Jedi master. This is the Dao of Doug on the trolleybus of happy destiny.

Loading Zone

IN THE EBB AND FLOW OF TRAFFIC, THE SPACE CUSHION BETWEEN VEHICLES goes up and down. As traffic turns from medium to heavy, the matter of inches can come into play as to whether traffic comes to a standstill or not. When a limo or ride share is picking up or the motorist leaves the vehicle unattended for just the few seconds it takes to get to an ATM or get a coffee, the attitude of the car and its distance from the curb can determine if the lane is shut down and blocked. This then creates an abrupt left merge situation to lane two and brings both lanes to gridlock. This setup for a backup is completely avoidable if the first parked vehicle would stay within six to eight inches of the curb.

The pecking order of when and how delivery trucks set up to off-load also affects lane closure and gridlock. The first-arriving number one truck may park in perfect order, but a second truck parks too close on the opposing traffic lane and makes for intense squeeze play that need not be if a longer gap is left open. Intending through vehicles build a backup line that prevents the oncoming lane from clearing truck one, thus preventing two-way traffic from clearing. This occurs in a commercial zone where lots of cafes and shops line the street. Upper Haight in the Haight Ashbury and Eighteenth Street between Delores and Guerrero are classic jam spots for the 33 Ashbury.

Once a delivery driver becomes familiar with his or her drop-off route, adjustments are made to the delivery schedule whereby no two vehicles create a rolling delay, because they wait for the other delivery to clear, going around the block to alter their drop-off time. Experienced UPS and FedEx drivers are good at this, mainly because they have another address close by and can adjust. Trash trucks can also go around the block and work on other houses or businesses if other trucks block their trash can pickup. This usually works for smaller bakery trucks and bobtails. But fifty-three-foot out-of-town tractor trailers from distribution hubs in the Central Valley can cause longer line delays.

The one line delay that can block both lanes in either direction is a loading dock zone. Fifty-three-foot tractor trailer rigs attempt to back into a dock perpendicular to a not-so-wide San Francisco street. These trailers take finesse and skill from the class A truck operator to make a pass in three moves maximum, else the blocked pedestrian, cycle, and vehicle traffic begin unsafe maneuvers. Office Max on Arguello Street near Geary, Big Lots on Mission near Thirtieth, the Whole Foods on Seventeenth at Kansas, Fulton Market Lucky's on Central between Fulton and Mc Allister—to name just a few. This just adds more delay to those patiently waiting in their lane. I have to pop the brake and relax and pretend I am watching a truck driver training video on how to back into a loading dock.

The solution to this is to paint a red curb clear on either side of two residential driveways across from the dock. This means taking away parking space. Here's the rub. Taking away parking requires a procedure that takes a long time. I cannot fathom why transit needs do not gain priority over the car, especially in a city like San Francisco. A truck making delivery to a grocery store can block commuters on the bus for up to six minutes because they can't back into the dock because of a parked car across the street. Our event marker button on camera may help by taking a screenshot of the offending vehicle.

The battle cry goes up along Chestnut Avenue when bus zones need to be extended for longer trolleys. Everyone loves the fact that new, larger equipment is to be added for service, but no one wants to sacrifice the three parking spaces necessary to increase the curb red zone. These delays add confusion to our general sign-up and cause some operators to have to pull out from an alien division or extend a pullout route from farther away from where our barn is or where we end our day.

The finale of long trailers in San Francisco occurs when a tractor trailer driver from out of town decides to go up Seventeenth Street from Market to access Cole Valley, or takes Leavenworth from the Tenderloin to access 101 North over the Golden Gate Bridge. The loading stanchions for hooking and unhooking below the trailer scrap on the dramatic elevation change before or after crossing a steep grade. The trucks stall going uphill or get wedged going downhill.

This recently happened when a truck got stuck crossing Union to go down Russian Hill. The only way to break free is to drag the tractor down the hill. The noise of the trailer's hitching posts dragging on the street definitely awakens anyone in a three-block radius! No alarm clock needed on this commute! Tour buses are also big offenders on Russian Hill.

During Super Bowl 50, a truck got stuck on Jones and California. Obviously this was a new driver on call for the extra work for the large visitor population we had hosting the Super Bowl. Tractor trailers at least have flexibility at the hitch joint. Buses are one solid mass, and damage to the frame may result. I'd hate to be in their dispatcher's office when this call comes in!

Also telling is when a new fleet of delivery trucks make to the streets. New employees are easy to spot by where and when they park.

They must adapt their parking so as to not create a car jam, so that cars waiting in the queue at a red barricade oncoming traffic stuck behind the newcomer. An exception are the new Amazon drivers in their gray vans; they know how to park, even though they are new! Could you guys please give the FedEx ground drivers a clue?

The simplest rule to keep the Zen is to leave a broad birth for smaller vehicles unable to see ahead, a space to move in front of my coach when they impatiently pass. I try to move to the right as much as possible so they can see the obstacle ahead, but many times this is unsafe for door openers and bicyclists. Even when passing a double-parked truck, with my high beams flashing, oncoming motorists appear oblivious to my move and block me from returning to my lane. I remember I am the paid professional on the clock, and a *no worries* attitude heals the block the fastest! I can find my Zen at any loading dock or any hill!

Blocked Zone—Bus Bunching

WHEN I GET INTO TROUBLE, IT BECOMES DIFFICULT TO KNOW WHAT action to take, especially if I am in a rush. Paradoxically, it is when I am in a compromise that my choice needs to be decisive and clear, but if I am not in a good space, I am apt to be in an accident. This is clear when operating large machinery with lots of souls on board, and a rescue vehicle or ambulance emerges on the scene.

A car tries to overtake on the left or cuts in front from the right to make a right turn at a congested intersection. This one ideal, to sit back and watch the show, allows us to avoid the odds for a need to back up or make an abrupt maneuver that could cause danger or collision.

Meditation or quiet time on a regular basis about our show in life has helped me immensely in knowing that when the time comes, I am ready to make a choice. Experience in driving a Muni bus has given me that intuition that can also arise if I take quiet time before my day opens and when I retire at night. The patterns of my daily journey on the road become predictable, so when I see something different or out of place, I immediately adjust so as to keep a space cushion around the impending threat. When I was new, I would charge ahead of a taxi picking up or dropping off in the zone, but I have since realized that by pacing myself to the pull in to the curb, the taxi customer usually alights or departs, and the taxi has room to move away, thus giving me full access to the zone. I also find it easier to find a cab when I am in uniform going home from work!

I now try to avoid blocking any vehicle in the zone by slowing and see if the extra time cushion works. Nine times out of ten, it does. And then the key was for me to be sparing on the horn. And sure enough, I rarely need to use it. And when I do, I try to keep it to a friendly toot and not a ship-to-ship foghorn! Blaring does nothing for keeping my serenity, and I usually get a blast back later in the day, as the equation always needs to remain balanced. I would get awful angry horns when my tail end blocked an intersection because I had rushed ahead in to the zone behind another coach. I became aware of the frequency of the angry horn directed at me, and I looked at my part leading up to that situation. I also recalled the last time I gave an angry blast at another vehicle, and the hostile energy seemed to be about the same in intensity and force.

I stopped using the horn and got light on the power pedal. And sure enough, the longer the time passed with me not using the horn, the fewer horns I got. I started applying this invisible karmic ledger to other behaviors I found offensive to me. on the road. When shocked about a car cutting me off or a flyby or drive-by that seemed scary, I tried to recall when I made an action that was not anticipated by pedestrians or motorists, which may have given them the same feeling. And my compromising situations decreased dramatically. The suggestion to "sit back and watch the show" started to be a working part of my mind, and I got it.

The biggest and hardest part of all of this was to be able to check and scan left-right-left every five to eight seconds and see what was amiss. Construction delays and lane closures were a biggie in realizing that I had to shift my mode of thinking, drop speed, and allow others behind me to react and have time to make the decision to pass before squeeze play became too immediate and required sharp turns. I really hate sharp turns in life.

Vision Zero

THIS IS A GREAT NAME FOR A COMMITMENT TO REDUCING PEDESTRIAN collisions. Perhaps there is no way San Francisco will see not a single pedestrian collision in a year, but this does not preclude having a collective conscious vision to move toward a perfect goal in which no one makes contact. High-Injury Network, HIN for short, is the term for listing hot spots where collisions are high. As a person interested in transit planning, I absorbed the Vision Zero data with a passion, as though I could make a difference with my experience on the road.

I have noticed several categories of factors leading to collision: unfamiliarity, off-ramp, mental illness, signal walk cycle, senior housing, visibility, and downhill speed.

Unfamiliarity

North Point and Hyde and Francisco and Taylor are two HIN intersections that fall into the pedestrian and motorist unfamiliarity category. Setback triangles (shark's tooth) from the crosswalk help transit operators stop back from the stop line to give a big-picture view of intending sidewalk pedestrians a space cushion to avoid pushing too close to the crosswalk, which limits reaction time to stop for a stroller or senior. LED flashers would be indicated at these locations. These intersections are located close to a high visitor population by Fisherman's Wharf.

Freeway Off-Ramp

Seventeenth and Vermont could also use pedestrian-activated crosswalk flashers for the reason of unfamiliarity but also because of the category of downhill speed and proximity to the freeway off-ramp.

Motorists, frustrated by the Central Freeway and Bay Bridge backup, exit 101 and book to try to make up for lost time. Indeed, making Bryant an alternate arterial for freeway overload might be a good release valve to help the Essex/ Folsom merge downtown. This Vermont off-ramp also suffers from downhill speed, as motorists regain clutter-free traffic once leaving the freeway. Two early-morning fatalities have resulted when drunk drivers entered the freeway in the wrong direction. Flashers at the exit off-ramp by Slovenian Hall might also help when pedestrians attempt to cross this first stop line off the freeway. The same could be said of Folsom and Ninth by Bed, Bath, and Beyond in SOMA. Pedestrians crossing right by a freeway off-ramp need to be mindful that cars coming directly from the freeway may not have adjusted from a suburban mindset to an urban one. Two people have been killed crossing this off-ramp.

Downhill Speed

Seventeenth and Roosevelt, Fourteenth and Noe, Jackson and Spruce, also identified as an HIN, suffer from visibility problems, either from hills or large tree canopy. Lights at night are obvious to any owl or twilight bus driver. Motorists can't see pedestrians, particularly after dark, because of limited sight distance as they gain speed going downhill. Street stencils and pedestrian barriers would help, as would chirpers on a button, mainly as a warning to pedestrians that they are crossing at a high-injury location. Another idea I have is to use baby signs oriented toward the sidewalk with a red exclamation point in a yellow inverted yield sign, alerting those who cross this is a dangerous crossing.

Signal Walk Cycle

Too few intersections have isolated pedestrian cross cycles, such as Main and Mission, Mission and Beale, along Second Street between Market and Folsom, and at Grove and Gough near Davies Symphony Hall and Opera Plaza. I understand the necessity to keep heavy traffic moving, and this is exactly why the walk cycle needs to be isolated, called pedestrian scrambles. Traffic cannot make turns or proceed smoothly due to laggards and distracted walkers consuming the green for traffic to start moving. Dear engineer, here's a concept to consider: during peak traffic hours, from 3:30 p.m. to 6:30 p.m., only allow pedestrians their four-corner crossings every other or every third green cycle for all SOMA, Hayes Valley, and Van Ness intersections. Give them those precious extra five or ten seconds to cross diagonally during their cycle. Oh we can cross both walks at once, killing two birds with one stone, a bird in hand, and not in the bush, and not on the evening news or in an operator's transit safe driving record.

When the Third Street Bridge was closed and a single lane was permitted to turn from Townsend, only one or two cars could make it through the green. This bottleneck took an extra thirty minutes to crawl on Channel Street, when an isolated pedestrian signal would give Fourth Street a solid twenty-five seconds to clear cars from the single-lane choke point. Seeing DPT controllers standing by useless doesn't go over big after waiting thirty minutes to pullout from Woods to start my afternoon run.

Isolated pedestrian scrambles at Kearny and Post, Kearney and Bush, would help us make the green without any life histories flashing across the memories of late runners blocking the green for transit and cars trying to clear the crosswalks. Deny pedestrians a cycle for uninterrupted flow of traffic and then give them a four-points crossing.

Fourteenth and Folsom also needs a pedestrian flow isolation as seniors and those with groceries from Foods Co. and Rainbow Grocery need time without fear of turning cars.

Solutions

Chirpers, LED flashers, syncopated signal crossings using a two- or three-interval cycle for pedestrians, electronic speed limit signs with MPH red flash for speeders, pedestrian barriers, SFMTA signage and baby signs in line of sight with eyeballs sitting in a car, and stencils are all good changes to reduce high-injury network intersections. Granted, pedestrian barriers are often ignored, but it reduces claims when a pedestrian violates the law. Most No Parking signs are ignored simply because they are too high up from line of sight from a driver's view in the car. Lowering signs to bike sign size is a great visibility change, and

I get why engineers are hesitant to use them—defacement and graffiti and outright removal, such as the Muni flags on Market.

We need a vigorous sign-replacement team to keep the message clear. Destructive urges, by passing angry individuals, need to be addressed, and those damaging signs and barriers need to realize their actions are not in a consequence-free environment. I saw this anger firsthand when an angry youth did not understand why my 21 bus would not open the door while stopped on the island at a red light. Most of the damage to our Muni flagpoles occurs during the wee hours after a pass-up. If I can't get on the bus, then I'll be damned if anyone can either. The hell with these useless signs!

Kudos to the extra police presence on Market during peak afternoon hours; this helps save our peace of mind and can maintain a happy destiny to get home from work without any drama.

Leading Green

THE HAMPTON ROADS AREA BY THE CHESAPEAKE BAY HAS A NICE SIGN under its signals. The sign below an overhead signal is marked Leading Green or Delayed Green. This signals to motorists who get to turn first or last at a major intersection of four lanes or more, and with a four- or six-way cycle, including left and right turn arrows. Adding the Leading Green sign can keep a simple two-way cycle and preclude installation of a left- or right-turn arrow. The city of San Francisco has not upgraded its traffic signal flows or timetables with safety observers for years, maybe decades.

Note to traffic engineers and planners. The timeworn tool for data is to station human counters at intersections to monitor turn signals, lane changes, and traffic storage over various hourly day parts on weekdays, weekends, and holidays. This helps in detailing when changes in the signals should occur and gets the ball rolling to see when more cars are waiting at the end of a cycle for a green than those in cross traffic on a stale green.

When seconds tick by—with no cross traffic passing by during a stale green, a queue of cars sits waiting on a red—the timing of the green becomes noticeable. By counting signal changes myself while waiting at the red, I find that light cycles come in ten-second packs: fifteen-second greens, twenty-five-second greens, thirty-five-second greens, and forty-five seconds. The first and last, the shortest and longest, are the rarest. Haight and Fillmore is a fifteen-second cycle; Van Ness and Market, the longest, at forty-five seconds. In putting in a request for a cycle change, I understand that keeping these cycles is important due to the other signals at intersections near the affected change, as timing may get thrown off by the flow.

Cyclists are the first to become aware that cars travel in packs. Transit operators and veteran truck drivers come to know the lights and distinguish themselves from motorists by the way they drive. Even on the freeways, notice how pods of cars form on the road. It makes little sense from a safety point of view to try to speed or push through a knot of cars in the pack or speed up to be at the rear of a pack. Being in a relatively empty stretch of cars is great: less stress and better odds of avoiding conflict.

Very few arterials in San Francisco have timed lights, such as Oak and Fell, Golden Gate and Turk. Now, Green Wave streets such as Valencia are timed for bikes and not cars. Many cabbies and folks from out of town are not too thrilled when auto lanes are removed for bikes.

Indeed, making leading green changes at an intersection is not as simple as it may first appear. It isn't just car or bus flow that needs to be considered. Pedestrians need to cross safely during a sequence, and when they cross is important. Giving the walk signal at the end of a stale green on a one-way arterial may be extremely dangerous if motorists try to speed up and make the light before it goes red so they can tailgate at the end of a pack of cars making steady greens on a timed light arterial like Gough.

Gough and Sacramento is one such intersection that requires special attention. Transit inbound needs to make a leading green left turn on Sacramento, but the far side crosswalk on Gough to Lafayette Park abounds with moms and strollers and dogs on a leash charging into the street.

Putting in a bus bulb to shorten travel time to cross may be good in theory, but trolley turns don't seem to be considered, such as at Fillmore and McAllister. Our wheels roll over the sidewalk when we make turns at the Webster Street turn-back and pull-in loop. Leading greens are slowly being input around intersections in San Francisco. Most of our intersections have remained without left-turn storage or arrows to make turns, but this is gradually improving. Losing the light and losing the Zen need not be a given with new traffic lights and pedestrian bulbs and medians!

Lane Closed

THIS IS A COMMON ORANGE CONSTRUCTION SIGN FOUND ALL OVER THE city. Fortunately, I am driving the white 2004, 2005 ETI Skoda trolleybus from the Czech Republic, and I have sixteen-foot trolley poles for maximum travel maneuvering.

Not so with the new sixty-foot Flyer trolleybuses with 14'6" yellow poles limiting their lane traveling space whenever construction cones are found. Indeed, this was one reason I decided to change trolleybus barns and keep using the buses with the longer poles.

Sure, the new flyers have a poles down and cradle function, which means the operator does not have to leave the cockpit to switch to battery power, but it is always preferable to not have to stop and change power modes, much less get out and put the poles back up manually. The pause in having to brake to switch to the auxiliary power unit and then to stop and brake to return to 600-volt power does put a crimp in the beats of flow during a green light cycle of the traffic lights—even with inspectors on the scene to help. This is especially true when three lanes are crimped down to one.

The green ahead at a major intersection is timed assuming three lanes of flow, not one. If the lead car in the queue wants to turn, they have to wait for the pedestrians to clear, and so do all the other cars blocked behind the lead car. A five-, ten-, and fifteen-second add setting could be programmed into the signal box for such occasions, and delays could be reduced. The standard answer for such nonaction is that this would adversely affect other nearby lights and intersections, but because traffic is constricted, the artery is unclogged and free. True, cross traffic would build because they may have ten less seconds to cross, but because their lanes are all open, their backup is not as pronounced as the blocked street. The answer as to why no change can occur sounds final and predetermined and usually makes me frustrated and then angry.

When the 30 X gets caught in the Broadway Tunnel, and I hear riders at Clay and Drumm relenting of their tales, I know the delay is critical to their job start time. Creating a wide bypass along Bay to Embarcadero instead of going through North Beach may eventually be added in a bulletin in our paddle when we pull out, but having to wait two or three days after complaints to make the change is poor planning. It's like there is no understanding about the consequences of single-lane inbound backups on Columbus Avenue to Stockton Street.

The great news is when street inspectors are added to get motorists' attention to start moving forward at the end of a cycle and to hold back pedestrians when a sixty-footer has to clear the crosswalk and turn. I realize it's easy for me to be an armchair complainer as a passenger stuck in traffic, and with our resources pushed to the max with construction everywhere, I understand the road of happy destiny is found by relaxing and understanding that everyone, including the flagman, is doing their best. It is here I do notice the backhoe guys get orders to stop digging and move out of the way when I pass. I then see it is obvious they are under strict orders to let trolleys go by and clear the wires from their backhoe or blade.

I see it must be incredibly frustrating for the construction guys to keep stopping and dropping what they are doing to allow a bus to go by. They must be surprised at how often we pass by in either direction. Indeed, allowing us to go through slows down their work and adds days to the work order.

Manual control of the signals should be used more often, such as when a major arterial is reduced to one lane, especially on the inbound morning peak, should a traffic control officer man the box and give the arterial more time green to flush motorists through the congestion point. My division trainer points out that management is very aware of my published blogs on Muni, and I do hope this point gets hammered home for change.

One traffic control officer with the button on the box to manually override the green for a longer cycle on the impacted transit arterial can do wonders to save reroutes and traffic delay. The fear about impacting other signals' traffic patterns is overblown, as traffic on the other streets is minimal and should not be given the full cycle.

Indeed, our traffic engineers need to consider double-cycle programming built in to signals for traffic lane closures. This is to say that one pedestrian cycle is eliminated every other cycle, and, or, cross streets miss a green so the impacted transit arterial gets a full twenty-five-, thirty-five-, or forty-five-second green every other cycle. I don't know how you could code this into the lights for a switch, but I need to stress that our engineers are not using this harm reduction in their traffic cycles.

I laugh when I say harm reduction, but this is exactly what it can do. Two SFMTA inspectors were tending to a motorist's fender bender at Sutter and Mason during a single-lane turn and single-lane narrows for over a block, and this gridlocked traffic all the way back from Union Square to the Financial District. The fender bender could have been eliminated if the green light flow was opened up for a longer green. Too much stopping and starting creates more confusion and leads to the dead man's pause of who goes first, which eats up time and causes split-lane blocking. The blind man's bluff of who go, you go, first, eats up the clock and piles more gridlock backup.

I had the delight of seeing our engineering team proudly standing by a completed curb clear at Polk and Union, and I smiled back. Little did they seem to know I was headed toward the jam of the month at Columbus and Green. This is a classic location for cutting out a pedestrian cycle and giving Columbus a longer green as our Skoda trolleybus creeps along through the green on battery power.

With all the construction going on around town, I need longer poles. The construction workers seldom place the cones with the correct space needed for our poles to clear. Truck drivers also park too far away from the curb, and their trailer box also interferes with the ropes attached to our trolley of poles. There seems to be no route or line that avoids Lane Closed signs because they are literally everywhere in the city.

Whenever a lane is closed and I can't make it safely through, I pop the brake to engage the parking brake. I go out and rearrange the cones correctly or step out of the coach to talk directly with any flagman or street supervisor. Staying put in the cockpit is usually not a good idea because I can't be seen or heard by the person in control of the closed lane. I can get in trouble fast if I don't understand what lane they want me to cross over to or when it is safe to pass. Bulletins in our daily timetable let me know where the problems are.

Passengers get confused about where to stand when lanes are closed. I try to signal them with my lights or by hand gestures when I see them standing by a closed stop in a lane under construction. Sometimes my bulletins don't match up with the signs, and the construction sign dates marked on the temporary zone signs don't coincide with the how far the project has progressed. The dates and bulletins don't match the actual scene.

In these cases, I have found it best to pick up intending passengers at both the nearside and far side corners and make sure they get a ride or get off where they need to go. Passengers can become impatient if the bus zone has been moved a block down the road and I am stuck in traffic, only made worse because a lane is closed.

On Hayes Street, lane closures make for an interesting game of chicken, as we must pass by a block with only one lane open. If the flagmen are distracted, they miss the oncoming bus entering the gauntlet in the other direction. They will wave me on when it is not safe, and I ultimately am responsible for my passengers and my safety record by ignoring the wave from the inattentive flagman and staying put.

If they don't really change heart and pay attention, I can always play with lawn bowling or bocce ball rules, whereby the cone is the marker and I try to see how close I come to the cone at my rear tire without knocking it over. The most awesome week is when I can touch the cone and spin it to move into the correct position without anyone having to move it. This is one of my reminders I am having a great day, even in a line delay. I got past the narrows and am on my way to the gold, just like a skier in the Winter Olympics.

The road of happy destiny is coupled with manually operating signals on the box, especially during Christmas rush at Fifth and Mission. When I see two meter maid electric scooters blocking a left turn from Third Street to Geary at Market during the Christmas tree lighting in Union Square, I pick up the handset to TMC and make a call of gratitude. Saving fifteen minutes of delay on Black Friday is truly an early Christmas present from Operations!

The trolleybus of happy destiny is definitely not a bus that is rushing down the road! Especially with a lane closed!

VTT: Verified Transit Training

THIS IS WHY I AS BUS DRIVER, PARTICULARLY A TROLLEYMAN, AM USUALLY the last motorist stuck in traffic to talk about your mama. I am the professional! I give turn signals well in advance, know proper use of the horn, and change lanes in advance of hazards I see a block away. We operators have a better vantage point than those of you in cars. Motorists would do well to follow a Muni bus through a single-lane detour or when we straddle the lane. We know how to trail blaze, and we will let you see ahead of us as soon as the next bus stop at the next light.

Also, I have signal preempts, which means my bus sensor keeps the light green longer than normal. Please allow me to keep the green on for you when you follow me! Our buses communicate with those traffic lights that have a small white panel located on the mast arm of the overhead signals. This is a great use of global positioning satellite technology, and our director of transit notifies us of such improvements.

This rush by cars to cross the yellow line to get around at a four-way stop is just cray-cray. This action seems to be happening more frequently. So is the attempt to pass when I am in a long queue of traffic waiting at a stop or a red.

So it is the VTT, verified transit training, card I possess, next to my license and my medical certificate, that places me at the professional level on the road. I take classes on a regular basis to be reminded of how to handle the public on a city bus.

These classes are led by a state-certified safety instructor who often asks probing questions about various scenarios or has a senior operator answer questions from junior operators. Unlike the informal conversations in the Gilley room back at the barn, the discussions are usually led off by a video or training film. Accident review in the

215

collision avoidance class is very similar, but the conversation or topic is usually a round-robin of the description of the events or conditions leading up to an accident or a passenger complaint.

Though this may seem boring or pointless, I do always try to see if I can gain a new tidbit or technique from someone else. I usually do—how to adjust the windows to reduce the smell of a stinker was a biggie. Leaving a small crack open behind me helped with the crosscurrents. Thank God for the fog! Placing the doors for a flag stop at certain locations and the art of making the radio call were juicy tidbits I would not have discovered on my own.

When to call was also a great by-product of VTT class. Calling during afternoon peak period did not result in a quick response from Central, but early morning did. Also, the art of when to call for a switchback. I was calling in too early. The shift change of the shop for a road call, the acceptance of a variable end time, and how to handle late runners were all great learning points at a VTT class. The list goes on.

And in collision avoidance class, or accident review, I got to learn the basic food groups of accidents and could see that contact made with the coach was either SSL, sideswipe left, SSR, sideswipe right, SP, squeeze play, TBR, TBL, T-bone right or left, or RE, rear end. Mirror positions come into play for each line. Once I got my mirrors just right for each type of traffic, I stopped getting into trouble. Having mirrors high on the way to Daly City is not the same as going downtown on the 1 California in Chinatown, with mirrors down and close.

Crosstown 22 Fillmore line has different mirror settings and a different style of driving than the 24 Divisadero—even though they are only five blocks apart in Western Addition. The 24 travels along a four-lane street and has long stretches without boarding in a residential area. The 22 is all about the art of the stop at the curb and saving the knees.

In my opinion, the 22 is closest to the 1 California, and the 5 Fulton is much like the 14 Mission. The 49 seems to be in a class by itself. The fact that you do the Mission and then turn on to Van Ness is intense. Keeping the Zen on the 49 means taking a full ten at North Point, even if arriving late! Amen!

Range Sheets

Posted in the Gilley room, our break room, at our bus barn are the range sheets. These are the shift schedules that tell you when you report, pull out, make relief, go on break, begin your second part, and finish. The second part is usually only on certain day shift assignments or runs. Most early-starting or late-starting runs are straight through. The general pattern of the runs on the range sheets goes as follows. Straight-through runs pull out in the early morning and get relieved after lunch. These early-morning straight throughs begin as early as 4:00 a.m. and go to 1:00 or 2:00 p.m. There is no pull in, so you may finish somewhere other than at the bus barn from where you pull out. The next work shifts are split day shifts. These runs start a little later in the morning, from 6:00 a.m. or 7 a.m., have a two-hour break in the middle, and then work to 6:00 p.m. or 7:00 p.m. Their range is twelve hours. Hence, the name of the sheets is range sheets. They tell you your shift range per run.

A sample line on the range sheets looks something like this:

106 *6:36 1408 118/11:52(SR12:52)
164>2:02 602 6:36**

Reading across, this says, Run 106 pulls out (one asterisk) at 6:36 a.m. and is the eighth bus out on the 14 line (train 1408). At 11:52 a.m., the operator of run 118 is waiting for you (backslash means inbound) at Eleventh and Mission inbound to relieve me. I get paid an extra ten minutes (SR standby relief from 11:52 a.m. to 12:52 p.m.). Then, after lunch, I meet run 164 on the 6 line at 2:02 p.m. outbound (greater-than sign means outbound). I pull in (double asterisk) at 6:36 p.m.

On the range sheets are the columns of pay that are not just platform time. Platform time is the time spent in the cockpit. Other forms of pay listed here are lunch, standby detail (SD), standby report (SR) as seen in the above example, travel time (ICT), overtime straight (OT), and overtime night (OT after 6:00 p.m.). Lunch has been cut from several runs posted on a new sign-up and equals twenty minutes anytime you are in the cockpit for more than six hours.

Standby time used to total almost one hundred hours a day for all Potrero and Presidio runs, but now it is less than five hours a day. This looks good in cutting payroll costs, but I believe this cut can actually lead to longer-term staffing problems in finding enough bodies to fill all these runs. Running time between checkpoints on our paddles and recovery time at the end of the line also get chopped, so that platform time becomes a challenge to make ends meet, especially without a switchback!

These other forms of pay become less accurate when buses are missing, as any regular rider can attest. Travel time takes longer to get to another relief point in heavy traffic. Standby detail (SD) accounts for those waiting in the Gilley room to be detailed at the last minute if another coach needs to be taken to a relief point as a coach trade. Standby report (SR) usually is for those operators taking over an open run that has not been detailed by the regular operator. I would standby on report, waiting for the dispatcher to call my cap number over the PA. OT and night shift differential are other extra types of pay shown on the range sheets. OT starts after eight hours, and night shift begins after 6:00 p.m.

On the range sheets are the columns of pay that are not just platform time. Platform time is the time spent in the chair. Other forms of pay listed here are lunch, standby detail, standby report, travel time, and overtime straight and overtime night. Lunch has been cut from several runs posted on a new sign-up. These other forms of pay become less accurate when buses are missing, as any regular rider can attest. Travel time takes longer to get to another relief point in heavy traffic.

After these middle-of-the-day runs come early twilights. They start around two to four in the afternoon and go straight through with a pull in around nine at night. Late twilights start after four in the afternoon and go as late as two in the morning. Then come the owls, which may start around dinnertime, 5:00 p.m., and go through till almost sunlight, or after an inbound, early-to-work run.

The great thing about all this is the diversity of start and finish times one has, as with days off. Days off are connected and are paired in any combination of days off: weekends are Saturday and Sunday, and then Sunday/Monday, Monday/Tuesday, Tuesday/Wednesday, Wednesday/Thursday, Thursday/ Friday, and Friday/Saturday. Sunday/Monday and Friday/Saturday are very popular as a number one choice in days off other than weekends. Choices are made by seniority in three-minute bid windows on the day of the barn sign-up that falls on your rank with the other operators at your barn for a barn sign-up, or system wide for a general sign-up, GSU, which permits a five-minute bid window.

The distribution of days off is not equal. Monday Tuesday, or Tuesday Wednesday may be the fewest groups of days off, with Thursday Friday being the greatest number of days off. This can have an effect on those of us with lots of seniority with weekends off, because it means that if we have a junior operator in front of us with days off in the middle of the week, their days off may not get covered by the dispatcher. This has the effect as an open run, so I am less sure of who, if any, will be in front of me and what my headway will be. Thinking seniority comes with easier headway and less gaps between buses may not be so.

I call Central for a line check. This is the professional way to ask for help: *call for a line check.* It took me years to call calmly and use the correct language to ask for help on the radio. The hard part is to end the call quickly and with thanks. With an operator out for five weeks in front of me, the risk of complaints against me goes up. The first week without a leader, Central did not acknowledge a problem. The dispatcher could say all runs were out, and this would be true at the start of my second part. What they weren't telling Central was that a car parker or early report person filling in reaches maximum hours and pulls in early. This creates a triple headway situation that can extend for over four hours.

By the second week, Central said they would check, and after a pause, allowed me to move up five. By the third week, they would call and ask me to move up five. And by the fourth week, I checked the daily detail in the morning and saw a blank by the runs that were in front of me. This is where doing a great job without complaining seems unfair, in that the dispatcher fills holes with squeaky wheels.

The dispatcher is telling me not to stress out second desk by putting in for premium pay for not having a leader. I say that her stress is nothing compared to four to six hours of no leader on the 22 in the afternoon! We are entitled to extra run pay if we are working without a leader, but it has to happen for more than two consecutive days and for at least two hours or more in a shift. Good luck with that!

Today I can do this with a smile on my face. It would be my expectation to let the chit of a safety warning be dismissed, but the caution and reinstruct for a rescheduled conference still hangs in the air like ripened fruit needing to be picked. This is the emotional constitution we must have to stay at the job—to let things go and know that all we have to give to change a situation is love and not anger. Acceptance is the answer and the key to not getting in the bog of being a victim behind the wheel.

I have found working weekends to be much more relaxing than, say, working on a Tuesday. Having weekends off may not be such a great thing after all. By working a twilight, with two weekdays off, I have found I can schedule doctor or dentist appointments with ease and without having to resort to a run trade or time off in the middle of the week. Indeed, finding a great block or run with weekdays off could be a solution to keeping the Zen at work on a trolley in San Francisco!

Splits

Of the three shifts an operator can choose to work, the day shift is usually a split shift. Senior runs during the day report at a time interval between 6:30 a.m. and 7:00 a.m. and get off twelve hours later. In the middle of the platform, or drive time, is a two-hour lunch. I try to plan these break times in a way such that the direction the bus is headed when I am relieved is favorable to where I choose to take lunch, meet friends, or run some errands. Nothing is as simple as staying on the same bus I was just driving to shave off wait time or travel time to my lunchtime destination. If I have to go to another place to start my second part, I choose to make sure the bus I am going to get on is also headed in a direction favorable to where I make relief.

If I have to step off my bus to take another one in another direction, this extra cost in time adds up over the life of the sign-up. Also, the travel time to the second point can be half an hour away, so that together, almost an hour of lunch could be consumed in transit riding on other buses. I try to avoid this and pick break times that start and end close to places I frequent for lunch.

The Potrero Barn seems to be in the best location for finding the most diverse places to eat, shop, or meet friends on lunch. And from what my coworkers tell me, parking is not too bad. I try to get as much done on my lunch break as I possibly can. The great thing about a twelve-hour range as a work schedule is that you really don't ever have to buy or maintain any street clothes! I put my uniform on at 5:30 a.m. and take it off around 10:00 p.m. after dark. I don't have the time to change after work if I am en route to meet friends or go to a meeting.

I am in my uniform all day, five days a week. The good news is that I have new uniform parts waiting for me in the receiver's office.

After several years, we build up enough time to add to uniform pieces to make do with our long days and busy schedule, so we don't have to keep washing them constantly. Splits also make time to do laundry if I can get the inbound feng shui right on the dot when making relief! Staying on the same coach after relief helps. Is the bus headed in the best direction from the barn or from my house? These little nuances in time and direction add up over the life of a sign-up!

Pulling Out

THERE ARE CERTAIN KEY POINTS AROUND THE SYSTEM WHERE OPERATORS begin and end their shift that are not at the bus barn. Market and Van Ness is a relief point. It is a place where drivers take over the seat and relieve another operator per the run schedule. And at this corner, it is also where defective coaches can pull in along Eleventh Street to Bryant and park the coach. It's also where buses from five lines pull in from revenue service to the bus barn. Because Seventeenth and Bryant is also a pull-in/pullout location and relief point, it is somewhat of a congregation point for bus drivers waiting to make relief. Coaches get new operators in staggered time slots, where successive buses on line get relieved. This occurs midmorning around ten o'clock. Later around 2:00 p.m. Knowing what peak periods are, when buses are entering and exiting the line, helps with understanding why headway between buses increases and decreases. There are also runs between those getting relieved so that if a bus arrives without a relief operator, hopefully the driver who passes through without relief will stay in service. These relief times, controlled by scheduling, filled by dispatchers, can become a factor in spacing and wait time between buses. It can also cause gaps and overcrowding if there is not an operator or a coach to make relief.

One key point about relief points and pullout wires is the awareness of where they are. Sometimes a few blocks makes a big difference in how long you have to wait. If you are getting off BART at Twenty-Fourth Street and going outbound to Geneva and Mission or to a stop on the way to Daly City, then it pays (in time, and time is money) to know that just one outbound stop away at Cesar Chavez, all the morning pullouts to Daly City make their first stop after they turn off of Twenty-Sixth Street. Someone passing up the 49 at the Twenty-Fourth Street BART

Station is missing the chance to get on any number of 14 Daly City coaches pulling out and making their first stop at Twenty-Sixth and Chavez. There sometimes is a shadow period of very few buses in the morning as owl coaches pull in and fresh buses pull out. This is one of those cases where it pays to get on the wrong bus to transfer later on down the line. The important thing is to get past the pullout wires on Mission and Twenty-Sixth, where plenty of empty buses are heading outbound to the Excelsior and Daly City.

If you wanted to go crosstown on the 22 Fillmore and were waiting at Harrison inbound, you would find a nice empty 22 going your way. If you were waiting at Potrero and Sixteenth, you might end up being late and become angry as you saw a 22 turning off route before your stop and going home to the bus barn. In this case, just three blocks determine the difference between getting on a fresh, empty bus or seeing a bus turn off right before your stop. This can have a big impression on how one views Muni service.

There is lots of knowledge about riding Muni that once understood reduces the wait time to get somewhere and adds to being in the Zen as a rider.

Pulling In

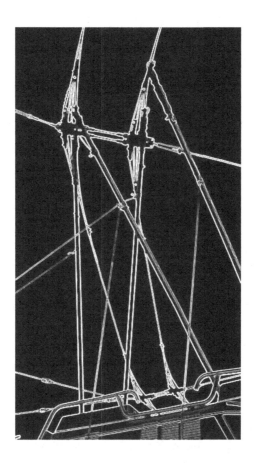

One common comment people make when waiting for the bus is "How come I see like three buses going in the opposite direction when I have been waiting fifteen minutes for a bus and nothing is coming?" This has to do with where the buses come from and where they are headed when they pull in. "Are you a forty-nine?" is asked a lot when buses along Van Ness have the head sign that reads, "Market." There is no line number displayed on the left of the head sign, just the words in bold, "Market." The truth is that this coach could be a 41 Union, a 30 Stockton, or a 49 City College that is pulling in to the wires on Eleventh Street and ending its run for the day.

Trolleys do not magically transport from their last terminal to the bus barn. They have to return to the barn on the wires, usually along a corridor that connects to the pull-in wires at various locations, like Seventeenth and South Van Ness, Sixteenth Street and Bryant, Eleventh and Mission inbound, or Tenth and Howard outbound. So when headway, the distance or time between buses, is gradually increasing after rush hour ends, knowing which direction the pull-in coaches are headed helps, because service is superior in this direction. Someone waiting at a big corner like Van Ness and Market at 6:00 p.m. would see three times the number of buses headed outbound along Van Ness, because these buses are pulling in.

The good news is that if you know the pull-in direction of buses heading back to the barn in the early evening, you get great service with buses that are almost empty and quiet. This is a great spot to find the Zen zone. Working a run that has pull-in coaches that do work is a great way to start a twilight shift with a gentle beginning—if your leader is a working leader and stays in service. When operators do not pick up, or I am missing a leader, the load on Van Ness becomes an impatient, angry drag down.

When I pull in from the 30 Stockton or 41 Union or the 49, I always try to pick up those waiting along Van Ness, even though I am a short-line coach. Technically, based on the information on our paddles, our run's timetable, we are a 49 line coach. I have found that if I pick everyone up, it helps the bus driver behind me going all the way to City College because he or she only has one major stop to pick everyone up—at Market. Sometimes I get permission to go down to Fourteenth Street so that my passengers can connect easier with a 14 to continue outbound. It doesn't cost me anything in time to do this, as a pull in from Fourteenth Street is actually sometimes faster than Eleventh, and it prevents a huge group of people from waiting at Market by Van Ness station. There is nothing worse than having a huge group of people waiting for the next through bus when I am pulling in. By picking up folks willingly and taking them to a transfer point on Mission, it reduces delays for my follower and helps those waiting. Having a PA microphone that works and makes my voice easy to hear and understand really pays off and eliminates the battle cry going up from angry passengers on board when I turn off the line to go to the barn.

In these cases, the right to remain silent is actually the best policy. If it has been one of those days, I have found it best to remain silent. *Anything I say can and will be used against me* in a passenger service request (PSR). I have learned as an operator that staying in service to get folks closer to a transfer point doesn't always work. More drama does not mean better service!

When new at Muni with a high cap number and low seniority, the probability is high that the time available to me during my three-minute bid window shall be in the afternoon and with a pull in at the end of your day. When I have a lower cap number and want to work days with big money, I may have to choose a day run split whereby I also have to pull in after a long twelve-hour range during the day. The point being, after working for many hours, the last trip is a short-line trip, which involves taking the coach off the regular route and switching over to wires on streets that lead to the bus barn, and I'm tired and not as willing to wait for you to realize you have to get off the bus.

Interestingly enough, no matter how many years a San Franciscan has under their belt in living in the city or riding Muni, if they don't have a friend or family member who has worked for or is working for Muni as a transit operator, they are clueless about what happens in the morning hours from 8:45 a.m. to 10:00 a.m. and around 6:15 p.m. to 8:00 p.m. Certain runs' buses end service during the end of a peak period of frequent service, to fewer buses and a longer headway.

Most people don't understand when peak period is or that the headway between coaches changes every four hours and is clearly marked at any shelter with a map. Most riders have confusion about express and limited service. They are unaware that the express service operates in only one direction, depending on the time of day, what lines go downtown, and which lines go crosstown and never see Market Street.

Express coaches run inbound in the morning and outbound in the afternoon, and this of course requires that you know which side of the street you need to wait on to catch the bus in the correct direction of travel. This is not as easy as in most cities because the hills and fog obscure the tall downtown buildings.

Most of this knowledge about pull ins also includes that toward the end of any peak period, one intending for a Muni coach headed in a direction toward the bus barn *should look not at the line sign but the destination as well.* The ratio or number of people looking at the destination sign of the bus has remained about the same, with less than one in ten standing on the sidewalk waiting for the bus actually acknowledging the bus destination before boarding. If I inform those boarding about the destination of the coach, patrons are clueless about why the bus is a short-line coach. Just as in the run from hell I worked in 2007, there seems to be an unlimited well of new, misinformed, or confused passengers about bus pull ins after peak periods.

If I could wave a magic wand of desire to change behaviors that chronically delay or add to tension between riding public and our union members, it would be this issue. *It is simply a matter of awareness and pattern.* And no matter how many years or how many hours at work I have been in the seat, the patience must be mustered to quickly and clearly explain that this bus is ending at Market and Van Ness, Sutter and Divisadero, or Seventeenth and Bryant.

Not My First Rodeo

DENTS AND DINGS NOTWITHSTANDING, ONE CAN TELL HOW MUCH TIME one has behind the wheel by looking no further than the defect card after making relief. Senior operators can roll with whatever they have been given. Others take "safety significant" to levels seen only at the National Security Agency. The biggest variable to accepting equipment is the personality and style of who is behind the wheel.

We have terms for the style of movement an operator has during his or her run. I have a reputation as a runner. With Mars in Aries and my second house rising in Leo, I have a charismatic demeanor that may come across as nondiplomatic, though I love to show my sunny side. In training, the only hint at personality is within the three points affecting safety: weather, traffic, and operator.

When I ask a mom with a screaming or crying baby to move back, other passengers in the rear sound disbelief and shock that I would ask a mom and baby to move back or leave the coach and wait for the next one. Once again, it is operator, my sense to drive safely, that cannot be judged by another. I am driving a ten-ton vehicle in heavy rush hour traffic, and yes, any number of noises can be distracting: a relationship breakup over the cell phone, using the metal stanchions as a drum set, arguing about a deal, talking about where to buy product, and a whole assortment of goodies.

Anyway, I see how what may be a good schedule during one sign-up can become a setup for failure in another, depending upon the headway between transfer coaches, leaving time of a leader, and how fast one can push stale greens. I have learned to eat fresh greens, and this pause at a stoplight has turned my style into that of being a good guy. By stopping well behind the crosswalk or stop line and looking at the show on the street, all is calm, all is well. Turk, Eddy, Post, Harrison, and Kansas are streets, just to name a few, where I do a self-check-in to see if I am pushing ahead or laying back.

Relief time at relief points does add the characteristic of a Russian roulette when filling out a choice slip during a general sign-up. I try to find a split day shift that has two equal parts, with the second part hopefully being shorter. Five hours in the morning and four and a half in the second is ideal. Except when it is not. Sometimes, time does seem to pass by faster in the morning than in the afternoon. A busy trip can make time pass by faster. It is a fine mental and spiritual and physical balancing act that becomes not unlike the ballet of life. At some point, I have to let go and let God be the dancer. My will gets me into a rock and a hard place. Better to look out over Alcatraz from the 41 line at Leavenworth on Russian Hill on a beautiful sunlit morning than be assigned to "the rock" in a hard place on a seat that loses air and will not adjust!

The answer to the question at relief, "Is this a good one?" can be like carrying a loaded weapon. The response "The coach runs smooth" means no flat tire, hard steer, or good braking. But oh, by the way, your mirrors shake like a wooden roof shingle in a windstorm, and you will find your butt on the floor as the chair slowly loses air on the way to Daly City! Hey, but it isn't safety significant. Really?

Keeping Zen means keeping quiet! Especially on a Friday on the last trip! Sometimes the best relief is a pull in! No one to ask, "Is this coffee cup yours? Are these your papers?" Some operators build a nest around them when they occupy the seat for many hours, and it takes some doing to ask them to leave the coach as they found it. One can only wonder what their closet or kitchen looks like at home! "Get your stuff out of here!" may not be the best bet to start the day at relief!

Indeed, diplomacy with coworkers is perhaps, at the end of the day, the biggest challenge to face with time behind the wheel. Did my hand signal to move up to the top of the zone at the terminal actually show an angry, hostile flip off with fingertips down, in a condescending brush-off motion, or was it an alleluia, praise God, hands up, palms facing, show of grace? I am reminded of how often it is not what is said but the tone with which it is said.

Owls and Twilights

OWLS START AROUND 5:00 P.M. AND GO TO SIX O'CLOCK THE NEXT morning. Some late twilight runs start around 4:00 p.m. and get off in the wee hours of the morning after midnight. When starting these late shifts, a relief is made during a busy time. The bus is full, and the air is stale. The coach is fully warmed up and ready to go. Usually a quick check of the mirrors is all it takes. The day starts out busy, but traffic thins as the shift goes on, and this makes for less stress as the shift continues.

I have found these runs to be quite enjoyable and easy on the life outside of this job. I don't have to set an alarm, and I get regular business hours to make appointments and get things done. The problem is with my social life, as the middle of the shift is during prime time for socializing and going out. I have known a few owls (operators who work nights), and going to breakfast is a nice time to catch up. I guess the best things about working nights is staying out of trouble and not spending money!

Calling Central

One of the common comments I get from operators, even those with time and lots of experience, is "I never call Central." Or "Those guys are clueless." And I have found that those operators on the extra board fall into this category more than the average operator working a regular run on the same schedule every day. Extra board operators get to be assigned a new run on a daily basis. This is great when a sign-up drags on for months; it keeps monotony and boredom at a minimum, and it also prevents an attitude to develop from regular problems or passengers, because I am not on the same schedule day in and day out. I believe some operators are hiding out on the extra board so as to reduce their accountability with the regular riding public. But for me, I like the regularity to plan my time off by having a fixed schedule. Also, if there are recurring problems on my run and line, I get to take a look at what I am doing to cause these problems and see if I can make them go away. That's why I like to do my homework during a sign-up and see if I can make a choice that prevents headway problems or overload, though this is not always clear.

"Central" is shorthand for OCC: Operations Central Control. Even though nine of ten interactions with Central may not appear fruitful or necessary, it is that one in ten times when a call to Central, or from Central, is immensely helpful. And it is this one in ten that makes me keeping a professional, calm tone on the air really pay off. Central operators come to identify us not by run or coach number but by our voice. Yes, Central cannot necessarily see what is going on in and around my coach, so bearing this in mind, I don't get upset if they state something contradictory to what I know or can see.

A lot about what Central can see has changed recently. The new drive cams mounted on the front windscreen (windshield) have helped, as do the newer cameras in the newer coaches. Central Control is no longer in the dark about what is going on in front of our coach, and I believe this to be a good thing. Some would say that this is an invasion of privacy, but I disagree because I am a civil servant in a job serving the public.

Cameras are being installed around the common areas at our division for security purposes, and the drama queens are upset. If you are a public servant and carry yourself professionally throughout your day, what is the problem? Yes, I do believe George Orwell is right: big brother is watching us in more and more places, but I try to keep this aspect on a positive note, hoping that these images would capture an event that would protect me from abuse and falsehood about what happens. Much of the cost of litigation can be stopped dead in its tracks by the images captured on the coach. I look at the drive camera as my friend.

I said that only one in ten calls may appear helpful, and these calls usually end in a tagline from Central I've come to know all too well. Below are a list of the taglines Central gives us and the emotional component that goes along with them. These phrases may seem simple and innocent enough on this paper, in your armchair or desk as you read this, but believe me, when I get these directives, I am under a much higher level of stress or unusual headway.

See the Inspector

It usually occurs when things are very busy. Central Control may be having high call volume, sometimes due to a major line delay, such as when the tunnel gets blocked. We are silently expected to work an extra load without a break, and we need a switchback for a mental break or because we have been working for over two hours without a break. Sometimes on a straight-through run, we may have gone for four hours without a fifteen-minute break. So we call for a switchback, usually ten minutes short of our final terminal. The answer from Central Control is to see the inspector for time and place. But nine times out of ten, there is no inspector! I usually pop the brake and wait and see. If no one comes to the door, I can call again, but this adds to the delay, and other coaches may be blocked behind me. "Take it to the end and call back later" is the usual response. Not getting the break I need when I need it adds to the frustration.

Take It to the End

Usually a Central response after "See the inspector." And even if I do make contact with the inspector, he or she says, "Take it to the end." Good is the day that I can follow this instruction without a problem. If I am all alone—that is, without a coach behind me—I follow this order, but if my follower catches up to me by the time I reach my last short route switchback, I call again. Many operators wise to this make sure they stay four minutes or more, so that the lead coach doesn't get a switchback. This makes for a long day unless I can turn it into a game or my coach shuts down and I need a road call.

Do the Best You Can

When I cannot take on any more passengers because my bus is full, I call to let Central know I am beginning to pass up stops. This phrase comes into play when we are late and heavy. Many of our coaches have defects that are not safety significant but are randomly occurring and cause delay, such as slow doors and slow brake release. Fare box problems and lack of heat or air can also cause us to not feel that we have been given what we need to do our job properly. Not being able to use the wheelchair lift or kneeler due to low air is just another curse to hear, "Do the best you can." But at some point, going out of service may soon become reality. This most frequently occurs when a bus is already missing in front of me. I am taking on more people, which adds to the bus performance issues and adds to needing relief.

Put It on the Defect Card and Continue in Service

This usually pertains to a bad fare box or Clipper card service not working. If a defect concerns our ability to pick up wheelchairs, it is mandatory that I call. Many times, the bus won't move if the lift does not stow. This is a bummer to have to clear the coach and tell everyone that the bus is out of service. So most times, of all the orders, this one is usually the fastest and easiest to follow. Hopefully I can continue in service, but this is usually an order before another call to state that we can't continue.

Getting out of the bus to push the wheelchair lift to stow is one technique. Resetting master control and shutting off the bus sometimes makes the problem go away. I am amazed at those who can make it to the relief point on time and not break down. So the lack of writing anything down on the card and bringing it to the relief point is an honor in and of itself, even though many take issue with this and feel that the relief operator is not being honest. But given my own situation to end a part of our shift on time, bringing the coach to a relief point is better understood. Breaking down and having to pull out may not be any easier than calling Central at the relief point and calling the shop. So the decision to stay in service is up to me and not Central, and the order to continue in service lends itself to conflict with others—passengers and coworkers alike.

Help Is on the Way

I make sure I have something to drink or eat. I have a pair of reading glasses or reading material also. I never know when my shift will end or how long I will have to wait in the dark or cold wind for a road crew to assist me in getting back on the road. We are required to call back at regular intervals to check and see when help will actually arrive. There are some good times and some bad times to ask for help, especially during a shift change. Faced with the prospect of waiting in the cold, I do try to keep going as best we can, without delay. Many times, this is impossible because the bus will not move. "Help is on the way" can have my eyes rolling because it seems like a bad joke.

But to remember that I never know who is listening, it is best to remain calm and stay professional. Doing so has given me that switchback or that pull in I really need to go home at the right time.

Shoes

"BABY NEEDS A NEW PAIR OF SHOES." THAT'S WHAT I SAY WHEN I AM hitting hard and I see sparks at night off my collectors. Shoes are the carbon blocks that sit inside the brasserie or metal brackets that form a slot at the end of our trolley poles. This is the point at which I collect our power from the overhead. The shoes sit inside of the collectors. Six hundred volts of direct current are fed through the feeder wires, which come from certain utility poles that carry the wires upon which I travel. Next time you are on a hill by some trolley line, look for the poles carrying the power. You can see the wires coming directly out of the pole and on to the overhead.

If too many buses are too close together, especially on a steep hill, the power breaker will go off, and I will temporarily lose power because the feeder wire cannot handle the load. This shutoff of power, or a tripping of the circuit breaker, can occur leaving Chinatown on Sacramento Street heading outbound up the hill to Nob Hill, and also on Union Street leaving Van Ness inbound. It didn't take me long to learn this fact.

Heading inbound on the 41 line, I was not too far behind two smaller coaches that started across Van Ness as I pulled into the zone to pick up a few runners. Because the next stop at Polk is on a steep hill with a short green light, two buses did not clear the Polk Street stop as I crossed Van Ness and began to climb. Sure enough, as I got close to Polk, they started to move on to Larkin. This is one of the steepest grades in the system. Since no one was waiting at Polk, I did not kill the light but proceeded ahead before the light turned red. I figured that the other buses would be on to the next block before I crossed Larkin—business as usual, such as in the Mission line I was familiar with. Big mistake. My pull on the power caused the bus in front of me to slow down dramatically, and I put the pedal to the medal, but the bus came to a stop. There were now four buses in three blocks, loaded with passengers getting to work, and two of us were stopped.

I put on the parking brake and waited for the bus in front of me to start moving. Fortunately, he was able to start moving forward once I stopped draining energy from the wires. Another bus behind me was starting to climb from Van Ness, and sure enough, I saw the bus in front start to slow down as the bus behind me started to hit the steep grade. I won't follow too close from now on. The feeling of powerlessness when I put my foot down on the power pedal and start to lose power on a hill, with a full bus, is not something I would like to experience again.

Having a traction brush fail is also another scary movie. In departing Chinatown for Nob Hill, I lost all forward traction on the bus. The parking brake would not hold the coach either. All I could do was hold my foot on the service brake and call for help. One thing I did forget about was that when the air in lines reaches a certain point below sixty pounds per square inch, the emergency brake will pop up and hold the coach. This is a small comfort when the air in the lines is not holding the coach at a higher pressure. Did I really want to test the pop-up and see if it would hold? Luckily, it did. But I sure hope I never get that coach again when I am leaving Chinatown during peak period!

After rain for a week, all the carbon dust that has built up on the wires gets washed away. This is great for keeping our hands clean, should I need to use the ropes to replace my poles on the wires. But not good for wear and tear on the carbon shoe. It cuts faster into the wire because there is no more dust to act as a lubricant. The groove in my shoes gets deep. My collectors hit the hangars and crossovers with a loud noise, and my poles drop down off of the wires. I need new shoes.

There is a special slot in the range of the poles where I can hold the pole down to look at the shoes. This is at about a forty-five-degree angle from where the pole attaches to the roof of the bus. I can look to see if the carbon is cracked or deeply grooved. Sometimes when I look, there is no carbon at all in the collector! I cannot drive the bus forward from that point and must not move until the shop arrives and replaces the carbon. When we have new carbons, I still have to be careful in crossing other wires, because the slot in the new carbon is very small, and the poles can fall off of the wires easily.

Paying attention to how hard the coach is hitting the wires is good for staying in the Zen of driving Muni.

Wheel Blocks

"Unbelievable, just unbelievable." This is the statement of a resident near the La Playa bus terminal by the Ocean Beach Safeway. It was recorded for the *Jon Stewart Show*. This was a comedy show, and the occasion for the recording was based on the fact that this man's garage was hit by motor coaches more than once. Buses rolled away from the terminal and ran into his house. Not once, not twice, but three times (a lady). On the video, he replays the incident of how he fell out of his chair when the bus hit. This vision is hilarious for a television show, not so funny for the operator of the bus and in training class. Our training department shows this video to make a point about the importance of using a wheel block to prevent an unattended coach from rolling away.

Ocean Beach is not the only place where buses rolled on the loose. In Daly City, at the end of the 14 line, buses have also caused much damage to buildings and cars. The front wheels can roll over the curb and run into parked cars, or if the wheel is not curbed, it can roll all the way down the hill and into a building at the first intersection after the pullout from the terminal. One may wonder how this could happen. Inattention to detail is usually the first line on a disciplinary letter I receive when I am in trouble. There really is no excuse. I sometimes forget to use the parking brake when I am in a rush.

If I am adjusting a mirror on track four, I sometimes only open the doors instead of setting the brake. Whenever the seat is vacated, the brake must be set. I can only imagine what could cause an operator to forget to set the brake. Perhaps there was a distraction from someone asking a question or the rush to get to the bathroom. In any event, it is hard to justify any reason why the brake is not set. I have not found anyone who agrees that this could be excused.

239

When I was out with an inspector being requalified, we came to the outbound terminal on the 1 line at Thirty-Third and Geary. *Requal* occurs after we have a chargeable accident. We have to be graded and evaluated by a training inspector to make sure we are doing everything correct to ensure safety. Every now and then, it is not the operator on the training coach who gets in to trouble. Case in point. Out at Thirty-Third and Geary at the 1 California line, a coach was all the way back in the zone and had not been moved up.

I could not clear the crosswalk on the turn before the terminal, so the inspector grading me asked to be let out and to move the unattended bus up to the lead space in the zone. The door was closed, so he put his hand in the driver's window to open the door from the door dial. As soon as he pushed it, the bus released the air brake and started to roll back into my coach!

In one sweaty moment, the instructor was able to collect himself and rush to the open driver's window and stop the coach by opening the front door using the door dial. The bus stopped within two feet of my bumper. After overcoming the initial shock, we waited for the operator to return. Although words were said, no write-up occurred. Later found out that disciplinary action was taken, and I saw that operator one last time before he went into the superintendent's office for his hearing. I never saw him again.

There is no excuse for not wheel blocking the coach or for not using the parking brake. He had about ten years with the company at that time. With good eyesight and hearing, it doesn't matter how old you are to start working as a driver with any company. Inattention can rear its ugly head at any moment, and with it comes the loss of the job.

Staying in the Zen zone means being focused and adds to job security!

RDO

REGULAR DAY OFF. IF A WORKWEEK GOES BY AND I HAVE KEPT MY sanity, I can test my body and mind and see if I can work on my day off, my RDO. If I haven't turned crazy by working my run during the week, I can see if I can make extra money on a day off at the overtime rate of pay. I know I have mastered the Zen of Muni if I can work my regular run and still have the energy to try more work, if it is available, to get ahead of bills or save for a vacation or toy. One of several things can happen. If I have had a good week, a few hours of work on the weekend can take the Zen vibe away really fast if I am working an intense line without a leader. The good news is that folks who would have to wait twice as long to get picked up have the service they expect, because operators work on their day off.

The best thing about RDO is going home after the day is done. Just made bank at fifty-two dollars per, and it's over! The law of diminishing returns does make itself apparent on payday though. And I have seen that if overtime hours exceed twenty-six per pay period, the amount of fatigue or hangover from working on a day off becomes not worth the extra hours due to taxes. Working three days of overtime in a two-week period takes such a toll on personal time; I can be no fun to be around on or off the bus. I have to be careful I don't get a PSR, passenger service request (complaint).

Trying to explain my life to my loved ones at home or anyone who tries to reach me by phone is a chore. I am not sitting at a desk in an office. My schedule can change at any time with traffic, construction, fires, parades, protests, and equipment failure. If I have a jealous lover, this job may not be for me. *Sorry, got to go!* I have to move my bus up because my follower needs room at the terminal. I have only three minutes to take a bite. *Can I call you back later?* I am sorry my phone is off; I am not allowed to have it on!

I now try to say, "I gotta go," or, "I won't be able to call you back for an hour." Voicemail is great for leaving a message, but don't expect us to be on the line if you call right back; we are already on the road! "Video killed the Radio Star," my favorite song on MTV in the eighties, has now become iPhone killed the (Voiceover Star) voicemail machine (and returned calls).

Most of my friends now know what to expect when it comes to unavailability on the phone, but it does take some getting used to. Sometimes months. Sometimes years. I can't just call whenever I like. The schedule is just a guideline really! Kind of like the pirates' code on *Pirates of the Caribbean*! But just as Captain Jack Sparrow, I too have to make it up as I go. So if you do have me in your address book, know this: I never know what is going to happen next. If you wonder why I am not arriving at the arranged time, hey, I took Muni! Now I know what the letters SFMTA stand for: Sorry, folks. May take a while!

Keeping it Zen adds that sixth sense, that intuition that helps our loved ones and friends understand dinner may get cold before we get home!

The Fare Box

Surveys of time use show that much time is spent in the bus zone, loading passengers. Though this would seem to be a revenue loser, as those who board in the rear would be evading the fare, my experience has been that most riders are honest and pay their fare by coming to the front door to get a receipt or transfer. Those who enter in the back because of wheelchair boarding or a kneeler request do come to the front from the aisle to get a transfer and pay their fare. By believing that most people are honest and abide by the unofficial honor system of paying for their ride, I have reduced almost all problems and dwell time delays at the front door and fare box.

This surrender on my part has made my job a lot easier, and I always try to be of service if someone is a little short but needs a ride. This took me several years of discovery, as I am somewhat of a perfectionist. My Mars in Aries has reared its ugly head with some fare disputes that got me into trouble. Being rude or appearing nasty is a fast behavior modify if ever there was one. How riders react to my statement of what the fare is, over time, gives me an idea of how I am to handle myself, or set the tone of requesting the fare, without getting into an argument.

The first and most obvious dilemma one first realizes as a transit operator for San Francisco is how oblivious passengers are in expecting us to see their fare in the first place. If I had one magic wand or wish that I could click my heels to make come true, it would be that boarders see how impossible it is for us to check their fare. If it were a problem with fewer than 10 percent of people riding, then it would seem like I am being picky or controlling, but over half of the people boarding do not show their fare in what I would call a thoughtful or honest way.

Granted, as two columns of people board at major transfer points, they pass by quickly if I am lucky, but the way in which I am to look at their fast pass or transfer is ridiculous by any standard. Injecting humor into the situation by stating that there are two lines, fast track and exact change, and motioning to imaginary two lines at the front door helps interrupt the pattern of blocking that occurs from tagging in on the one side, and the fare box on the other.

So there should be no surprise why the majority of operators appear to not be looking at the fare when it is presented. Almost no one appears to be concerned that we have a chance to actually look at their hand. I'd say less than one in ten boarders actually shows me the fare in a reasonable way. I've learned that if I turn in my seat to face the door and appear genuinely interested in looking at what's in your hand, then odds do increase for proper fare presentation. What the majority don't seem to understand is that front door boarding is no reason for a reduction in fare evasion. People showing fare properly at the front door are such a small fraction of the total that, to us as operators, it makes no difference what door people enter. Hopefully, with the newer cameras, if anyone is actually viewing images, they would see it is virtually impossible to see most fares, even at the front door.

This brings me to the various styles of impossibility of fare evasion by those coming to the front door. There seems to be a paradox. And indeed there is. While I said that most people are honest in paying the fare, I also said they are clueless about how useless their presentation is for me to see. Bereft of knowing what they are showing, after countless times being berated by them for asking for their fare, taking my request personally such as an attack on their character, I have learned how to ask for the fare without too much backwash.

Here are some of the major food groups of fare evasion. Remember, I am not saying that these passengers don't actually have a valid fare. What I am saying is for the purpose of checking the fare, these maneuvers constitute fair evasion because we cannot determine if the fare has been paid.

The Wand

Like Merlin the magician, or something out of a *Harry Potter* movie, these people move their arm in such a wide swath it is a miracle that anyone can see what the hell they are holding. We have over thirty-eight types of pass ID that are acceptable for fare, and I've never seen management post all forms of pass in one bulletin. Ironically, it doesn't matter, because I can't see what the hell people are showing me anyway. But that does not mean I should not make an effort to look at people's hands when they board, and it definitely does not mean I should just rationalize not checking at all. If I get distracted by another question or something else, these small rituals throw me off, and I get mail. I get a letter for a review about my behavior when I can't see why this is so. But if I talk to other drivers about this at the relief point or in the receiver's office, I usually get the right answer.

I would rarely ask for help or feedback when I was new, and this added years of distress that did not really need to be there. So when the wand goes by, I need to always be ready to do the correct action. Ask for the fare, even if the person whipping by us never stops. Most times, the person or persons behind the offender questions me as though I was asking for their fare; the wrong person usually stops to question me. "No, I wasn't asking you. The fare is three dollars." And that's usually the end of it. Just as in calling out transfers and destinations, it matters not that the right person hears me. I was following the rule.

Our most honorable mayor, Mr. Gavin Newsom, when riding on a cable car, made the observation that the conductor was not checking fares. What he may not have known is that I become accustomed to my regulars. I know who has their fast pass, and after the fourth of the month, it is not necessary to see the fast pass every day. Just because it is not apparent that I am checking every fare does not mean that I do or do not know who is paying.

The Jackknife

In all fairness, there are those seniors and those with mobility problems who may make coming up the stairs a balancing act. I have to be mindful of being of service, especially toward those with mobility problems that may not be visible; however, can a rider at least make an attempt, once in a blue moon, to at least show me that they have a current, valid monthly pass? If the month is new and you are a regular, isn't it reasonable to show me at the beginning of the month that you have your new pass?

The jackknife is accomplished like the wand except for an excessive up and down motion with the arm holding the pass. Made to look like the arm is a counterweight to the balancing act of climbing, there is no chance in hell that my eyes can focus on a pass that is moving up and down at or near the speed of light. Just because you are holding the pass does not mean I have the ability to see it. When I explain that this is the fourth of the month and many old passes have expired, this usually helps.

If a regular rider becomes offended that I am asking to see their fare, I respond by saying, "Yes, I know you are a regular pass holder, but I haven't seen you with the new pass yet." If the fourth day of the new month is after a holiday, I give grace for this. "Are you going to get your new one today?" Then things get better. "You need this transfer until you purchase your new pass. I don't want you to get in trouble." This heals all wounds and prevents me from being perceived as a heal. The great reward at first impressions was when days turned into weeks turned into months without anyone taking my fare checking personally. It took me over five years to be able to say this truthfully.

Toll Booth

Having been a Jersey boy, I pride myself on being quick to pay a toll. If you have ever been headed to points south from NYC on the Garden State Parkway on a summer weekend, and you have successfully crossed the Raritan River Bridge crossing and toll booth, you know how paying the toll in the bucket in a timely fashion can contribute to delays of those behind you.

The one thing about Californian's being laid-back, is the cluelessness about how action, or in this case inaction, has a cannonball effect on others. I have never met a native New Yorker who was completely clueless at the fare box. Some Californians who have grown complacent and accustomed to not showing their fare are the biggest offenders with the toll booth method of fare payment. Should they be asked to show their fare by the fare inspector, they become grudging payers. It fast becomes obvious at the box that they are unfamiliar with actually paying a cash fare. I need to remember everyone is doing the best that they can, given what they know and what they have.

I find I lose my balance and fall back into a familiar pattern of not liking you if you don't behave like I think you should. The toll booth method involves dropping the coins over the slot in a dropping fashion, using the thumb or pointer finger as the feeder for the coin drop. Most people take the slow drip method instead of the fast pour because they are counting out their fare as they pay. This method is a bummer on morning peak inbounds if people haven't counted out their change in advance. This really slows us down and is the best reason to eliminate the fare altogether.

Dump Truck

These folks have learned that a single coin drop by drop is too slow, so they count their change ahead of time. This is a great first step to making Muni flow. But dropping the whole wad at once plugs up the coin slot. And those who have perfected this style usually also know how to fish with their fingers to stir the pile and let the coins trickle past the slot. I need to be willing to show them how to clear the slot. If they aren't willing to wait to see this, I need to surrender and clear the pile anyway. And so I need the humility to wait another day to find the right time to see if they will learn. After all, their rush to move back is my desire. And so I have to see my part in creating the dump truck. This patience to resist change upon them is something I have to constantly guard against in picking up folks who are slow to the door placement. And if I don't allow them the grace to do their thing, trouble soon follows. So I review my day and make sure I don't resist what I fear is to be a constant, unchanging dilemma upon my daily trips. And God, or the Muni gods, give me grace in making a mistake once or twice. If I create a patient and loving attitude when a jam occurs, the situation rarely repeats itself.

Tissue Deluxe

I was always seeing granny holding her fare in a wrap of tissue. And the tissue would break up and fall into the coin slot and lead to a coin bypass. Or there was some hair that fell into the coin slot along with the coins. Hopefully, I could dump the whole lot with my dump button and make the problem go away. But over time, if not caught right away, the fare box would stop counting coins, and the coins would build in the neck and cause a constant distraction. But it wasn't until I asked why seniors wrapped their coins that I got the answer. Their hands were dry with age, and the coins would stick to their palm and not go in. They had learned to put the coins in a wrap so that they would not stick to their skin and go in. They were only trying to be ready and be fast, but I didn't see it this way. So they had a good reason for this. And so I don't stop them when they put the tissue over the coin drop.

Whenever I see something happening over and over that is not to my liking, if I stop to ask, I get my answer, and the distraction goes away. Finding the right time and place to get the answer doesn't occur when I think it should. Only after I take a prayerful pause to be ready to accept that I may not have the answer does the answer soon come. This gets me excited about my job again.

If I take the role of a detective and try to unravel a mystery, I am back in the right mindset to discover the answer. And the answer is not one of arrogance or hostility to make my life as a driver miserable but because they are only trying to do the right thing after having problems paying the fare the regular way with their palm and fingers. Most operators are not so controlling as I am, so they haven't had to worry about how someone pays the fare. But for me, it was a big deal. I was not a good person if I ignored what I thought to be the most important deal for keeping my employer in the black, collecting as much fare as possible. In reality, this tightrope actually was reducing my job security and my paycheck, as I was being perceived as a dick or a mean driver. So the comment, all conflict arises from misplaced desire, really hit home here. I am not the Gestapo or the police. I am not an inspector. I am simply required to state what the fare is and let it go. Passengers' actions or reactions are not my responsibility. And once I got over this, my job at the fare box got easier.

Dollar Curl

I have always had a recurrent idea in a dream state regarding a life purpose here. And it revolves around a seemingly impossible task, such as in *Horton Hears a Who*, whereby the elephant has to go through a field of flowers to find the one flower with the one speck containing Whoville. The enemy drops the one flower into a huge field of flowers off a cliff. Amazingly, our hero begins the daunting task without a single hesitation.

In my design, it is like cleaning up a huge trashedout stadium after a game alone—such that no one would ever agree to start such an enormous task—with a passerby later to remark, "You're done already? I can't believe it!"

I have had some success in this area—including the dollar curl. Muni does seem to offer this ultimate challenge. My hope is like a candle being able to light an entire cathedral—in a purposeful, peaceful manner—not like the match used to trigger a wildfire!

My goal or purpose in life is to begin the impossible task and to be successful in the task, with someone coming by later to remark, "You're done already? I can't believe it." And I have had some success in this area. Except for the dollar curl. Muni does seem to offer the ultimate challenge. My hope is that like one candle being able to light an entire cathedral (or one match to trigger an immense wildfire!), I hope I can actually start one task or action that eventually leads to a permanent change, whereby that first once thought impossible task is basically removed forever. And having the knowledge that I was there at the beginning. That one person can actually make a difference. That it isn't about the impossibility of ever finishing but about being willing to try and see what happens.

And so I trudge with the dollar curl. Not all fare boxes are created equal. I found out from a coworker in the revenue department that the slots on some of the bill meters are narrower. I made the effort to make a revenue appointment with my coach to see what I could learn. It seemed that few operators would ever consider calling Central Control to get a fare box fixed while in revenue service, but I did so anyway. I learned something about what causes the fare box to fail: hair in the coin slot, tobacco and cotton from pockets that were mixed with the coins, and just the regular dust on dollars. When I learned about what to look for that would set the ball in motion to begin to clog the fare box, my problems of fare box failure went down. If I got owl coaches assigned to me in the morning from another run, such as an owl, I would go through a period of days where I would get several coaches in a row that had bad fare boxes. I kept calling to get revenue to meet me at Ferry Plaza, or Cal train, or Howard and New Montgomery. I learned the good times and places to ask to meet. I never would have figured this out if I never called. Around 9:00 a.m., in an off-peak direction by the inbound terminal, where other coaches collected, was a good time and place.

And so my journey about cause began. Then on to offer help when and where the problem started. When someone put a dollar or coin into the box. If a dollar has a bent corner or if the edge is creased, the dollar will not go in fare boxes with a narrow slot. It became easier to look at their bill before they put it in the slot, rather than watch them struggle and hold up the boarding cue. Saying to them to flip it over didn't work because they would try the other side of the bill rather than a simple flip, and the other side had a crease up in the same direction. Using my hand as an example doesn't work because they are focusing not on my hand but on the slot. Showing them how to put it in is the fastest and best. Most don't care or seem interested in knowing this, but over time, I noticed fewer and fewer people having problems. I started seeing more people with worn bills having them already folded to put into the machine, I also learned from them that two bills together work and that other operators had told them about how to crease the bill before putting it in the slot. By using my hand in a curl, pointing my fingers down, stating that the dollar moves into the machine going down through the roller, I saw the light go off in their head and declared it another victory of the day.

The Question

These are the pros. The don't have the fare and usually don't intend to pay, but by framing the greet by asking a question about where I go, they get me to tell them the correct answer, and they thank me, passing without showing a fare. They have made me look good. Doing service. They get to pass by without a delay. And there isn't any humiliating or hostile story about asking or needing a ride. And I have since gotten less offended at the those who do the drive-by. That is, those who don't look, talk, or indicate that they have a fare but use the others paying their fare as a smoke screen for passing by without fare. But after realizing that I am here to be of service in providing a ride, I became less angry at the drive-by folks, because, in the end, they were saving me time in the zone. "Do you need a transfer?" is the best one liner to get their attention and see if they have some money to put in the box. Sometimes they only have a penny to put in. I'll take it. Hey, it's one penny more than Muni would have gotten. And the sense of self-esteem that seems to manifest from this does make for a friendlier coach and a friendlier ride. Better than those who ask the question are those who say …

I Have It

There are creative ways to get past the fare box and not have to pay at all. If I am very busy, I let some of these transgressions pass by, but it doesn't mean I am not aware you are scamming the system. It begins by saving your transfer from yesterday. If you boarded the coach later in the day, you have a longer transfer, and if you place your thumb over the date, it looks like a good transfer. This doesn't work on the first of the month when the transfer changes color. Still, there are a few diehards who try it anyway.

The other way to block the ID of the transfer is if you purchase a transfer earlier in the day. The transfer is held like a cup, so that your hand blocks the bottom strip indicating the time of expiry. Finally, there are those who have been burned in the past who hold the transfer in such a disguise mode and then lash out at the driver when asked to pay the fare. They move their hand to show that the transfer is valid and attempt to train the operator not to question the fare. This is how riders train operators not to check the transfer.

My spiritual research has indicated that I have the freedom of choice in how I am with respect to what is going on around me. I may not be able to think my way out of the ninth level of hell, but I can choose at any time how I feel. And when I can't get into the Zen zone, I better take a deep breath and reboot.

The fare box was jamming up, and I needed to keep resetting it.

Passengers were complaining about being pushed and shoved. I was without help in front or behind, and no buses were in sight. I was losing it. I made a decision. *I can't stay in this mindset.*

The Eighteenth Street switch was right in front of me. I clicked right on to Eighteenth and left Mission. "This coach is out of service," I announced. "Awww," came the response from the packed bus. Unauthorized pull in. I opened all doors, and people slowly streamed off the bus. Not without some comments about my abilities or my mother! This was the only time I recall that I defied procedure and went out of service without permission. At this time, I lacked the ability to control my load and check in with myself about my mental state.

Fortunately, I had another senior operator on board, and she told me what I needed to do and what to say to the dispatcher when I went to ask for another coach. She had boarded and was returning to the barn to pick up her car. Her day was over. I had forgotten about this ninth level of hell and how she may have saved me from suspension or dismissal.

I remember when I was new to the city and put in coins every trip. I did not want to commit to a whole month pass. But as soon as I did, I found I used the bus more often than not. The simplicity of a pass was worth the freedom to not look for money every time I boarded. The rub is having enough money to buy the pass when rent is due. Humility goes a long way as an operator in remembering the challenge to pay for transportation in such an expensive city. I would also do well to remember that our city fathers also have serious challenges in making ends meet to pay for the maintenance on all of our fleet. It is not just the cost of buying something but the expense of keeping it.

Keeping the Zen can be the hardest part of staying calm in the seat behind the wheel!

Always in Service

U<small>NLIKE MOTOR COACHES, TROLLEYS ARE ALWAYS IN SERVICE</small>. T<small>HIS IS IN</small>
the Muni rulebook, although very few people understand this. If I put
up the sign that says Garage, it does not mean that I will not pick you
up. I am putting up Garage so you can see my destination clearly. Many
times when I put up the line number with a short destination, riders
don't see my short-line destination and become upset or don't exit when
I reach my last stop. I have been written up for posting Garage. I am sad
that the street inspectors don't understand that when I put up Garage,
it does not mean I am out of service.

We do have the sign Ask Driver, but on the old coaches, the line
sign still stays up. I know I sometimes put up Garage when I have had
a long day and am tired. If I have been missing a leader for more than
a trip and have carried a heavy load and been late on schedule, I have
been known to put up Garage because I believe I have done more than
my fair share for the day.

I don't feel like dealing with more questions about where I am
going after a killer day. The last thing I want to have happen is to get
in an argument with someone who wants to go farther than my pull-in
point. I believe my garage is a hard-won benefit after being of service
all day. I would like to think I have built up credits for being in service
on most days when I pull in.

There are times when I announce my last stop and someone comes
forward to ask if it is okay if they go with me, say to Seventeenth and
Bryant, which is two blocks from the gate, and I am always happy to say
yes. I don't fully understand why I cannot quickly answer yes to other
questions asked throughout the day, when a yes would be the simplest
and quickest answer. I can say that when I am pulling in and someone

asks if I go near to where they want to get off, I have always and without hesitation said yes when I am going home.

I am a trolleyman. And trolleys are always in service. This is the one rule I can say I have honored in all my years with Muni. For example, when I have an Eleventh Street destination outbound from Ferry Plaza on the 14 Mission, and I pull into the zone at Ninth Street, I announce that this is my last curb on Mission. Notice I say last curb. This is accurate and simple. I did not say this is my last outbound street stop. I click left at Tenth and turn on Howard before we turn left on to Eleventh, but I don't have a sign that says Ninth.

Eleventh and Howard is closer to the major transfer point of Van Ness and Mission. But to let people out there seems like kind of a waste. It seems short of the mark. In just two blocks, there is the option to get on four buses during the day, or two buses at night, and I have always been particular in letting my passengers get as far as they can get on my bus, or at least make a smooth transition to their next ride, with as much possibility in getting the next bus most likely to pass in as short as time possible.

I heard another operator getting into some trouble for passing up a wheelchair or lift request, such as at Fourth Street or at Sixth, because "I am only going to Ninth," just as I had done on an earlier sign-up. This was the same man who, time after time, got passed up or brushed off because we operators assumed he was going to ride beyond our pull in to Sixteenth or points beyond, and we never waited to hear that Ninth was okay for him. He was fast boarding and departing and really did not take up much extra time.

Over the years, he became adroit at getting the coach and run number of coaches that did not pick him up. This led to many complaints for many different drivers. Our rush to be done caused us to get a complaint, a letter, or mail from the dispatcher, a love letter, so to speak, because this was a valid complaint since we passed up a customer with a right to get to our short-line destination. And I remembered that those requiring a lift just a few blocks away should not have to wait for my follower when I was able to take them a short distance. Especially if no bus was in sight behind. I had to learn to create this space the hard way. After the angry cry from those I shut the door on during my quick passes outbound to Ninth, I realized eventually that it was emotionally a lot easier to take my time and let everyone board, but let them know I was a short-line coach. If they did not understand after I turned onto Tenth, at least I made an honest effort by pausing at each block and stating that I was pulling in on Eleventh.

I left open the possibility that maybe some people did want to go on to Bryant or to Costco at Harrison and Eleventh. For an out-of-towner or someone not from SF, all these street names may sound confusing, but the point is that if trolleys are always in service, our pull-in routes do offer easier connections, even if we are traveling off of our regular line route.

I have found that I almost always have one or two passengers who are willing to travel beyond my last regular stop. I have never had a problem doing this.

A wonderful recent victory was a nice man in a wheelchair from Larkspur, who rode the ferry into my terminal at the Ferry Plaza. After small conversation, I found out he wanted to go to Costco at Eleventh and Harrison. This was on my pull-in route. What a great feeling to take him beyond Mission Street and drop him across the street from Costco, without him having to make a transfer and waste time looking for the 9 line or 47. Being able to get to this point of finding a joy that remains hidden when most of us pull in with a one-track mind has a lot to do with the spirit behind writing this how-to manual on the Zen of Muni. One thing our car culture lacks is the sense of community that can be built on the bus when we talk and communicate with one another. I still have this man's business card that he gave me when he got off at Harrison and Eleventh.

I found out about the history of his nice apartment complex and his life after retiring to a great place to live. All this richness would have been lost or reduced to a piece of mail warranting a conference with my superintendent for possible discipline, when instead I got a connection from another passenger who got great service.

Pulling in on the Mission wires from the other direction is the same dilemma at Twenty-Sixth and Mission. Sure enough, I have a passenger who desires a location within one block of the Potrero gate, such as by the KQED television station across from our yard, or in some other residence or business in nearby media gulch. All the hurry up and go home energy becomes a relaxed, enjoyable ride for that one person I make special by dropping them off within a block of their destination.

The knowledge that I saved them time without additional transfers instills in them that our system is great and that they are a part of the Muni family. This goodwill can have expansive positive effects on the perception of drivers as a whole group and goes a long way to hopefully preventing calamities or funding arguments down the road. Instead of an angry or unfriendly tone repeating that I am not going somewhere, this is a much lighter, happier way to pull in.

Straight Through

I WORK A SPLIT. THESE RUNS ARE FROM 6:00 A.M. TO 6:00 P.M., MONDAY through Friday—or from 7:00 a.m. to 7:00 p.m., weekdays. The question remains, how can I have a life (hah) by working a twelve-hour range during the day and keep my sanity? My answer has been to cram as much as I can into the two-hour break in the middle of the day. Just like school bus drivers, many city transit companies break up the day with split day shifts. I take people to school or work, take a break after the peak period, and then come back to take people home. As I live in the city, I try to make this work. I try to get something done over lunch so when I get off at 7:00 p.m., I can feel like I accomplished something, without having to do more after work. I can be totally drained after a twelve-hour range of driving in the city! There used to be standby time built in to these ranges, but this has evaporated from our run choices.

This is politically unfavorable to pay a driver when they are not in the seat, but I would like to point out that the cost of not offering some of this standby time may be increasing costs not directly on the payroll books. Right now, higher cap numbers are filling these day run splits. Can this be sustained, or will it result in more breakdowns and sick days? The dispatchers with experience say no. *Give them an inch, and they'll take a mile* seems to be the philosophy when it comes to paying senior operators standby report or standby detail. I would disagree, mainly because I am a senior operator, and I have seen this standby pay go away! There used to ninety hours a day built into this standby report (SR) or standby detail (SD) on our barn range sheets. This had an effect on a few senior operators during a sign-up posting. They saw the new range sheets and decided to retire! *Reduction of standby pay can reduce the longevity of operators.*

One way to avoid this huge day part of taking away a life is to do a straight through. This means coming in really early, say at 4:00 or 5:00 a.m., and getting off before school gets out. Or make relief during a school trip in the afternoon and work till midnight or later. This of course means picking up the bar crowd or those with no place to go who fall asleep and use your bus as a shelter. In the morning, you pick up folks with a purpose in their life. At night, you get the denizens of the deep. After 10:00 p.m., inbound on Mission, I see no purposeful souls waiting for the bus. Same is true for inbound on the 49 after Market. There really are no paying customers with any sense of good, orderly direction, going to any perceivable destination with purpose, except to sponge off of others, or intending drug buyers.

Straight throughs have also gone through pay cuts. They have shorter recovery time at the terminal and get off sooner. My point is that at some point, the schedule cannot be met, because the shaving of time and money becomes too extreme, and on time performance falls below 60 percent. This seems to be the effect that causes gaps in service. The harmony of a fifteen-minute recovery time, which allows buses to leave on time, would allow for more even distribution of buses on the line. The cost of shaving down run pay has its price in bunching and missing coaches, and a lack of operators available to do the job. There should be a direct correlation between run pay, time off, and on-time service, but by keeping scheduling underfunded and understaffed, accountability is lost, and blame can be assigned in a nebulous way, directly or indirectly blaming the operator.

As I update this chapter (2018), a massive set of training classes are underway to augment 160 new hires into the system.

The Tower

THE SECOND HAPPIEST MOMENT OF THE DAY IS THE TIME WE SEE THE tower in our front windscreen because it means we made it back to the barn! We completed another day of revenue service without creating more incident paperwork or having trouble meet us before our day is done. Oh, just a minor piece of paperwork to be turned in to the tower, the defect card. How long could this take? How bad could it be? Do you guys remember the recent movie title *There Will Be Blood*?

The blood, the sweat, and the tears are rarely shed at the tower. These are found during the special event when the bus is packed at 36 Avenue by Golden Gate Park and there are another three miles of bus stops with people waiting to get on to go to BART at Fifth Street! No, the tower is usually a sweet spot without drama.

The tears will come in the next week, or the next month, when you get the bus again on a cold and windy morning, and it still has no heat. Or the chair still loses air. You hop in and see perfectly through the eight mirrors, but halfway to Daly City, you become a low-rider in the seat and wish you had the hydraulics to lift your ass up out of the seat to see what lies ahead. Or the horn goes off any time you try to turn the wheel. That poor little Chihuahua may never be the same again. Glares and stares from cyclists and pedestrians who think you are a regular horn honker. No, the art of the pull in is to know what I can and cannot put on the defect card and what will or will not get fixed. This is much like reading tea leaves. But in this case, the leaves are the three parts of the defect card: yellow, pink, and white.

If I see lots of hanging chads by the door to the tower, I would do well to smile and let things go. After all, the logic within the hallowed walls of the tower may go something like this: if it was okay for you to drive like that all day, it couldn't be all that bad. If it *was* broken, you would have called for the road crew, and if it was unfixable, they would have sent you in. Unspoken to be sure, unwritten to be sure, but can I get my defect card on the windshield wiper, with the order of "track 22"? Track 22 is code for that sinking feeling sometime in the next day when the next operator realizes they have been had. That the manufacturer's maintenance schedule does not coincide with the parts budget allocation!

"Good one?" is the late-night request that comes forth from the tower worker when pulling in during the wee hours. A thumbs-up means advancing to the happiest moment of the day, the fare box collector. Do not pass go. Do not collect $200. But on to free parking! (Actually no, parking is now paid, and it just went up.) Being able to get something fixed without breaking down on the road is truly a God-given gift. And to get the defect card on the wiper and to be assigned the same coach the next day, with no problems, is perhaps an Eighth Wonder of the World in keeping Zen as a transit operator in San Francisco!

Nowhere in Particular

ONE OF THE HAPPIEST ZEN ZONE TIMES I HAVE EXPERIENCED DRIVING the bus is at the end of a swing shift, or the shift that Muni operators call the twilight. After completing my last full trip on the 49 Van Ness, I had a pull in to Eleventh and Mission, so I remained in service along Van Ness outbound from North Point and Aquatic Park to Market Street. We can usually put up the Market Street destination sign. On the old Flyer trolleys, there was the sign Nowhere in Particular. Usually, no one pays any attention to the destination sign. Intending riders only look at the line sign and board, assuming the coach will continue to its regular terminal destination. One of the social experiments I like to try is to see if various head signs work to my favor by getting attention or by limiting the number of questions I get asked about where I am going.

Often, when I have had a long day and am exhausted, I try to see if I can pull in without delays with confusion at the front door and fare box about my short-line status. Sometimes, one brief announcement is all it takes, and everyone departs willingly and knowingly without any confusion.

Other times, when I inform them at the door that I am a short-line coach, it creates confusion about what choice to make and if there is another coach coming. And I sometimes can't tell in advance if I will have to expend more energy overcoming a lack of understanding, trying to make clear over and over my out-of-service stop, or whether I can keep quiet and wait till the last stop. Sometimes people get angry when I go out of service, and the sense is that I have failed them or am not doing my job. It's as if I am intentionally stopping short and am scamming the system and cutting out early. I have to adjust my thinking to realize that they may have had a bad experience on an earlier trip that day, or they have been cut short by some other run or pull in where the operator did not follow the rule of announcing the pull in correctly or without regard for their need. And this understanding took a while to get used to. Any anger is not about me but about some other time and place.

So one night near Halloween, on my pull in from North Point, I saw that the paper in the scroll roller was torn and would get caught and tear a bigger rip. I had to look for another sign to put up that would make it clear that I was not going all the way out to Ocean. And, being in a playful mood, I decided to scroll all the way up to "Nowhere in Particular." And this was a good decision. I got a lot of smiles along the way. Even some toots from coaches going in the other direction. People were noticing the sign more so than if I had put up the standard sign of Mission or Market. I did not have to waste any impatient energy with all those I came in contact with who were waiting at the bus stops along Van Ness. And they waited for the next bus to take them beyond my pull-in point. I didn't have to say anything. The few who did get on were in a good mood and obliged nicely by getting off at my last stop without a peep. "I wish I could go where you are going! Good night." Wow. What a difference from the usual groans or sighs.

My playful energy transferred perfectly, and no one complained. I was in the Zen zone on my pull-in trip instead of getting stink eye or endless questions. The biggest test of the Zen zone is on a pull-in trip without incident or delay. I am sad that this sign was not included in the new digital readout of the new head signs. I have always wondered who gets to make the decision to encode the destination roster and who gets to program in the automatic announcements. Most riders believe that, as employees for the railway, we know about many details—such as when the next bus is coming.

When I was new, I did not have much to go on. Now with the bus shelters displaying the waiting time between coaches, some of the confusion has gone away. I try to look to see the next bus display in the shelter to see if I can read the next arriving time. I am always hopeful that new tech can solve Muni problems. I am sad when some of the humor and creativity is taken away as an older tech, like the paper scroll, is removed. The newer LED lighting is not necessarily easier to read than the old black-and-white paper signs. Although the GPS technology helps customers a lot, sometimes I think that adding computers or chips to buses was a dumb idea.

Oh well. Nowhere in Particular was a fun sign to put up and seemed to get a good response from everyone when I used it. There are those few precious times when it seems okay to put up a more unusual sign, and it was neat to have had that option.★

★*Some or all of the views expressed herein do not necessarily reflect those of the SFMTA.*

How I Got My Job

On my trail to be fired by my previous employer for poor job performance, I was given an ultimatum: show up at EAP office at 9:00 a.m. sharp on Monday or be fired. I rang the security bell at 8:58 a.m., and no one answered. I rang again at 8:59 a.m., and still no answer. I left with my tail between my legs. Two weeks later, I received my termination letter for failing to appear. *But I showed up,* I said. *No, you were instructed to show up at 9 a.m.* They must have really wanted me to go! Talk about being on a schedule!

So about two weeks later, I got up the courage to file a grievance with our union rep. She got on it right away, and she had an urgency to her voice. Sure enough, the time to file a grievance was within two weeks of the fire date. Fortunately, the Thanksgiving holiday happened to fall within this two-week period—and the contract states ten *business* days. The holiday didn't count as a business day! I successfully saved my old job!

Sure enough, almost to the day, I got the new job at Muni two years later. This timing coincidence was incredible. I heard an inner voice that told me my time with the old employer was done. *What's all this got to do with sitting back and watching the show?* It means as long as I keep my purpose clear and my direction and motives honest, nothing but good follows. This spiritual law seems to hold as true as water seeking its own level and the law of gravity dropping an apple off of a tree. I have become adept at valuing my physical laws, but spiritual laws are just as valid. We are spiritual beings in a physical body. So when I pause to sit back and watch the show, I can keep my bearing and all will turn out well.

And this concept of watching the show can be applied in the macro world of our life goals. I don't know how many times I applied to jobs because I was in a financial crunch and dumbed down just to get a job I could get right away to pay rent. To be sure, there is a wisdom in this. Get immediate needs met, then go on to bigger and better later on. I never seemed to get this. Once employed, I became too busy to think bigger. But as the months turned into years, I realized I was content to maintain my status quo by rationalizing that life's simple pleasures as a worker among workers was enough. I never gave a thought to moving upstage in my goals.

As long as happy hour beckoned after shift, that was enough. Until my life got hit with a reboot at age thirty-nine, I began to get a place where I could actually *sit back*. Not lazy, as some would say, but to avoid the drama without being the lead actor on stage. I finally made the split between getting a job for paying rent now and putting in for a job that would take longer to get and pay more with a long-term future. My answer was to be a civil service worker in the Department of Transportation in the city and county of San Francisco.

I was always too worried about what others were doing and always sought the lowest common denominator rather than bringing up the equation to a new, more aware level. It's been found that when an angry or pessimistic person enters a room with a group of people, such as a break room early in the day, productivity is reduced by all for the rest of the day. The energy I bring to a bus full of people can sometimes make a difference. Is riding the bus a drag, or is it fun?

I noticed early on in my bus-riding days some drivers looked relatively relaxed. Nothing seemed to faze them, and some were actually fun to talk to. There did seem to be a way in which to make their work look easy and relaxing, yet a high-paying job. So the seed was planted early on that this might be a good job for me. As a Gemini sun sign, transportation and continual movement fit my sign. My fourth-grade art project, *What do I want to do when I grow up?,* was a picture of the silver GM coaches that serviced the NY Port Authority from Jersey during the sixties. Bus driver was a job I wanted to do since the fourth grade. I have heard those who are successful in their jobs later in life had a passion for those activities or skills from an early age.

Sure, it would take some doing, but in the meantime, why not put in for it and wait and see what would happen? I got menial, easy jobs in the meantime—construction delivery, housecleaning, and nonprofit residential pickup truck driver. This sense of service kept me going as I put in and waited for the better job. Indeed, when my number came up with the Municipal Railway, I was ready to move.

Unlike civil engineer, medical doctor, dentist, or lawyer, bus driver did not seem to appear on the success roster. I didn't really care. Ralph Kramden was my hero. I saw no matter how half-baked an idea was that I could hatch, as long as I had my friends and made a connection with others, everything would turn out okay, just like a thirty-minute sitcom! When Jackie Gleason would exclaim, "How sweet it is!" I got it. I guess you could say the in a way *The Honeymooners* was my imprint version of *The Wonder Years,* which many followed in their youth in the eighties.

I applied as truck driver with a nonprofit retailer for the upcoming Thanksgiving-Christmas rush. I was so grateful for the timing in getting that truck-driver job when I needed it most that I refused my first training class with Muni and finished out the holiday season. I got one first refusal when starting with the city, and I took it, knowing that I was close to starting a training class.

Fast-forward to San Francisco and the late nineties. Newly elected Mayor Willie L. Brown Jr., Esq., was mandated to fix Muni in his first one hundred days, and he took immediate action to hire more bus drivers. I went to the Moscone job fair and put in to get on the list. Finally, at age thirty-nine, I was making a plan about choosing a job that seemed more like a career or occupation than just another paycheck fast.

I encourage anyone living paycheck to paycheck, or between jobs, to pause and look deeply about what kind of service they want to provide to others. I would always sit in the front seat when I rode the bus with Grandma, and I liked it when the bus drivers would talk to me. I still do that now, conditions permitting, and I feel like I am actually in a recruitment mode. Early first impressions can and do have a lasting effect on our life decisions later on down the road. I got them when I was young, so I present myself as doing a fun job.

The events around this hire date are so incredibly unusual that I think they bear testimony that when our motives are pure and not self-seeking, God has a way of showing up and helping.

Watching the show can also take on a religious tone. I have heard that the path to a God-given life is broad and wide and very much unlike a tightrope. Yet my life to this point seemed just that. I put in for the truck-driving job on Friday. I prayed. I kept the faith. I took a deep breath and said, "This is it. Am I just doing another wishful thinking? Or am I on sure footing?" Indeed I was. Next Monday, I got the job. I had asked with a non-self-serving attitude and got a good response. This last-minute breakthrough was only another series of coincidences that seemed as though there were forces at work that were beyond my control, helping me.

When Muni notified me that I had been selected as an applicant, only a two-week window existed in which I had to answer, or I'd have to start over and reapply. At this time, in 1996, job apps were not online as they are today, so I put in a card that was self-addressed, and when the window for application was open for those two weeks, I had to send back a mail-in response that I was available for hire.

Luckily, I still had a post office box near my old house so that my address would be stable and not change. One big problem many applicants have when applying for city jobs is that the address they use when they first apply changes during the time frame until the hire notice arrives. As I went about my business, I forgot about what address I used when I applied. This has been the cause of many an idea I am not good enough, or I have to know someone to get in. This just is not true. If I put in for a city job, I will get a response.

Just as a thank-you letter can be as good as gold after a job interview, a follow-up letter to a new employer is always a good idea and really has no downside. What negative could develop if I checked back to see how my name on the list was progressing? So, when I went to make a journey to my mailbox in another neighborhood from where I was staying, I saw the last letter in the pile. It was from the city, and as I tore it open, I dropped my jaw. The deadline for applying had passed. It was last Friday!

I rushed on the bus to the address on the letterhead. *Oh, well, I* thought, *if I have to reapply and start over, then so be it.* As I was riding on the 43 bus to the Presidio Division, I forlornly looked at the cancellation stamp on the outside of the original envelope. When in the heck did they mail the letter? Oh, not too long, only about two weeks ago—I couldn't believe my eyes.

There were two different dates on the cancellation stamp: November 16 *and* November 17. I did the math. November 17 meant I had one more business day to report my positive response to agree to be hired. I couldn't believe this last-minute hope. When I got to the hiring office, I was all smiles. "Sir, I realize the deadline for the next class expired last Friday, but take a look at this." I showed him the double cancellation stamp. I was in! He accepted the cancellation date of the seventeenth and allowed me to start. I knew there was a power greater than myself at work here.

It has been said that a spiritually fit person has no regrets about the past. And so, by trying over and over to not be resentful about why I was let go or quit in the past, I looked to where I had success and what I enjoyed about what I did. Even if the job description seemed lowly or without promotion, what had I done in those jobs that was helpful to my employer, and how could I carry this forward? My job evaluations were mediocre and average. When I took an honest look at my part and how I had become my own worst enemy, I saw that when I could reflect upon the stage of my life and see the show, I would excel.

I have been doing this ever since and now have an abundance level I never thought possible. I was always too worried about what others were doing and always sought the lowest common denominator rather than bringing up the equation to a new, more aware level. It's been found that when an angry or pessimistic person enters a room with a group of people, productivity is reduced for the rest of the day. The energy I bring to a bus full of people can sometimes make a difference.

I've heard time and time again that my worst moments can be the turning points for the best. It's easy to type this now and to talk from a platitude point of view over coffee, but this spiritual law seems to hold as true as water seeking its own level and the law of gravity dropping an apple off of a tree. I have become adept at valuing my physical laws, but spiritual laws are just as valid. We are spiritual beings in physical bodies. So when I pause to sit back and watch the show, I can avoid dramatic choke points and keep my bearing, and all will turn out well.

Printed in the United States
by Baker & Taylor Publisher Services